the BIG PICTURE *of* BUSINESS BOOK 4

Praises for *The Big Picture of Business*

"Hank Moore is a thought leader. Cognizant of the past, he weaves the accomplishments of others into dynamic strategies. I've worked with him and admire his writings."

—**George P. Mitchell**, Chairman of Mitchell Energy & Development. Developer of The Woodlands & downtown renovation in Galveston.

"Whether I'm at the office, at home, or on the road, I always have a stack of books I'm looking forward to reading. We all need people who will give us feedback. That's how we improve. Success has really been based on partnerships from the very beginning."

—**Bill Gates**

Hank Moore truly embodies the concept of the Renaissance Man, from his worldly connections and involvement to his almost eerie sense of business acumen, in forecasting trends and patterns of commerce. To those of us who deal in the often delicate balance of customer and company, it is blessing to have, in Hank Moore, a resource we can depend on for fair, statesmanlike and balanced observation. I count him as a valued business friend."

—**Dan Parsons**, President, Better Business Bureau

"Every book that Hank Moore writes is a keeper. That's because of his thought leadership and ability to target what is paramount. His books are not only required reading, but they are blessed reading. Hank Moore brings out the grits and guts of these pioneers like nobody else could. You will be recommending these books to your friends."

—**Anthony Pizzitola** MBA, CFM, CBCP, MBCI, Quality Assurance Manager—Jones Lang LaSalle.

"You can have brilliant ideas, but if you can't get them across, your ideas won't get you anywhere. Management is nothing more than motivating other people. The speed of the boss is the speed of the team. Get all the education you can, but do something and make it happen."

—**Lee Iacocca**, past-Chairman, Chrysler Corporation.

"Hank Moore knows more than most, and more importantly he knows how to bring out their traits. I don't know how he does it."

—**George W. Strake Jr.**, Chairman-President, Strake Energy, Inc.

"Hank Moore works miracles in changing stuck mindsets. He empowers knowledge from without by enthusing executives to reach within."

—**Dino Nicandros**, past-Chairman of the Board, Conoco.

"Mr. Moore is one of the true authority figures for business and organization life. He is the only one with an Ethics Statement, which CEOs understand and appreciate."

—**Ben Love**, Vice Chairman, Chase Bank.

"Hank Moore's Business Tree™ is the most original business model of the last 60 years."

—**Peter Drucker**, business visionary.

"Always ahead of the trends, Hank Moore's insights are deep, applicable beyond the obvious."

—**Lady Bird Johnson**, former First Lady of the United States.

"Hank Moore provides fresh approaches to heavily complex issues. His step-by-step study of the business layers makes sense. It shows how much success one could miss by trying to take shortcuts. There cannot be a price put on that kind of expertise."

—**Roy E. Disney**

"How can one person with so much insight into cultural history and nostalgia be such a visionary of business and organizations? Hank Moore is one of the few who understands the connection."

—**Dick Clark**, TV icon.

"Hank Moore is a million dollar idea person. He is one of the few business experts whose work directly impacts a company's book value."

—**Peter Bijur**, Chairman of the Board, Texaco.

"30 minutes with Hank Moore is like 30 months with almost any other brilliant business guru. He's exceptional, unlike any other, and with a testimonial list to prove it. As a speaker, he's utterly content rich, no fluff, no 'feely-touchy' nonsense, right to the point and unashamed to tell the truth. There is nobody better. Every CEO needs him."

—**Michael Hick**, Director, Global Business Initiatives.

"I could not have wished for a better boss and mentor in my first professional job than Hank Moore. He leads by example, and taught me valuable lessons not only about business, but also professionalism and ethics that have stood me well throughout my career. Indeed, when I was in a position to mentor others, I've often repeated 'Hank Moore stories' to my staff, and they've all heard of my first boss. Over time, I grew to understand more and more that Hank Moore treats others with respect, and thereby commands respect. I was privileged to be trained by this creative and brilliant thinker who gets more accomplished in a day than most do in a week."

—**Heather Covault,** Media Relations Manager, Writer, Web Editor at Kolo, Koloist.com.

"Hank Moore brings alive the tales of these important individuals in a rich and detailed way that affords us all the opportunity to appreciate their contributions to our world and way of life. Well researched and experienced, Legends reflects Hank's personal relationships with those legends shaping the past, present, and future. Legends is a must read."

—**Nathan Ives**, Strategy Driven.com.

"Hank Moore has a wealth of knowledge. Not only is he fascinating to talk with, he's a fabulous writer as well. I'm so glad that he put all of his extensive knowledge of pop culture and business history down in a book for generations to come. Now we can all have access to the amazing stories behind many of the histories, corporations and who's who. Thanks Hank for sharing these wonderful stories. You Rock."

—**Kathryn C. Wheat Wiggins**, author, *Networking: Naked and Unafraid.*

"Important Ideas Efficiently Presented. Hank Moore is a real king of business strategy in a time when there are all too many pretenders to that throne, and he knows how to write. The Business Tree is not for those who like their information presented slowly and interlaced with fluff. Moore's ideas are clearly and concisely presented. The book is all meat; and therefore needs to be read and pondered, then read again. Hank's books contain an enormous amount of useful information that will help any executive to function more effectively. Highly recommended."

—**Daniel Krohn**, attorney at law

"Hank Moore writes this book from a fascinating and unusual point-of-view. He is both an advisor to top-level managements of business and non-profit organizations, and an avid student of popular culture, especially of pop music. Combining these two perspectives, he offers valuable and entertaining insights about motivating excellence in organizational behavior. Hank's book is full of warmth and good humor, as well as keen insight. It is also stuffed with facts. This book is an enjoyable and thought-provoking read."

—**Thomas J. Perrone**

"Hank Moore is one of the legends of business, as well as pop culture. He connects the genres for ultimate wisdom. This is an adventurous book, his 13th. The next one, "Pop Music Legends," will go out of the stratosphere. This book series is a major undertaking. Hank Moore has crafted them masterfully."

—**Nancy Lauterbach**

"Hank Moore is a prolific writer with an amazing knowledge of his subject. Everyone will love this book."

—**Douglas B. Gehrman**

the BIG PICTURE *of*
BUSINESS
BOOK 4
THE VALUE YOU DESERVE
Innovation, Motivation &
Strategy Meet Tomorrow

HANK MOORE
PULITZER PRIZE NOMINATED

NEW YORK

LONDON • NASHVILLE • MELBOURNE • VANCOUVER

the BIG PICTURE *of* BUSINESSB O O K 4
THE VALUE YOU DESERVE
Innovation, Motivation & Strategy Meet Tomorrow

© 2022 HANK MOORE

Published in New York, New York, by Morgan James Publishing. Morgan James is a trademark of Morgan James, LLC. www.MorganJamesPublishing.com

Proudly distributed by Ingram Publisher Services.

Morgan James
BOGO™

A **FREE** ebook edition is available for you
or a friend with the purchase of this print book.

CLEARLY SIGN YOUR NAME ABOVE

Instructions to claim your free ebook edition:
1. Visit MorganJamesBOGO.com
2. Sign your name CLEARLY in the space above
3. Complete the form and submit a photo
   of this entire page
4. You or your friend can download the ebook
   to your preferred device

ISBN 978-1-63195-637-9 paperback
ISBN 978-1-63195-638-6 ebook
ISBN 978-1-63195-639-3 hardcover
Library of Congress Control Number:
2021909359

Cover Design by:
Rachel Lopez
www.r2cdesign.com

Morgan James is a proud partner of Habitat for Humanity Peninsula
and Greater Williamsburg. Partners in building since 2006.

Get involved today! Visit MorganJamesPublishing.com/giving-back

Dedicated to Joan Moore.

Hank & Joan Moore

TABLE OF CONTENTS

ACKNOWLEDGEMENTS

Remembrances to some of the business legends whom I knew and worked with: Malcolm C. Baldridge, George R. Brown, George & Barbara Bush, Winston Churchill, Dick Clark, John & Nellie Connally, Stephen Covey, Philip B. Crosby, Michael Dell, W. Edwards Deming, Roy Disney, Peter Drucker, Michael Eisner, Bill Gates, Max Gotchman, Dr. Norman Hackerman, Gerald Hines, Ima Hogg, Lee Iacocca, Lady Bird Johnson, Lyndon B. Johnson, Ben Love, Clare Boothe Luce, J. Willard Marriott, Glenn McCarthy, Marshall McLuhan, Harris & Carroll Masterson, George & Cynthia Mitchell, Bill Moyers, Dino Nicandros, Earl Nightingale, Cactus Pryor, Anthony Robbins, Eleanor Roosevelt, Colonel Harland Sanders, Vidal Sassoon, Peter Senge, Allan Shivers, Roger Staubach, Jack Valenti, Dottie Walters, Jack Welch, Gus & Lyndall Wortham.

Also, acknowledgements to Imad Abdullah, Sharon Connally Ammann, Tom Arbuckle, H.E. Madame Sabine Balve, Jim Bardwell, Robert Battle, Judy Blake, Tom Britton, Dr. Lee P. Brown, Margie Nash Buentello, Neil Bush, Crissy Butts, Tony Castiglie, Glenn Chisman, Sandra Collins, George Connelly, Rob Cook, John Cruise, Hector & Arleigh De Leon, R.J. Diamond, Sue Ditsch, Deborah Duncan, Tony S. DUrso, Tom & Anna Dutta, Alan & Gay Erwin, Dr. Ron Evans, Margarita Farmer, Felix Fraga, Dr. Yomi Garnett, Martin Gaston, Douglas & Christine Gehrman, Andrea Gold, Diane Payton Gomez, Glen Gondo, Sonia Guimbellot, Phillip Hatfield, Bubba & Glenna Hawkins, Royce Heslep, Michael Hick, Mary Higginbotham, Bruce Hillegeist, Derrill Holly, Richard Huebner, Susan & Robert Hutsko, Hiett Ives, Chris Kelso, Dana Kervin, Soulat Khan, Jon

King, Kirby Lammers, Nancy Lauterbach, Torre Lee, Wea Lee, Steve & Barbara Levine, Mike Linares, Craig & Vicki Loper, Jayce Love, Anya Albert Lucas, Stuart & Laura Lyda, Jackie Lyles, Hon. Tammy Collins Markee RCC, Wayne Mausbach, Don McCoy, Bertrand McHenry, Kathleen McKeague, Bruce Merrin, Amber Mesorana, Julie Moore, Larry Moore, Phil Morabito, Jesse Mueller, Larry Mueller, Lizz Mueller, Bill Nash, Howard Partridge, Dan Parsons, Monte & Linda Pendleton, Leila Perrin, Tom Perrone, Joe & Courtney Peterka, Sue Pistone, Anthony Pizzitola, Travis Posey, Doug Quinn, Sally Mathis Ramsay, Roy & Gail Randolph, Connie Rankin, David Regenbaum, Ronney Reynolds, Tamra Battle Rogers, Donna & Dennis Rooney, Mike Rosen, Melissa Rotholz, Rob Rowland, Tony Rubleski, Monica Ryan, Jordan Rzad, Rita Santamaria, Rick Schissler, Jack Shabot, Lisa Trapani Shumate, Previn Sonthalia, Bill Spitz, Maggie Steber, Rod Steinbrook, Gail Stolzenburg, George Strake, Bill & Cindy Taylor, Deborah Taylor, Jon & Paige Taylor, Jane Moore Taylor, Jacqueline Taylor, Charlie & Laura Thorp, Rich Tiller, James & Carolyn Todd, Linda Toyota, Candy Twyman, Mary & Paul Vandenberg, David Wadler, Cameron Waldner, Jack Warkenthien, Louie Werderich, Kathryn & Chris Wiggins, Jennifer Wilhelm, Sara Wilhelm, Robert Willeby, Melissa Williams, Ronald Earl Wilsher, Kyle Wilson, Beth Wolff, Dr. Martha Wong, R.D. Yoder, Tom Ziglar.

Special dedications to the Silver Fox Advisors and the Better Business Bureau.

Chapter 1

THE VALUE YOU DESERVE

Ultimate Leadership Chapter

T here are many kinds of influences out there. How influences stick with us build character, which is transferred into the influences that we shape for others.

See the value in others that they cannot see in themselves.

When you give, you also get your share.

Self worth is not equal to or determined by net worth.

Persistence beats resistance.

Footsteps in the sands of time are made by moving forward.

Choose the road to go where you wish to grow.

Tonight is the night to be bright.

Every company represented here needs mentoring.

Things that were not achievable in early careers are now yours to master.

Opportunities will come your way when you believe they will start happening today.

It's almost tomorrow. Today will be yesterday tomorrow. The minutes into the future will soon become the cherished memories of the past.

Tomorrow might not come, when dreamers dream too late. How can you know what's possible, until you try.

Use the system for the betterment of society. When business does the right thing, it's good for society and for business. Right things matter and pay back in goodwill.

Define who you are. Do not let others define you. Be stronger than your excuses.

May you always be a dreamer. May your brightest dreams come true.

People worry so much about the cost of living. Concern yourself with the value of life. Ask yourself: what more do you want. You've earned it.

Recall and build upon the teachable moments that influenced you.

Hope for the year: healing, recovery and valuing each other. Hope inspires us to do the impossible & carry on during difficult times. There will be tough times, and they will pass.

Mentoring guides your success. Effective leaders don't have to be lonely at the top.

You are not alone. Learn to know, grow and share the success.

We are all caretakers of something. Show gratitude often. Notice other people. Reward yourself. Prepare for and nurture your future. Serve your community.

It's about time, place and attitude. People who are adaptive and adaptable get further. Celebrate others. Stand up for others. Learn the secrets of successful people.

The more that we remind others of the worth of life and positive opportunities, we remind ourselves as well.

Reinforce truths everyday. Otherwise, vacuums will be filled with lies and misinformation.

Quote from Winston Churchill: "All the great things are simple, and many can be expressed in single words: freedom, justice, honor, duty, mercy, hope."

Quote from Albert Einstein: "Learn from yesterday, live for today, hope for tomorrow. The important thing is not to stop questioning."

Quote from Dr. Martin Luther King, Jr.: "We must accept finite disappointment, but never lose infinite hope."

Early Sum Gain, Salad Days Lessons

Everything we are in life and business stems from what we've been taught or not taught to date. A career is all about devoting resources to amplifying talents and abilities, with relevancy toward a viable end result. Failure to prepare for the future spells certain death for businesses and industries in which they function.

Many of us were great kids with promises they have since fulfilled. Our early years form the basis for contributions throughout life, mentoring others and serving communities. Saluting the current youth, who will do and accomplish magnificent things.

Young school years showed bright promise for future leaders. We must constantly reflect upon what we learned, the leadership values instilled and the great people with whom we grew.

Fuel You and Propel You

A rich and sustaining Body of Work results from a greater business commitment and heightened self-awareness. None of us can escape those pervasive influences that have affected our lives, including music and the messages contained in songs. Like sponges, we absorbed the information, giving us views of life that have helped mold our business and personal relationships. These include:

1. Expertise, including talents, skills, education, training, resume credits and industries served.
2. Core Values, including ethics, standards, level of professionalism.
3. Track Record, including experience, accomplishments, professional reputation and level of career achievement.
4. Work with Colleagues, including people skills, executive and leadership abilities, collaborative team experience and references.
5. Business, including marketplace practical knowledge and understanding, business savvy and participation in the business development process.
6. Body of Knowledge, including original ideas, self-created expertise beyond formal education and writings.
7. Vision, including uniqueness, substance, creativity, value-added business relationships and contributions to the Big Picture of Business.

What sets this series apart from other business books:

- Discerning sources of business advice. Collaborations, partnering and joint-venturing. How to create and change corporate cultures. Vision that transcends hype and pretense.

- Understanding and dealing with distractions. Avoiding the rabbit holes to stay focused. Getting the success that you deserve. Properly mentoring the next generation of leaders. Results based planning.

- Taking the offensive to be strategic. Creating a career body of work. Customer focused management. The business leader as community leader. Keeping it real and sustaining success in the long-term.

- Getting, keeping and inspiring stakeholders. Performance based budgeting. Learning from the past to master the future. Branding and marketing under the umbrella of Big Picture strategy.

- Mastering the Big Picture. Escaping the partial-niche mentality. Meeting marketplace demands with innovations. Learning from failures in order to succeed. Fine-tuning people's behaviors into collective strength.

- Why businesses go bad and how to avoid the traps. How to succeed beyond previously-held beliefs. Evolving the workforce into professionals who go the distance. Cause related marketing as a definitive success strategy.

- How to innovate. Creative business after-markets. Benefiting from change. Discerning true business consultants from vendors. Creating business partnerships that previously did not exist.

- How and why to move the future. Understanding trite expressions in order to create real strategies. Why good organizations click. Professional development they are not getting. Communications strategies.

- Crisis management and preparedness. Quality control. The path from innovation to success. Businesses in transition. Public company obligations. Charity involvement. How good companies do great things. "The Big Picture of Business" is an encyclopedic set of books covering all aspects of business. Categories of chapters in each volume include:

- Strategy development, planning and business overview.

- Original cutting-edge essays on topics not covered by other books, publications or websites. These include "Doing Business in a Distracted

World," "Behaviors in the Workplace, Protocols on the Job," "Dangling Carrots & Rabbit Holes," "Loyalty Programs," "The Medium is the Message," "Kick the Can, Check the Box," "Concepts, Models & Strategies," "Significances of Seven," "Power of Three," "Questions," "It's About Them, Not the Customers," "High Cost of Doing Nothing," "The Book of Acronyms," "The Value You Deserve."

- Business niche topics from the Big Picture perspective. These include "Where They Go to Get Business Advice," "Professional Services," "Encyclopedia Knowledge Bank," "The Seven Lists, Stages-Progressions to Business Success," "Training & Professional Education, You've Got to Be Taught."
- Informational chapters. Case studies of strategies.
- Leadership and people skills chapters. Motivations to succeed.
- Legends chapters highlighting trends & innovators. These include "How the Automobile Transformed Business & Society," "The Masters of Repurposing," "How Businesses Got Their Names," "Cities in Transition," "Small Inventions, Little Things That Make Big Things Work," "The History of Business," "The History of Volunteerism and Non-Profits," "Pop Culture Wisdom," "Lessons from Recessions and Corporate Scandals," "Business in the Internet Age," "My Own Experiences and Memories in Working with the Business Legends."
- Process chapters, including fiduciary responsibility, ethics, quality management, etc. Words and terms, expanding and further defining business.
- Appendix sections encompassing the author's previous writings, including classic magazine article reprints.

Key Takeaways from this Book Series
- Never stop learning, growing and doing. In short, never stop!
- Offer value-added service. Keep the focus on the customer.
- Lessons from one facet of life are applicable to others. Learn from failures, reframing them as opportunities. Learn to expect, predict, understand and relish success.

- Contribute to the Big Picture of the company and the bottom line, directly and indirectly.
- Prepare for unexpected turns. Benefit from them, rather than becoming victim of them. Realize that there are no quick fixes for real problems.
- The path of one's career has dynamic twists and turns, if a person is open to explore them. Realize that, as the years go by, one's dues paying accelerates, rather than decreases.
- Put more focus upon running a successful business. Plan your business.

Chapter 2

WISDOM FROM NAPKINS, BAGS AND SCRAPS OF PAPER
Where Great Concepts Started.

Insights into Creative Idea Generation.

Great ideas do not develop in a vacuum. One must constantly observe, interacting with sources outside your normal environment. Read a lot. Take notes. Keep files of these notes and review them periodically. Creative people have energy and vision. They spend time observing, thinking and analyzing. At some point, the creativity translates into pen or pencil on paper.

When you least expect it, the idea flows, and it is written down, usually at a place and circumstance of unique dimension.

When we think, we jot things down on whatever piece of paper is at hand. Many of the great ideas were put to paper on scraps of paper.

People who are idea machines jot down ideas in quantity. The best ones are pieced from others. Those scraps of paper become goldmines of creativity the more they are reviewed. Great ideas often become more relevant after multiple readings, growing into effective strategies.

Physicist Paul Lauterbur scribbled ideas for the M.R.I. while in a Pittsburgh diner. Novelist J.K. Rowling wrote her ideas for Harry Potter on a napkin while on a train. Abraham Lincoln's Gettysburg Address was first outlined on a restaurant menu.

Concepts that started on cocktail napkins included the Voyager airplane, the fire nose nozzle, Seattle's Space Needle, Reaganomics and the Discovery Channel's annual Shark Week. Pixar's characters started on paper scraps at restaurants.

Other companies that started as writing on table napkins included AC Business Advice, ProWorkflow and Southwest Airlines.

Tech companies that started as writing on napkins included Algorithmia, Arivale, Bump, Compaq Computers, Ethernet, Facebook, Indix, OfferUp, Peach, Photo VR, Qumulo, Spare5, Textio, Twitter and Unikrn. Sound United Design Officer Michael DiTullo enters creative ideas into his smartphone.

Nike CEO Mark Parker constantly takes notes on a Moleskine notebook. In meetings or at home, Parker jots down ideas and makes drawing of new shoe designs. While in a meeting with cyclist Lance Armstrong in 2009, Parker was doodling through the entire presentation. At the end of the meeting, Armstrong asked Parker what he was doing. Turns out he was sketching another show design with cyclists in mind.

Reviewing My Own Ideas, Going Through the Archives

I keep file folders of paper, showing the genesis of great ideas. I often revisit those files for creative ideas. The old notes spark new creativity, where ideas can be expanded for modern usage.

On a slip of paper from a 3x5 memo pad, I scribbled "The Big Picture of Business," which evolved over 20 years into the title of this book series. Other notes on the same sliver of paper included: "Confluence, for executives who successfully go the distance. Compact disc reference for business knowledge." This book series started as white papers, many of them published, beginning on those note pages.

The creative floodgate opened. On that program, I jotted acronyms for other key business words, including Change, Technology, Service, Progress, Business,

Finance, Research and others. The Technology acronym then inspired my monograph for Harvard.

Hotel notepads are great places to jot ideas. On an Omni Hotels tablet, I wrote: "Address current needs as part of a strategic approach. Budget controls do not equate to an effectively run company. Easy solutions are not worth having, nor do they last. Vision cannot work in a vacuum." This is stuff that I advise companies about everyday and is laced through these books.

I found a notepad from a company retreat. The name on the notepad is L.B. Foster Company, with the product lines pipe, piling and rail. This 5x8 pad is filled with my notes. One said, "Characteristics of Viewpoint, using TV screen analogy. People react to what they know. How to think differently, what to think." That page evolved into the covers of this very book series.

The next page listed "Levels of Worker." That evolved into Chapter 15 of Book 1 in this series, "People in Organizations, The Work Force."

Two pages later is the phrase "Lessons Learned But Not Soon Forgotten." That later turned up as the title of Chapter 31 in Book 3 of this series.

On that same notepad, I wrote: "Always carry notepads to meetings. Never make the customer wrong. Thank people for correcting mistakes. Everybody can benefit from public speaking experience. Make three times more compliments than criticisms to have your points made." That is good to remember.

People of a certain age remember VHS videotapes. Inside the tapes were sheets of labels, I found a stack containing ideas that I wrote down, including: "Levels of answers to questions vary. Efforts made today have a relationship to tomorrow's success. In reviewing choices, decisions and change, one movement affects the others. The wise one looks at others as a mirror and profits from their mistakes. Greed is a universal quality, a shortcoming we can all potentially succumb to, given the circumstances. Making no decisions is like making the biggest decisions of your life."

Also in the files, I found a program for a children's theatre production of "Winnie the Pooh," dated Oct. 25, 1997. While Pooh was onstage talking about getting ready to do things, I scribbled on the program: "The Busy Work Tree, concepts of a person's job, profession and career." I tested these concepts for 20 years with corporate clients. This work resulted in Chapter 24 of Book 3 in this series, "The Busy Work Tree, The Learning Tree and The Executive Tree." These concepts were derivatives of my Business Tree concept, which was scribbled down years before on an air-sickness bag while in flight.

While waiting for an oil change, I jotted on the flyer: "Problem solving, accountability for consequences. Seven ingredients of a fulfilled life, for individuals and organizations. Values, ethics, boundaries and standards."

On the back of a Thunder Cloud Subs menu, I wrote these ideas: "The Growing Pains of Small Business. The Loneliness of Leadership. Why People Do It, reasons for organizing. Pitfalls to avoid, drawbacks and opportunities." Small business needs the best ideas and consultation from the brightest mentors.

I was in a hospital Emergency Room waiting area recently and heard "code pink" over the PA system. I asked: "what's that." I began asking about other codes. That sparked the creative urge to jot down ideas for a chapter on the subject. I grabbed the first piece of paper at hand, which was a promotional flyer on the hospital's Obstetrics and Gynecology program. I jotted down an outline for a chapter that would included medical, police, environmental, financial, government, technology and manufacturing codes. The result was a chapter in this very book, "Codes, Categories and Standards." It began by writing "code pink" on a medical flyer.

I was shopping with my wife at a department store when inspiration hit. I grabbed sale flyers and sketched out what became Chapter 7 of this book, titled "The Masters of Repurposing."

I sat in the audience for a college graduation ceremony. I drew on the program cover to amuse my young granddaughter. Then, the commencement speaker began. She used the word "reward," which got me thinking. I had started using words as acronyms for business strategies. I wrote down "reward," then many others. That evolved into my chapter, "The Book of Acronyms." I reprised the acronym idea at the end of the next chapter of this book, using COVID as a series of fresh acronyms for business comeback plans.

I attended a luncheon. The speaker discussed demographic trends and population shifts. He opined that the automobile affected such growth patterns. Intrigued, I grabbed paperwork from the center of the table and sketched out what became Chapter 6 in "Big Picture of Business, Book 3." That comprehensive chapter was titled "How the Automobile Transformed Business and Society." In it, I reviewed the histories of auto manufacturing, oil companies, drive-in movies, shopping centers, fast-food restaurants, auto spinoff industries and retailers.

Note Cards

Index cards are used for a wide range of applications and environments: in the home to record and store recipes, shopping lists, contact information and other organizational data; in business to record presentation notes, project research and notes, and contact information; in schools as flash cards or other visual.

These cards are 3" by 5" and were invented in 1760. Part of standard stationery and office products, they symbolize organizing ideas and information. Common uses of index cards are library index systems, files of business contacts, research notes and home recipe boxes. Furniture was designed to hold archives of index cards. In the days before computer databases, business information was archived on index cards. They were replaced by indexing software in the 1980s.

Index cards were part of my career at various stages. I began my career in 1958 at a radio station in Austin, TX, as a disc jockey. Adjacent to the studio was the music library, containing shelves of records and a filing cabinet with contents of the library, artist information and record numbers listed on the cards in the catalog. Inside the studio, we had a box containing public service announcements, printed on note cards and for us to read in rotation. The news department had card files containing content and contact information. The business office had card files on advertisers, community supporters and technical information on the operation of the radio station. We also kept a Public File that included forms, memos, letters of support and note cards, utilized as reference when we renewed the station's license.

In 1965, I attended a dinner party in Washington, D.C. In a private reception room, I sat on a couch. To my left was Walt Disney, who said to me, "Kid, don't forget this. There are six ways to creatively regenerate a good idea. If it doesn't have that many arms and legs, it's not a great idea." Sitting to my right was Howard Hughes, who said, "Kid, my advice is for you to keep a pocket full of note cards. You can write down these things that people like us tell you. Some day, you'll wind up with a series of books." True, as this is book #13. This event is why both Disney and Hughes appeared on the cover of my eighth book, "Pop Icons and Business Legends."

Through the years, I kept jotting on note cards, as well as other slips of paper. I kept most of those scraps, thus feeding ideas for client strategies. Among those corporations that I later advised were Disney and Baker Hughes.

Note cards came up again in 1980. I advised Lee Iacocca, chairman of Chrysler Corp. He joined Ford Motor Co. in 1946 as an engineer, in 1960 becoming VP-GM of the Ford Division. He championed the design and introduction of the Ford Mustang, Ford Escort & models of Lincoln-Mercury. He left Ford in 1978 and went to Chrysler Corp. Iacocca worked with Congress to negotiate a bailout for Chrysler, working to turn the company around and repay the loan. New models released included the Dodge Aries and Plymouth Reliant. In 1987, he engineered acquisition of AMC, including the Jeep lines. He retired as chairman-CEO of Chrysler in 1992. President Ronald Reagan appointed Iacocca to head the Statue of Liberty-Ellis Island Foundation.

Mr. Iacocca asked me for ideas on instilling employee pride in workmanship. I recommended that he visit plants and assembly lines. I recommended that he carry index cards containing specific information to convey his interest in the employees as individuals. Often, he autographed the cards and gave to the workers as keepsakes.

Lee Iacocca served as chairman of Chrysler Corporation for 14 years. He delivered 663 speeches to articulate company values, internally and externally. In his mind, great communicators motivate, rehearse, are storytellers and keep it simple. He had fond memories of my note card idea, evidenced by his endorsement of this book. Today's CEOs carry such valuable information on their cell phones, as they visit workers to thank for their service.

Pieces of Paper Contained Great Ideas
and Led to Inventions and Concepts

The kids' meal debuted in 1973 at Burger Chef, known as the Funmeal. It was sketched out on the back of a placemat.

Daniel Adamany and Aaron Nack consumed three martinis each and wrote on 10 cocktail napkins in creating the business plan for their IT company.

When the green chiles they had ordered from New Mexico didn't arrive at their home in Tampa, FL, Allison Rugen and Carlo Marchiondo went to a bar and on a cocktail napkin they still have jotted the plan for Southwest Chile Supply, a company that now includes restaurants, wholesale accounts and chile merchandise.

George Ballas was the inventor of the Weed Eater, a string trimmer company founded in 1971. The idea for the Weed Eater trimmer came to him from the spinning nylon bristles at a car wash. He jotted ideas on a notepad at the car wash. He thought that he could devise a similar technique to protect the bark on trees that he was trimming around. His company was bought by Emerson Electric and merged with Poulan, which was later purchased by Electrolux.

Benjamin Franklin loved to swim and was 11 years old when he invented flippers for the hands, later adapted as flippers for the feet. He sketched the invention in his school notebook.

Curt Swan was a comic book artist most associated with Superman. Swan made a quick small drawing for an airplane employee in the 90s, drawn on a barf bag. It reappeared in comic books.

Thomas Alva Edison was 17 in 1862, producing as his first invention a telegraphic repeating instrument, while working as a telegraph operator. His designs were written on a telegraph log pad.

Param Jaggi was 15 in 2008 when taking a driver's education course in Plano, Texas. Watching the car exhaust, he got the idea for a small device that plugs into the muffler. In his driver's education handbook, he sketched a device to utilize algae to convert carbon dioxide from automobile exhaust into clean oxygen. In 2011, his sustainable design won the International Science Fair, beating out 1,500 other applicants.

Cyrus Hall McCormick was 15 in 1824 when he developed a lightweight cradle for carting harvested grain. In 1831, he invented a horse-drawn device to cut small grain crops, known as the reaper, sketched in a note pad.

The original fortune cookies were introduced at a tearoom in Los Angeles and a Chinese restaurant in San Francisco, CA. The original messages were handwritten on scraps of parchment. They were later printed, as distribution of the cookies spread worldwide.

Steve Chen, Chad Hurley and Jawed Karin founded YouTube, a video sharing website, in San Bruno, CA, in 2005. The original office was above a restaurant, and they wrote the plan on the back of takeout menus. The first video posted was Karin at the San Diego Zoo. More than 100 million views per day have been realized, with videos uploaded by individuals and companies.

Samuel Colt worked in his father's textile factory and went to sea in 1830. He conceived the idea of a repeating firearm, utilizing a revolving set of chambers, each brought into alignment with a single barrel. He wrote the ideas on the back of textile order forms. He received the patent in 1836 and opened a factory to manufacture his guns. His other inventions included an underwater mine system for harbor defense, telegraphy and submarine cable. The westward expansion created demand for his guns, and Colt's firearms were essential in military service.

Some of the more glamorous and non-techie napkin idea stories involve writer and producer Aaron Sorkin, who says he wrote the play-turned-movie "A Few Good Men" on cocktail napkins while working as a bartender at a theatre. Sorkin didn't write his screenplay for the Academy Award-winning "The Social Network" on napkins, but Facebook, the subject of that movie, also started on the back of napkins.

Kimberly Fowler was drinking a mojito at a bar on James Beach in Venice, CA. Her Yoga for Athletes classes were popular, and many of her members had to maintain a second gym membership for weight training. When she overheard a waiter at James Beach say "just add mint," she realized she could just add weights to YAS. She jotted down the ideas on cocktail napkins, and Yoga for Athletes Ripped was born.

Berry Gordy was an assembly line worker at Ford's plant in Detroit, which inspired his musical career. On the back of assembly line timesheets, he wrote songs for friend Jackie Wilson, including the hit "Lonely Teardrops." In 1959, Gordy founded his own record company, following Ford's lead to create a mass production system for hit records.

Hitsville USA produced the Motown Sound, which revolutionized pop music and radio listening in the 1960's and 1970's. The Motown Sound featured a dynamic roster of artists, including Diana Ross & the Supremes, Marvin Gaye, The Four Tops, Smokey Robinson & the Miracles, Mary Wells, Junior Walker & the All-Stars, Stevie Wonder, Michael Jackson, The Temptations, Martha & the Vandellas, The Marvelettes and many more. Berry Gordy hoped that his stable of stars would headline New York's Copacabana Nightclub, and all achieved much more stellar fame, influence and respect. The Motown Sound inspired soul music, broadened the radio airplay configuration and inspired generations of soul superstars, songwriters and music producers.

Will Keith Kellogg started by selling brooms, then moved to Battle Creek, MI, to help his brother run a sanitarium. As part of the diet for patients, the Kellogg brothers pioneered in making flaked cereal. The original recipes were written into charts for the patients. In 1897, Will and John founded the Sanitas Company, commercially producing whole grain cereals. In 1906, he founded the Battle Creek Toasted Corn Flake Company, later becoming the Kellogg Company. In 1930, he formed the M.K. Kellogg Foundation.

Lisa Jeffries was asked by a friend in Raleigh, NC, for help on a New Year's Eve party and event planning recommendations. She met the friend for drinks at Sauced Pizza and came up with the idea for RaleighNYE.com, a one-stop guide to the city's NYE parties. Logistics for other events were added.

Jason Stenseth and Mazen Dauleh drafted a plan for their medical equipment rental company while sipping Crown and Cokes at a Denver bar. They wrote ideas on several cocktail napkins. They bought a domain and registered with the state while still at the bar. Their plan was to sell and rent equipment not usually covered by insurance. Their client base now includes hospitals, schools, doctors' offices and medical supply companies.

Eli Whitney worked in his father's shop, repairing violins and manufacturing nails and hatpins. On the back of sales tickets, he sketched a device to separate short staple upland cotton from its seeds. In 1793, he then built a hand-operated cotton gin, perfecting it to clean 50 pounds of cotton per day. His factory built the first milling machine. By 1795, U.S. exports of cotton were 40 times greater than what they had been before invention of the cotton gin.

Creative Idea Generation

Consider your consumers. Think macro (big picture), and ask questions. Explore the marketplace, and do your research.

- These are the methods of generating ideas:
- Brainstorming and reverse brainstorming.
- Research.
- Focus groups and test sessions.
- Problem inventory analysis.
- Creative problem solving.
- Study what worked for others and what did not work.
- Review the innovations before you and why they succeeded.

- Remember that we learn three times more from failures than from successes.
- Yesterday's bad ideas will become opportunities to improve.
- Engage others in your thought process.
- Develop ideas when others are unaware of the problems.
- Thought process progression.
- Applying principles and rules for thought progression.
- Free association collection of thoughts.
- Value analysis is where one conceptualizes ideas by evaluating the worth of other ideas.
- Matrix charting is where one compares the elements of ideas against each other.
- The Big Dream approach is where great ideas are juxtaposed against their constraints.
- Forced relationship ideas compare different product lines and how the new concept becomes the umbrella over other creativity.
- Synectics is a problem solving process. It means joining together seemingly different ideas. It considers personal, direct, symbolic and fantasy elements of the idea and how it will be utilized.

Here are my recommendations for business idea designs:

- Write things down as quickly as the come to you.
- Find meaning in your own scribbles
- Revisit the ideas later.
- Add additional content each time you revisit the ideas.
- See patterns in the kinds of things that you write down.
- Add pictures or symbols to the words.
- Form a brainstorm process to add meat to the thoughts.

I offer these rules for conducting creative idea brainstorming:

- There are no dumb ideas
- Don't criticize the ideas of others.

- Build on the ideas of others
- Focus upon quantity, not quality
- Focus upon results and impact
- Leave your ego at the door
- Feel free to challenge ideas
- Be prepared to defend your concept
- Always separate a bad idea from a good person.

  Some ideas are ahead of their time. Other ideas to consider are ones that others dismissed. Look to nurture those ideas whose time has come.

  Business is the whole first, then the pieces as they relate to the whole and then the whole again. Business is about cultivating relationships.

  It is our primary job and responsibility to be reality detectors for our organizations.

  Management cannot just preside over operations of a company. It must be an active part of it. We are the sum of choices made.

  Taking no risks and making no choices are not options.

  Corporate responsibility must be laced throughout every business decision.

Quotes on Creativity from the Legends

"Creativity is a drug I cannot live without." Movie director Cecil B. DeMille

"The secret to creativity is knowing how to hide your sources." Albert Einstein

"Frugality without creativity is deprivation." Amy Dacyczyn

"Creativity can solve almost any problem. The creative act, the defeat of habit by originality, overcomes everything." George Lois

"Creativity represents a miraculous coming together of the uninhibited energy of the child with it apparent opposite and enemy, the sense of order imposed on the disciplined adult intelligence." Norman Podhoretz

"Creativity is allowing yourself to make mistakes. Art is knowing which ones to keep." Scott Adams, "The Dilbert Principle"

"Above all, we are coming to understand that the arts incarnate the creativity of a free people. When the creative impulse cannot flourish, when it cannot freely select its methods and objects, when it is deprived of spontaneity, then society severs the root of art. In free society, art is not a weapon. Artists are not engineers of the soul. This nation cannot afford to be materially rich and spiritually poor." President John F. Kennedy (1963)

"Creativity is seeing something that doesn't exist already. You need to find out how you can bring it into being and that way be a playmate with God." Michele Shea

"Creativity comes from trust. Trust your instincts." Rita Mae Brown

"While we have the gift of life, it seems to me that only tragedy is to allow part of us to die, whether it is our spirit, our creativity, or our glorious uniqueness." Comedienne Gilda Radner (1946-1989)

"Curiosity is the key to creativity." Akio Morita, "Made in Japan" (1986)

"My curiosity is my creativity on the way to discovery. A hunch is creativity trying to tell you something." Proverbs

"Creativity is the power to connect the seemingly unconnected." William Plomer

"Don't think. Thinking is the enemy of creativity. It's self-conscious, and anything self-conscious is lousy. You can't try to do things. You simply must do things." Science fiction writer Ray Bradbury

"You must not for one instant give up the effort to build new lives for yourselves. Creativity means to push open the heavy, groaning doorway to life. This is not an easy struggle. Indeed, it may be the most difficult task in the world, for opening the door to your own life is, in the end, more difficult than opening the doors to the mysteries of the universe." Daisaku Ikeda

"When we are angry or depressed in our creativity, we have misplaced our power. We have allowed someone else to determine our worth, and then we are angry at being undervalued." Julia Cameron, "The Vein of Gold"

"Nothing can be created out of nothing." Lucretius

In 1981, Rod Canion sketched a plan on the back of a menu at the House of Pies diner in Houston. He showed an investor a design for an IBM-compatible PC clone that would form the basis for Compaq. The company became the world's biggest PC supplier and was acquired by Hewlett-Packard in 2002.

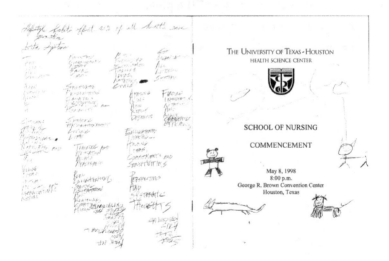

Here is a nursing school commencement program from May 8, 1998. There are drawings on the front that I made for a grandchild. At one point, the commencement speaker, amidst some dry remarks, suggested that the rewards of their chosen career should be redefined. I was drawn to the concept of repurposing the word Rewards. On that program, I jotted other familiar business terms, which became "The Book of Acronyms: New Ways of Looking at Familiar Words," which appeared in Book 1 of this series.

On a La Quinta notepad, I wrote: "The philosophy of one era is the common sense of the next. Compromise between friends is rarely regretted. A large measure of art is consistency." This evolved into the basis of my Legends book series.

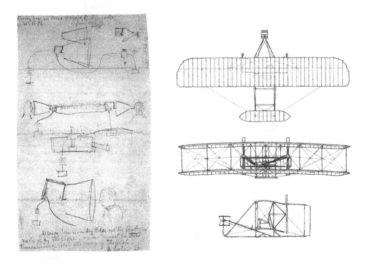

The original tablet sketch of Alexander Graham Bell's telephone concept and the original 1903 flyer airplane by the Wright brothers.

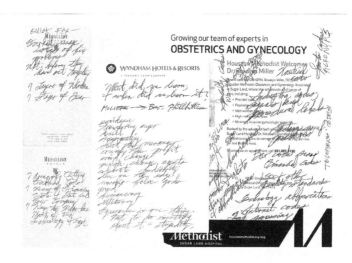

At right is the original outline for Chapter 10 of this book, "Codes, Categories and Standards," sketched on a healthcare flyer. On a Wyndham notepad, I wrote: "What did we learn, and when did we learn it? Ignorance is one thing, and not to do something about it equals stupidity. Doing nothing gets to be a habit. Let one thing slide, and another layer of problems appears." That evolved into "The High Cost of Doing Nothing," Chapter 10 in Book 2 of this series.

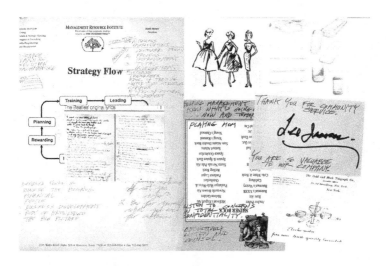

An original notecard signed by Lee Iacocca. Thomas Edison's original drawing of an electrical generator and power system in the 1880s. An original Beatles song lyric, from the back of an envelope. The original cell phone and fashion sketches.

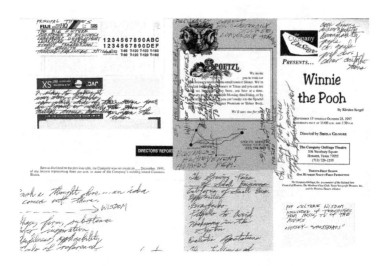

This is my original outline for "The Big Picture of Business" on VHS tape label sheets. My outline for leadership programs on a theatre playbill. My outline for creative idea generation, sketched on notes at a corporate board retreat.

Chapter 3

TYPES AND CATEGORIES OF COMPANIES TO SERVE BUSINESS

Not all companies are alike. They are created for different purposes. They fulfill several purposes. They occupy various niches, sometimes more than one. Their people differ vastly, including their motives for getting into business. Their staying power in business reflects a host of motivations, planning, actions and strategies.

Each business is governed by one of 10 types of business ownership and classifications. They include sole proprietorship, partnership, LLP, LLC, Series LLC, C corporation, S corporation, non-profit corporation, benefit corporation and L3C.

Though companies try too much to emulate others, they must be seen, run and utilized as unique entities.

These are categories of companies and organizations:

- Speculative.
- Test strategy.
- Spinoff of another company.

- Choice by the principal in downsized times.
- Creating a new widget.
- Improving someone else's widget.
- Utilizing new widget making processes.
- Rollup of widget companies.
- Representing expanded service niches.
- For show, investment or quick acquisition.
- Temporary business, meant to nurture and then sell to a rollup.
- Inherited company.
- Lifestyle choice by a principal to do something else.
- Ego driven industry.
- Not a real business but more of a hobby.
- Pick up where other companies left off.
- Meant for specialized services.
- New takes on old products and services.
- Online platforms that occupy perceived business niches.
- Declining niches that still need to be served.
- Designed to last.

Non-profit organizations face many challenges beyond the scope of providing core services. In the process of growth, membership, fund-raising, community relations and accountability activities, it is vital for each organization to ascertain its niche, constituent base, purpose and long-term potentiality.

This is my original examination of the varying levels of non-profit organizations. No analysis of this type has appeared before. This is for the purpose of pinpointing those unique probabilities, challenges and opportunities for the successful conduct of business:

1. Limited scope.
2. Niche-cause.
3. Advocacy.
4. Emerging.
5. Midstream.

6. Mainstream.
7. Premium.

There are seven phases in the life cycle of any company or organization:

1. Conception.
2. Birth.
3. Childhood.
4. Youth.
5. Maturity.
6. Avoiding the traps and downward movement, which includes stagnation, decline and death.
7. Going the distance successfully.

These the primary dilemmas and challenges of business owners and CEOs, per category on my Business Tree:

1. The business you're in. What the company started out as being is not what it is now. Many are not sure why and how to fully adapt. They are concerned what will happen to the business under new management.
2. Running the business. They are still thinking like the profession for which they were educated-trained, not like the organizational head that they have become. They are in the "lonely at the top" syndrome. Many are uncomfortable in administrating but not willing to relinquish full control. They either assume that all employees are fully capable of running the business and remain aloof from them. Or they don't give employees enough resources to do their jobs, thus becoming micro-managers and watchdogs.
3. Financial. If the interest is only on financial gain and profit, business owners will lose sight of the reasons for being and staying in business.
4. People. Many owners don't spend enough time with employees and then wonder why they're not an empowered team. Many delegate away most people skills responsibilities. They don't fully communicate company Vision. They don't put enough resources toward training.

5. Business Development. They don't participate enough in sales, marketing and promotions. They abdicate duties to others, losing sight of the marketplace.

6. Body of Knowledge. Owners understand one or two phases of company operations, without a symbiotic relationship of each branch to the other. They don't participate with Branches 1-5. They don't develop or champion the tools to change.

7. The Big Picture. Many owners and CEOs don't have a current strategy for the future. By sticking to a partial past blueprint, they may have never crafted or articulated a shared company Vision, with input from others. Many fear change, without understanding how and why to master it. They advocate certain behaviors for others in the company but don't always walk the talk.

People Propel Organizations

People under-perform because they are not given sufficient direction, nurturing, standards of accountability, recognition and the encouragement to out-distance themselves.

First comes Talent Acquisition, and then comes Talent Management. Talent Acquisition is about hiring candidates with the right skills and potential to evolve at your company. Talent Management is what follows after a candidate is hired. It involves training and developing current employees, keeping them satisfied and engaged and preparing them to take on more challenging responsibilities.

Each member of an organization must view himself or herself as having customers. Each must be seen as a profit center and as having something valuable to contribute to the overall group. Each is a link that lets down the whole chain by failing to uphold their part.

Human beings are not perfect and don't do everything right on the front end. We learn more workable strategies through trial and error. Organizations full of human beings need the impetus to think new creative thoughts, without the judgment of past mistakes. Those who continue to make the same mistakes thus become the case studies from which good companies learn the next round of lessons.

A major problem with many organizations stems from the fact that management and company leadership coming from one small piece of the pie. Filling all management slots with financial people, for example, serves to limit the organizational strategy and focus. They all hire like-minded people and frame every business decision from their micro niche perspective.

The ideal executive has strong leadership skills first. He or she develops organizational vision and sets strategies. Leaders should reflect a diversity of focus, guaranteeing that a balance is achieved. The best management team looks at the macro, rather than just the niche micro.

These are the classifications of jobs and employees in the workforce:

1. Unskilled labor
2. Basic jobs
3. Apprentices
4. Semi-skilled labor
5. Helpers
6. Servers
7. Entry-level worker
8. Base-level seller, including door-to-door, telephone, clerks and retail sales
9. Support staff
10. Journeyman laborer
11. Technician
12. Administrative
13. Entry-level professional
14. Mid-level worker
15. Mid-level seller, including consumer services, marketing, retailer and vendors
16. Tradesman serving as skill providers
17. Craft provider
18. Science and technology provider
19. Mid-manager
20. Mid-level professional
21. Career worker

22. Professional seller, including business-to-business professionals and financial services
23. Career manager
24. Career professional
25. Consultants for every level to this point
26. Senior professional
27. Executive
28. Seasoned professional
29. Beyond the level of professional
30. Knowledge creator, Inspiring force and wisdom resource

How Companies Evolve, Case Studies Working with Business

Most of the time, clients listen to my advice, heed it and benefit from it. These were times that they did not.

A friend of mine was a consultant to a restaurant chain. They were popular, yet kept believing falsely in their own hype. They asked me to analyze their prospects for going public on Wall Street. I discouraged that, saying they didn't have what it took.

When things were at a crossroads, he called me into meetings to help adjudicate conflicts. I went to their corporate office, sat at the conference table. The president opened the meeting with a jab at my friend. "He says that we only have three problems with our company. What are they?"

My friend said, "Your food is terrible. Your prices are too high. And your customer service is bad. Other than that, you don't have any problems." Their response was oblivious.

The board chair turned to me and said: "I know that you're going to phrase it more diplomatically." I replied, "It's worse than that. We need to talk privately."

She said, "I know. You're going to lecture me about diversity." I replied affirmatively and said the research showed they forgot where they came from. I suggested that they move the corporate office back to the original neighborhood, reconnect with communities and that she visit the branch restaurants more regularly. The changes worked for awhile. Then, they reverted back to the old ways. 12 years later, I told these anecdotes at their bankruptcy hearing, and it was sad for me to recount as expert witness.

Just as organizations start out to be one thing, as they grow, they often evolve into something quite different. What the founder started, if successful, will change over time and over generations of management. Disney started out as an animated movie studio pure and simple. It has expanded far beyond that, and now its core business is licensing its name: to retail outlets, cruise lines, credit card companies, ice shows and more.

As businesses change, management must be astute enough to re-shuffle its priorities. For example, the retail grocery store chain that has acquired so much property as it opened up stores—subletting space to other tenants—really must begin to run itself as a property management company. The local bistro that grew into a chain, found its core business becoming the selling of franchises.

I have worked with many businesses that had moved on from their original business model to something different at they grew and evolved. Case in point: the analytical instruments and equipment industry. Most of the niche companies in this area evolved and grew up because of chemical plant industrialization of the 1950s and 1960s. The founders worked in production environments where plants and factories had on-staff engineers, analyzer specialists, operators, lead chemists and other technical department managers.

Many analytical instruments professionals all came along in the same generation. They founded their companies to meet scientific niches. Their entrepreneurial efforts led to the research and development of the technology. They began serving a broad range of industrial, institutional and governmental client organizations, providing specialized equipment and services to assure accurate analyses and process control.

Cutbacks at chemical plants, water treatment facilities and such have all but eliminated the staff positions that utilize the equipment designed by these companies. Many of those people developed technologies at their plants and subsequently went into business to manufacture and distribute.

The client side changed, while many of these niche companies stayed basically the same. Over the years, factories, laboratories and plants merged. Their numbers have shrunk. Cost efficiency became the overriding factor. In industry, the analytical equipment buying decisions are made by purchasing agents rather than technically trained supervisors. As a result, equipment is bought, and vendors are expected to install. There is not as much follow-through. Equipment and systems are less integrated as they used to be. Development of operating software is usually done in-house or with their own consultants.

To address the needs, many of these technology companies have moved beyond the making of equipment and into training customers in the use of the equipment, consulting on chemical issues, environmental audits, monitoring and other professional services. I recommended that they expand their priorities toward selling consulting hours and contracting for projects, moving from being just a manufacturer to a consulting business.

They were able to expand in such a way as to show customers the connectivity of all equipment to each other. The by-product of being inside the plants was the uncovering of other needs, which resulted in the development and modification of other equipment to serve necessary functions.

During my work with a chain of credit unions, which were attempting to move further into the banking business, several priorities had to be examined, in order to expand the notion of core business.

We asked some key questions. Would small customers still come first? How do we compete with established banking companies? What kinds of additional services must we provide? Where do we find customers in previously under-served markets?

Having advised various independent banks in developing their strategic plans, I saw some common themes emerging. Each of the independents said they wanted to avoid falling into the pitfalls of the big bank holding companies, yet they really intended to grow very large. Achieving a healthy balance of strength, size of deposits and customer focus with the credit unions was the strategy. The planning process fostered a culture that was commensurate with their rich history and the assurance of plenty customer service, enough to draw customers away from banks that had gotten too big.

I worked with a large city airport system. Up to that point, large food service companies held the contracts, and the food was commonplace, predictable and offered little variety. With government bureaucracies being far too accustomed to awarding sole-source contracts, that practice precluded a food court format populated by subcontractors.

We identified a company that would serve as a managing agent. Though they operated restaurants, their charge was to build and oversee a strong network of subcontractors. Thus, a realignment of companies served to redefine the core business.

The mix of the products was based upon an objective panel of restaurateurs, hospitality industry veterans, hotel school faculty and other experts concerned with building teams that would supplant a sole-source contractor. The committee sought out companies that would bring new tastes and diverse restaurant concepts to the food court. We realized that participation in this high-profile enterprise would put many small businesses on the map.

The committee judged menu items, plans for restaurant operations and other aspects, followed by site visits to existing facilities. The recommended slate was presented to the city council for a vote. We proudly stated that 55% of the subcontractors were women and minority owned businesses. After achieving a winning vote, this coalition started serving at airport terminals, to great success.

Collaborations, partnering and joint venturing are the dominant trends in business today. The old model of a major contractor running most of the food service operation, with a smattering of subcontractors, was reversed, with the subs as a group holding the contract. In most cities, this food court model has created more food service revenue, and its participants have grown other locations in their expanded business. The localized menu items were now at the airports.

How Companies Develop Staying Power

1. Some companies stick around by default. Some are One Hit Wonders and have limited utility, not having what it takes to go the distance. Some companies live short lives because that's all they've got in them. Some stay around a little longer than they should have, not because they are doing right things but because they have just stuck around.
2. Many are needed for a particular niche. They don't try to be all things to all people. They have a specialized market.
3. Some show the potential to develop into a longevity company. They have made an effort to justify their niche, not just to fill it by default. They take pride in being the best in their area of expertise. Many do business with other quality oriented companies.

4. Some produce time-tested products and processes. They are good and plan to get better.

5. Some are willing to do the things necessary for growth. Products and processes only represent one-third of a company's picture. Growth companies take risks and address the other two-thirds on a regular, systematic basis.

6. Some amassed earned respect to continue in business. They dare to innovate. They have a commitment to quality improvement. They look outward, rather than focusing all resources internally. They view the products, processes and people as a wholistic organization.

7. Some make contributions beyond the bottom line. They understand other reasons for being in business besides the dollars. They make healthy profits, while creating the best products, being a learning organization, upholding standards and continuing to justify the leadership position.

Businesses cannot exist in a vacuum. They must interact with the outside world. They must predict the trends and master the issues affecting the climate and opportunities in which they function. This includes stimulating "outside-the-box" thinking, building customer coalitions and distinguishing your company from the pack.

Though companies try too much to emulate others, they must be seen, run and utilized as unique entities.

The future is met by journeys along a twisting and turning course, affected by what we choose to do and the priorities that we assign. Along the way, there are warning signs that we either recognize or pay the price later for overlooking.

Company futures are determined by choices that we make.

Chapter 4

BUSINESS RECOVERY AND REGENERATION
Lessons Learned from COVID,
Economic Crises and Other Setbacks.

B usiness recovery is much more than loans to tide things over. Businesses need strategies, plans and insights into the marketplace and their future role in it. They need to know there is a place for them in a changed landscape.

Businesses need what they already needed before the letdowns. Crises precipitate taking charge and moving swiftly.

No business can just get a loan to pursue a "more of the same" process. They need education on business growth, wise insights into new ways of looking at their companies and motivation to make necessary changes. They need more than fear to get through the crisis. They need mentorship and visionary help.

Moments of crisis carry with it moments of possibility. In times of crisis, business does what it should have done earlier: study, reflect, plan and manage change. Sadly, business adopts a "head in the sand" mentality when the crisis seemingly passes. Many rationalize that they dodged the bullet.

Signs are that our economy has somewhat recovered from the second worst recession in history. Many companies kept their heads in the sand during the economic downturn, fully intending to return to business as usual.

What the Pandemic Did to Business

In addition to the health effects, the COVID virus negatively impacted the economy, spurring a recession. The pandemic caused great dislocation in business.

Stopgap measures to recover business resulted in false starts, forced openings, forced closings and loss of customers. Those forced into shutdowns reported loss of marketplace, dislocation of clientele and forced spending cuts that harmfully impacted small businesses the most.

According to surveys, 50% of business owners believed that the crisis would pass within four months. As the pandemic and its economic implications got longer, the business failure rates increased.

54% of businesses closed short-term, and 47% were marked by unemployment. Declines were the highest in the hospitality industry, at 50%. Small companies generally had cash reserves to last up to two months.

Anticipated duration of the crisis played a huge role in the impact of COVID on business. In the first months, 72% of businesses expected to reopen in four months. After eight months, only 47% expected to recover and reopen.

70% of the companies expected to participate in the Paycheck Protection Program. As websites crashed, opportunities to apply reduced and funds dried up, less than 24% got to participate. Those denied the financial aid experienced bureaucratic hassles and an inability to verify access.

48% of workers in small businesses have their livelihood directly tied to the ecosystem caused by downturns during the pandemic. Many found new jobs, took stopgap jobs or gave up on careers.

Liquidity crunches with cash flow disruptions showed slower cycles in recovery. Small businesses employ 50% of workers. 43% of these businesses closed, and employment in them fell by 40%. This was the greatest shock to business and workers since the Great Depression.

Actions as a Result of the Economic Downturn

Many businesses suffered closures, losses, failed strategies and missed opportunities. Many workers saw career dreams dashed, lost career momentum and a reality that putting things on hold might encounter changed business dynamics.

Business happenstances during the pandemic period included:

- Broken teams and staffs.
- People dropping out of the workforce to stay home with children.
- Some companies cashing in on the pandemic.
- Disparity in the access to resources.
- Wasted time that could have been better allocated.
- Lies and misinformation that caused more fear and consternation around the system.
- New pockets of poverty among otherwise productive workers.
- Rationing of food and water.
- Food lines that drew many people who were not traditionally on the charity rolls.
- Spikes in online internet scams.

One important area of business that suffered the most was in customer service. When you heard the terms "contact-less" and "contact-free," I heard customer service sinking to new depths. Human interactions were minimalized, thus making the restoration of customer service more difficult on the back-end of the pandemic.

The longer that things were socially distanced had a direct impact on customer service and repeat business. The lost time and momentum negatively impacted the usage of people skills. The longer that businesses were closed did negative harm to the ability to quickly retool and reopen. Lost time impacted relationships that businesses were trying to build with customers and stakeholders before the pandemic hit.

Many businesses started adding COVID charges to their bills. Many cited increased cleaning and sanitation services, plus costs to purchase personal protective equipment. Many cited loss of business in other areas caused due to the pandemic, limited occupancy charges, paying workers when the business was closed and costs associated with re-launching businesses. Many claimed that rising food costs, expenses for shipping PPE, delivery charges, supplies and costs of finding new suppliers to make up for those who curtailed or closed. Necessitated COVID add-on charges.

Hidden fees are nothing new. Those who pay cable bills, healthcare statements and academic charges are often beset with recovery charges. Consumers who were also hit hard by the pandemic had to bear the brunt for pandemic charges.

$900 of the cost of a new car goes toward covering marketing and advertising costs of the automakers and dealers. During COVID, the auto industry ran more ads, addressing inventories they could not sell. The advertising message was targeted around re-starting engines and people taking road trips to recover from cabin fever experienced during the pandemic. The percentage of advertising associated with cars, hotels and travel increased. The auto industry thanked consumers for past business and encouraged them to buy more cars as a patriotic gesture.

Education was changed by COVID. Schools had to close, and students lost the personal touch of schooling experiences. Learning went virtual through distance computer platforms. Schools had to quickly produce content suitable for home service delivery, augmented by tutoring from parents. The quality, consistency and effectiveness of teaching techniques were put on the shelf while parents did their best to instruct.

Professional development was affected and altered during COVID. Business and professional organizations suspended live programs and went virtual, with varying levels of success. Many associations cut vital programs and services, met by losses in dues and participation. Conferences went online. Association member levels dropped off.

Stresses as a Result of COVID

Terms that we learned and utilized during the pandemic included essential workers, social distancing, lockdown, cave syndrome, drive-by rationing, super spreader, rolling blackouts, quarantine, essential business, response team, generation pandemic, zoom conferences, food insecurity, humanitarian crisis, distance learning, pandemic brain fog, PPE supplies, PEP loans, masking up, front line staff, preventable crisis, infra-structure, boil water notices, sanitizers, vaccine hesitancy, the New Normal, vaccine tourism, working from home, vaccine passport, zoom conferences and normalizing the trauma.

Medical terms that became familiar included asymptomatic, clinical trials, contract tracing, epidemic, flattening the curve, forehead thermometer, herd immunity, immunosuppressed, immune surveillance, incidence, incubation period, index patient, intensivist, pandemic, patient zero, presumptive positive case, respirator, screening, shelter-in-place, Spanish flu, symptomatic, vaccine and ventilator.

The mental health of citizens was stretched during the pandemic, exhibiting itself in:

- Fear of the future.
- Health and financial concerns.
- Family losses.
- Feelings of despair about the path forward.
- Feelings of something taken away from them.
- Worries about older family members.
- Concerns over furloughs and loss of work.
- Austerity politics.
- Humanitarian crises.
- Losses in self-esteem levels.
- Concerns about the changing scope of COVID relief.
- Worries over false restarts of the economy.
- Overly cautious about re-infusing into society.
- Stresses taking the forms of aggression or violence.
- Changes in energy levels, appetite, desires and interests.
- Sleeping difficulties and nightmares.
- Worsening of chronic health problems due to strains on the healthcare system.
- Worries over what's next and the next shoe to drop.

Coping with stress, grief and worry led many to virtual chat-rooms. Zoom counseling services served needs during the pandemic. Many people used isolation time to engage in creative endeavors, reconnect with old friends and show compassion for the hardest hit in communities.

Many community organizations that would otherwise help with the crises were themselves closed, limited and affected by the pandemic. These included churches, non-profit organizations, food banks, counseling centers and niche service providers. Other organizations stepped up to provide assistance, as many heart warming stories surfaced. In the worst of times, many sectors of communities came together and supported one another.

Virtual Conferences, the Age of Zoom

Zoom and other platforms had been used for teleconferencing and training for several years. As COVID forced most business to become distanced, the Zoom era was widely utilized.

Conferences, meetings, professional education and customer service began utilizing cubes of people to contribute to the business.

Some of the dynamics of early Zoom experimentation included:

- People lost attention fast.
- People logged in but did not always watch.
- Many dialed in wrong, did not understand the technology and caused problems for others who were doing their best to cope.
- It was easy to find fault with presenter quirks, fixate on backgrounds and lose interest too quickly.
- It became easy to criticize the content, get distracted with texts and other electronic devices and go down rabbit holes rather than focus upon meeting purposes.
- Many people expected remote conferences to be like the virtual events they saw on TV screens.
- Attention deficit affected how long people would stick with the teleconferences.

After Effects of the Pandemic

What happened in the post-COVID recession was that many businesses went under. In my professional opinion, 25% of those that faded away probably should have. A great many frail companies were not on firm foundations and had abdicated their abilities to improve and serve customer bases.

As fallout from the recession, many people were thrown elsewhere in the workforce. Many fell into jobs for which they were not suited. Many downsized, and out-of-work people were forced to reinvent themselves.

Many became "consultants" of one sort. Many fell victim to frauds and scams. Services and websites sprung up to capitalize upon the avalanche of new entrepreneurs. Some sites offered the platform to become a consultant with a national firm by paying them subscription fees. The already inflated world of "reputation management" websites lured people into buying advertising in order to create the facade of being a "consultant."

Distinctions must be drawn into three consulting categories (and percentages of their occurrence in the marketplace):

1. Vendors selling products which were produced by others. Those who sell their own produced works are designated as subcontractors. (82.99%)
2. Consultants conducting programs designed by their companies, in repetitive motion. Their work is off-the-shelf, conforming to an established mode of operation, containing original thought and drawing precedents from experience. (17%)
3. High level strategists creating all knowledge in their consulting. It is original, customized to the client and contains creativity and insight not available elsewhere. (.01%)

As one distinguishes past vendors and subcontractors, there are six types within the 18% which constitute consultants (with their percentages in the marketplace):

1. Those who still lead in an industry and have specific niche expertise. (13.5%)
2. Those who were down-sized, out-placed or decided not to stay in the corporate fold and evolved into consulting. (28%)
3. Out of work people who hang out consulting shingles in between jobs. (32%)
4. Freelancers and moonlighters, whose consultancy may or may not relate to their day jobs. (16%)
5. Veteran consultants who were trained for and have a track record in actual consulting. That's what they have done for most of their careers. (2%)

6. There is another category: opportunists who masquerade as consultants, entrepreneurs who disguise their selling as consulting, people who routinely change niches as the dollars go. (8.5%)

Clients are confused and under-educated, not able to discern the "real deal" consultants from the hype. That is why those of us who are veterans write these articles, speak and advise on best practices. Enlightened clients hire real consultants and get great value, as opposed to companies who fall prey to under-prepared resources.

New Ways of Learning from COVID

In Book 1 of this series, Chapter 25 was entitled "The Book of Acronyms: New Ways of Looking at Familiar Words."

Organizations are accustomed to looking at concepts and practices one way at a time. Clinging to obsolete definitions and viewpoints has a way of perpetuating companies into downward spirals.

By viewing from others' viewpoints on life, we find real nuggets of gold with which to redefine organizations. Companies that adopt new viewpoints and defy their conventional definitions will create new opportunities, organizational effectiveness, marketplaces and relationships.

As a Big Picture business strategist, I encourage clients toward adopting new ways of thinking about old processes, including those that brought past and enduring successes. Symbolic are phrase definitions that I created for familiar business words. I have created new acronyms for COVID, in order to help us visualize opportunities differently.

COVID: Community Operations Verify Intelligence Data

COVID: Collective Ongoing Virus Incidents Decreased

COVID: Corrective Organizational Visioning Involves Discipline

COVID: Corporate Organizations View Interests Differently

COVID: Courage Overrides Variance In Defeat

COVID: Creative Organizations Visualize Individual Decisions

COVID: Continuous Operations Validate Increased Demands

COVID: Coalescing Omnibus Value Intelligence Destiny

Lessons Learned Going Through Rough Times

Society must not be lulled into a false sense of security. The recovery phase of the recession has been steady and real. Much of the damage was done and will take years to fix. This could cause the next recession.

I believe that small business is resilient and will try its best to stay on firm grounding. Wise entrepreneurs will bring in qualified mentors, as opposed to wanna-be consultants. Cool heads will prevail, and small business will recover and prosper.

Small business has learned many lessons from the recession. While some will still fight change and adhere to the same processes that got them into trouble, I see great opportunities for forward-focused businesses.

Paying attention to quality can realize lower operating costs. Research shows they can be cut in half. Quality also affects customer retention, enhanced reputation, access to global markets, faster innovation and higher return on investments.

The biggest source of growth and increased opportunities in today's business climate lie in the way that individuals and companies work together.

It is becoming increasingly rare to find an individual or organization that has not yet been required to team with others. Lone rangers and sole-source providers simply cannot succeed in competitive environments and global economies. Those who benefit from collaborations, rather than become the victim of them, will log the biggest successes in business years ahead.

Empowerment, team building and other processes apply to formal organizational structures. Teaming by independents can likewise benefit from the concepts. There are rules of protocol that support and protect partnerships, having a direct relationship to those who profit most.

Professionals who succeed the most are the products of mentoring. The mentor is a resource for business trends, societal issues and opportunities. The mentor becomes a role model, offering insights about their own life-career. This reflection shows the mentee levels of thinking that were not previously available. The mentor is an advocate for progress and change. Such work empowers the mentee to hear, accept, believe and get results. The sharing of trust and ideas leads to developing business philosophies.

It's important to read beyond the headlines and remember that recessions are actually a normal part of the business cycle. Recessions do have a valuable purpose in that they clear away weak companies and force people to spend less and save more. While this recession appears to be lasting longer than a normal recession, history has shown we will eventually emerge to a new period of economic growth and the stock markets will eventually recover their losses and hit new highs.

Business and society have experienced eight recessions since 1967. While the COVID recession may seem "different" for various reasons, it is important to remember that recessions usually have "different" causes or related events new to our history.

Chapter 5

DIAGNOSIS AND TREATMENT FOR
BUSINESS SYMPTOMS AND CONDITIONS
Interpreting Healthcare Analogies to Business Success.

H ere are some definitions for key terms in medicine. They allow doctors, treatment specialists, laboratory personnel and the healthcare system to agree upon specific terms describing medicine. I then make business analogies to these same terms, in order to bring similar approaches to companies, service providers and the marketplace.

Each book in this series features Big Picture descriptions of business parts and processes. The goal is to look at the whole of business, then at the parts as they contribute to the whole and again at the Big Picture. Most niche business people took too much as small niches. As doctors advocate for proper healthcare, it is essential to look wider to the business health of companies and the customers they serve.

Diagnosis: The nature of a disease or the identification of an illness. A conclusion or decision reached by diagnosis. It is the identification of any problem.

The word diagnosis comes from the Greeks, where a diagnosis meant a distinguishing, or a discerning between two possibilities. In medicine, that corresponds more closely to a differential diagnosis.

Treatment, symptomatic: Therapy that eases the symptoms without addressing the basic cause of the disease. Symptomatic treatment is also called palliative treatment. To palliate a disease is to treat it partially and insofar as possible, but not cure it completely. Palliation cloaks a disease.

The Latin "pallium" referred to a cloak in ancient Greece and Rome and to a white woolen band with pendants. Pallium was modified to form "palliate," an adjective meaning "cloaked" or "concealed" and a verb meaning "to cloak," "to cloth," or "to shelter." Today, "palliation" implies the disguising or concealing of badness or evil and suggests the alleviation of the vile effects of wickedness or illness.

Treatment Plan: An electronic or paper document that describes the patient's individualized diagnosis, strengths, disabilities, problem behaviors, needs, long-range goals, short-term goals, treatment interventions and treatment providers.

Healthcare: Efforts are made to maintain or restore physical, mental, or emotional well-being especially by trained and licensed professionals.

Sign: Any objective evidence of disease, as opposed to a symptom, which is, by nature, subjective. For example, gross blood in the stool is a sign of disease, evidence that can be recognized by the patient, physician, nurse, or someone else. Abdominal pain is a symptom, something only the patient can perceive.

Symptom: Any subjective evidence of disease. In contrast, a sign is objective. Blood coming out a nostril is a sign, apparent to the patient, physician and others. Anxiety, low back pain and fatigue are all symptoms, and only the patient can perceive them.

Managed care: Any system that manages health care delivery to control costs. Typically, managed care systems rely on a primary care physician who acts as a gatekeeper for other services, such as specialized medical care, surgery and physical therapy.

Risk factor: Something that increases a person's chances of developing a disease. For example, cigarette smoking is a risk factor for lung cancer, and obesity is a risk factor for heart disease.

Remedy: Something that consistently helps treat or cure a disease.

Remission: The disappearance of the signs and symptoms of the disease. A remission can be temporary or permanent.

Health: As officially defined by the World Health Organization, a state of complete physical, mental, and social well-being, not merely the absence of disease or infirmity.

Health risk: An adverse health consequence due to a specific event, disease or condition. The health risks of obesity include diabetes, joint disease, increased likelihood of certain cancers and cardiovascular disease. All of these consequences are related to obesity and are therefore health risks associated with obesity. A health risk may be related to genetic conditions, chronic diseases, certain occupations or sports, lifestyle factors or any number of events or situations.

My Business Analogies to Healthcare Terms

Diagnosis: Looking at problems at solutions in waiting. Seeing marketplace shifts before they occur. Adapting companies to change.

Treatment, symptomatic: Addressing issues as their come up. Effecting as they go, with the view toward longer-range planning and strategy.

Treatment Plan: Fixing problems and aggressively planning for future growth, unexpected competition and marketplace imbalances.

Healthcare: Effectively run companies make the best use of their resources, including financial, intellectual property, perfected processes, valuable staff, loyal customers and growth strategies that last.

Sign: A business trend, challenge or opportunity that becomes evident. Often, the course needs to be changed, in order to take advantage of business growth.

Symptom: Increased competition, economic challenges, technological shifts and societal needs for products and services.

Managed care: A viable business landscape, where companies fine-tune their core business, produce products in the best manner, utilize top talent, exercise responsibility and develop business in an equitable way.

Risk factor: By spotting trends, the organization will not make the same mistakes. By adapting, each marketplace will be more creative, effective and profitable.

Remedy: The company or organization rendering the product/service sees itself as a champion of change, whereas competitors may fall the victims of change.

Remission: The problems tend to dissipate, and the opportunities to grow and measured success will multiply.

Health: The company realizes that it is in the right place to deliver products, is trusted to grow and succeed and creates paths for future growth.

Health risk: Business crises will occur, including market shifts, recessions and wrong missteps. By planning ahead of the crises, we can prevent most of them from occurring.

Results, Benchmarking, Measurements

Fundamental to strategic planning is that the goals and objectives be tied to measurable activities. Gaining confidence is crucial, as business relationships are established to be long-term in duration. Each organization or should determine and craft its own character and personality, seeking to differentiate from others.

Effective benchmarks must be applied to all aspects of the business: Core Business, Running the Business, Financial, People and the interrelationship of these five major business functions to each other.

Benchmarking usually shows that customer service suffers during fast-growth periods. They have to back-pedal and recover customer confidence by doing surveys. Even with results of deteriorating customer service, growth-track companies pay lip service to really fixing their own problems. Benchmarking for success is a factor of how diverse the company can and would like to be.

Diversity is an enlightened mindset that affects workforce dynamics, plateaus of professionalism, work ethics, jobs and careers. Diversity embodies what it takes to succeed long-term, by diversifying the product mix, marketplace and customer focus. Every company is affected by external influences, and a diversity of ideas directly leads to pro-active approaches and measurements of achievements. Diversity is about the organization being all they can be, attaining levels of standards and questing for more. The wider scope that one takes with diversity, then it will be more embraced and coveted.

Business Model is a term that some people use to criticize the business failures of others. Few businesses are ever modeled. Business models relate to financial structures only, which represent less than 10 percent of the importance of each business. Less than two percent of businesses have strategic plans, which are umbrella frameworks for success. Business needs to strategize and plan first, with models for each sub-heading (core business, running the business, financial, people, business development, body of knowledge and the Big Picture) are addressed.

Levels of Managing Past the Latest Business Crisis

1. Hype Doesn't Last. Gimmicks depend upon constantly changing audiences. They get your money and move on. Society unfortunately gravitates toward the "latest crazes," learns their lessons and then moves on.

2. Always Being Upstaged by Someone Else. The "number one at the box office" mentality is self-obsoleting. The week after next, someone else will be at their plateau. If the only value of a company or concept is this week's rating, then it does not merit your long-term trust, support and business.

3. Public's Tastes are Fickle. The streets are strewn with the bodies of "one hit wonders." Flash-and-sizzle concepts dare the public to knock them off temporary pedestals. The public tires of newness and prefers organizations with consistency and solidarity.

4. Artificial Measures Aren't Reliable. Sales statistics can be manipulated. Box office sensations do not always make projected profits. Thus, their reason for creation failed. Creative accounting and spin-doctoring are justifications and not strategic business concepts.

5. Deceptions Catch Up with Everybody. Truths are not always heard when first voiced. The public knows that much of what they're sold is "too good to be true." Only when it becomes their decision to seek and sustain the truth does it matter to them. Truths will always emerge.

6. At Some Point, We Become Accountable. Gimmicks run their course. Hard work and determination are the constant routes to success. As people see past the flash and sizzle, they move forward, and that's when they do their best work.

7. High Costs Cause Changes in Business. Overcharges, waste, neglect, hucksterism and mis-representation ultimately cost you and me. The high costs are tallied and, much to our chagrin, are passed along to customers, only until such time as customers stand their ground and refute these costs back to the vendors with whom they do business.

Chapter 6

TEAMWORK IS AS TEAMWORK DOES

T eams comprise people who work together toward common goals. Each member is responsible for contributing to the team, but the group as a whole is responsible for the team's success.

The biggest source of growth and increased opportunities in today's business climate lies in the way that individuals and companies work together.

It is rare to find an individual or organization that has not yet been required to team with others. Lone rangers and sole-source providers simply cannot succeed in competitive environments and global economies. Those who benefit from collaborations, rather than become the victim of them, will log the biggest successes in business years ahead.

Teamwork creates synergy, where the sum is greater than the parts. It supports a more empowered way of working, removing constraints that may prevent people from doing their jobs. Teamwork promotes flatter and leaner structures, with less hierarchy. It encourages multi-disciplinary work teams that can cut across organizational divides. It fosters flexibility and responsiveness, especially in responding to change.

Workplace teamwork pleases customers who like working with good teams, especially when the customer may be part of the team. It promotes the sense of achievement, equity and camaraderie, essential for a motivated workplace. When managed properly, teamwork is a better way to work.

These are the conditions for teamwork to occur:

- Compelling reasons for being organized.
- Direction for the team to participate.
- Have goals, with objectives and tactics.
- Structure of the team.
- Establish expectations.
- Supportive players and processes.
- Leverage team member strengths, as each brings skills and talents to the team.
- Shared mindset.
- Teams tackle more complex and substantive activities than do individuals.
- Internationally, team members comprise regional, cultural and other distinct qualities.
- The team has a culture unto itself.
- Benchmarking, evaluating and review of the team's activities.
- The chief functions of the team include trust, healthy debate, conflict management, commitment, accountability and focusing upon results.
- The top teamwork skills include planning, organizing, decision-making, problem solving, communications, persuasion and influencing, conflict resolution and feedback.

Research Statistics Regarding Teamwork
- 75% of employers rate teamwork and collaboration as "very important," though 18% of employees get communication evaluations at their performance reviews.
- 86% of employees and executives cite lack of collaboration or ineffective communication for workplace failures.

- 80% of businesses utilize social collaboration tools for enhancing business processes.
- 90% of employees and executives believe lack of alignment within a team impacts the outcome of a task or project.
- 39% of employees believe that people within their company could collaborate further than they do.
- 54% of employees say that a strong sense of community. Great coworkers, celebrating milestones and a common mission kept them at the company.
- 99.1% of employees prefer a workplace where people identify and discuss issues truthfully and effectively. 50% say that their organization discusses such issues.
- Organizations that communicate effectively are 4.5 times more likely to retain the best employees.
- 50% of positive changes in communication patterns within the workplace may be accredited to social interaction outside of the workplace.
- 33% of millennial employees want to have collaborative workspaces.
- 37% of employees say that working with a team is their primary reason for working there.
- 5.9% of companies communicate goals daily. 33% of employees said lack of open communication led to negative impact on employee morale. Businesses with effective communication are 50% more likely to have lower employee turnover.
- 27% of employees who leave within the first year describe feeling disconnected to the organization. 33% say the ability to collaborate with others makes them more loyal.
- 83% of professionals depend upon technology to facilitate collaboration. 82% felt that they would feel impacted in the absence of this technology. 49% claimed that they use mobile devices for collaboration.
- 59% experienced challenges while working together. 71% of millennial workers faced challenges, while 45% of baby boomers concurred.
- Knowledge workers spend 14% of their workweek in communicating internally.

- Improving internal collaboration could raise the productivity of interaction by 25%.

Team Building Training Impacts Companies

Team building must be part of the corporate Vision first, not as a series of exercises delegated to trainers.

Training is unfairly blamed and scapegoated for pieces of the organizational mosaic that Strategic Planning and cohesive corporate Vision should have addressed earlier. Trainers cannot reconstruct organizational structure, nor can other niche consultants.

Companies owe it to themselves to think and plan before launching piecemeal training programs. After carefully articulating and understanding direction, then training needs (including team building and empowerment) will stand a chance of being successful.

I recommend that team building be conducted as part of a company Strategic Plan, with top management participating. Companies must plan by predicting (rather than reacting to) strengths, weaknesses, opportunities and threats.

Professional development must be offered to every employee, including mentoring for top executives and up-and-coming young people. Education should show decision makers all phases of the organization and what it takes to succeed and grow, personally and as a team.

The following topics recommended to be taught to executives who wish to achieve longevity in business and success for their companies:

- Marketplace factors outside your company, how they can hurt or help your business.
- Generational work ethics and why young people need executive mentoring to "go the distance" in their careers, offering value to the company and profession.
- Understanding the value of conducting independent company assessments, other than the "bean counter" approach.
- Workplace literacy. Much of the work force does not have basic skills, nor reasoning abilities. They embrace technology, rather than ideas and concepts.

- Understand and celebrate diversity. This is a blessing, not a mandate.
- Accept and embrace change. Research shows change is 90% beneficial. So why do people fight what is best for them?
- Embrace what business the company is really in, why it stays in business, where it is headed.
- Know who plays a part in growth and how. This process is known as Visioning.

Encouraging Teamwork

Defining three terms will help to differentiate their intended objectives:

Collaborations: Parties willingly cooperate together, working jointly with others, especially in an intellectual pursuit. This represents cooperation with an instrumentality with which one is not immediately connected.

Partnering: This is a formal relationship between two or more associates. It involves close cooperation among parties, with each having specified and joint rights and responsibilities.

Joint Venturing: Partners come together for specific purposes or projects that may go beyond the scope of individual members. Each partner in the venture retains their individual identity. The joint venture itself has its own identity, reflecting favorably upon the work to be done and upon the partners.

I have observed the greatest successes with teams to occur when:

- Crisis or urgent need forced the client to hire a consortium.
- Time deadlines and nature of the project required a cohesive team approach.
- The work required multiple professional skills.
- Consortium members were tops in their fields.
- Consortium members truly understood teamwork and had prior successful experiences.
- Consortium members wanted to learn from each other.
- Early successes spurred future collaborations.
- Joint venturing was considered an ongoing process, not a "once in awhile" action.
- Each team member realized something of value.

These are the priorities in teamwork:

- Building good team members.
- Showing respect for each other.
- Benefiting clients and customers through shared resources and perspectives.
- Establishing and sustaining good communication with each other.
- Foster cohesion of the team.
- Encouraging innovation.
- Maintaining quality.
- Honoring promises made.
- Achieving efficiencies by an economy of scale.
- Encouraging team members to socialize and bond.
- Each player has the best interests of the team at heart.
- Recognize, reward and celebrate collaborative behavior.

The benefits for participating principals and firms include:

- Ongoing association and professional exchange with the best in respective fields.
- Utilize professional synergy to create opportunities that individuals could not.
- Serve as a beacon for professionalism.
- Provide access to experts otherwise not known to potential clients.
- Refer and cross-sell each others' services.
- Through demands uncovered, develop programs and materials to meet markets.

These are the truisms of teamwork:

- Whatever measure you give will be the measure that you get back.
- There are no free lunches in life.
- The joy is in the journey, not in the final destination.

- The best destinations are not pre-determined in the beginning, but they evolve out of circumstances.
- Circumstances can be strategized, for maximum effectiveness.
- You have got to give to get.
- Getting and having are not the same thing.
- One cannot live entirely through work.
- One doesn't just work to live.
- As an integrated process of life skills, career has its place.

Quotes About Teamwork, Collaborations, Partnering

"All for one, one for all." Alexandre Dumas

"Never ask that which you are not prepared to give." Apache law

Tsze-Kung asked, saying, 'Is there one word which may serve as a rule of practice for all one's life?" The Master said, "Is not Reciprocity such a word? What you do not want done to yourself, do not do to others." Confucius (551 BC-479 BC)

"Whose bread I eat, his song I sing." German proverb

"A chain is no stronger than its weakest link. Union is strength. United we stand, divided we fall." Proverbs

"It takes more than one to make a ballet." Ninette de Valois, choreographer

"What I want is men who will support me when I am in the wrong." Lord Melbourne, 19th Century British statesman

"There are only two forces that unite men: fear and interest." Napoleon Bonaparte

"When bad men combine, the good must associate. Else they will fall, one by one, an unpitied sacrifice in a contemptible struggle." Edmund Burke

"One man alone can be pretty dumb sometimes, but for real bona fide stupidity, there is nothing that can beat teamwork." Edward Abbey

"The finest plans have always been spoiled by the littleness of those that should carry them out. Even emperors can't do it all by themselves." Bertolt Brecht, German dramatist

"Everyone has observed how much more dogs are animated when they hunt in a pack, than when they pursue their game apart. We might, perhaps, be at a loss to explain this phenomenon, if we had not experience of a similar in ourselves." David Hume, 18th Century Scottish philosopher

Chapter 7

THE MASTERS OF REPURPOSING

Business in the Internet Age

The first known use of the term "repurposing" was in 1984. Its definitions and meanings include:

- To find new uses for an idea, product or process.
- Giving a new purpose or use to.
- Finding ways to change, adapt and take to a new dimension.
- To make more suited for a different purpose.
- To re-use for different or expanded purpose beyond its original intension.
- To re-use on a long-term basis without alterations.

Other words describing the concept of repurposing include: recycle, save, regenerate, re-apply, employ, exercise, exploit, harness, operate, direct, run, work, reprocess and remodel. Recycling takes usable items, including raw materials, and turns them into items that people can use.

- Repurposing involves compilations, reissues and highlights, including:
- New content juxtaposed with old content.
- Reissuing on different platforms.
- Combining with platforms that did not exist with the original issues.
- Adding new graphics, statistics, quotes and other data.
- Turning one product into a series.
- Writing about how the original product transformed into more.

Publications

Reader's Digest was founded in 1922 by DeWitt and Lila Bell Wallace. Each monthly issue was a compilation of material from other publications, including excerpts from books, short articles and pop culture tidbits. It was originally marketed by direct mail to teachers and nurses. At its peak, it had 30 million subscribers. In the 1950s, *Reader's Digest* developed a division to compile and re-release classic recordings. That activity is detailed in the next chapter, covering the repurposing of music.

Time Life Magazines began when Henry Luce was a reporter with the *Chicago Daily News* and the Baltimore News. In 1922, he and partner Britten Hadden formed *Time Magazine,* reworking articles from newspapers and including commentaries, forming the first news magazine. Luce carried on after Hadden's 1929 death, steering time and adding other magazines to the empire: *Fortune* in 1930, Life in 1936 and *Sports Illustrated* in 1954. His wife, Clare Boothe Luce, wrote plays and served in Congress. In the 1970s, *Time Life* developed a division to compile and re-release classic recordings. That activity is detailed in the next chapter, covering the repurposing of music.

Little Golden Books was founded in 1942 Georges Duplaix as a children's book subsidiary of Simon and Schuster. Bank Street College of Education's Writers Laboratory became source material for the books. One of its first releases, "The Poky Little Puppy," is still sold today and looks essentially the same. The company produced Little Golden records, tapes, toys, CD-ROMs and games. Some books were adapted from other children's icons, including Disney, Sesame Street, The

Muppets, Mister Rogers, Barbie, Power Rangers and youthful personalities. Ownership of Little Golden Books changed over the years, going in 2001 to Random House.

They Paved the Way for E-Commerce

Sam Walton became the youngest Eagle Scout in Missouri's history. He worked for J.C. Penny Co. as a management trainee, did military service in World War II and then took over management of a variety store. He established a chain of Ben Franklin stores, having 15 of them by 1962 and the Walton's store in Bentonville, AR. The first Wal-Mart superstore was opened in 1962 in Rogers, AR. When he died in 1992, the chain included 1,960 Wal-Mart and Sam's stores. In 1998, Walton was named by Time Magazine as one of the 100 most influential people of the 20th Century.

Sebastian S. Kresge was a salesman whose territory included several of the Woolworth stores. He decided to open his own 5-cent and 10-cent store, in 1897 in Memphis, TN, with a second added in Detroit. In 1912, the S.S. Kresge Corporation was chartered, with 85 stores. In 1962, the chain opened the first Kmart store in Garden City, MI, expanded to department store status. In 1977, S.S. Kresge Corporation changed its name to Kmart Corporation.

John G. McCrory opened his first 5-cent and 10-cent store in Scottdale, PA, in 1882. One of his early investors was Sebastian S. Kresge, whose Kresge chain of stores evolved into Kmart. At its peak, McCrory's operated 1,300 stores under its own name.

Frank W. Woolworth went to work as a store clerk. In 1873, he convinced his boss that a bargain counter he had seen in another store would work well in theirs. Overstocked and damaged goods were priced five cents. In 1879, Woolworth began a store of his own in Utica, NY, with a variety of goods priced at a nickel. He opened another in Lancaster, PA, offering goods up to 10 cents. Other stores were opened in Buffalo, Erie and Scranton. He rolled those and other acquisitions into the F.W. Woolworth Company in 1912. The Woolworth Building was opened in New York in 1913, then the city's tallest structure. By 1919, Woolworth had more than 1,000 stores. In the 1960's, the chain broadened into department stores, renamed as Woolco.

Eddie Bauer founded his first shop in Seattle in 1920 (when he was 21 years old), opening in the back of a hunting and fishing store. He expanded the line and renamed it "Eddie Bauer's Sport Shop." He developed heavy wool garments for outdoorsmen. He received more than 20 patents for clothing and outdoor equipment. In 1945, Bauer offered his first mail-order catalog. His principal business became manufacturing of clothing and catalog sales. In 1971, the company was sold to General Mills, who shifted the focus to casual clothing and expanded to 61 stores. The Spiegel catalog company purchased Eddie Bauer from General Mills in 1988. Eddie Bauer Home was launched in 1991, selling furniture, décor, linens and tableware.

John Wanamaker started working as a delivery boy at age 14 and entered the men's clothing business at 18. In 1861, with Nathan Brown, he founded Brown and Wanamaker, which became the leading men's clothier in the U.S. within 10 years. In 1875, he opened a dry goods and clothing business, inviting other merchants to sublet from him. In 1896, he purchased A.T. Stewart in New York and broadened the department store chain. In 1918, Wanamaker's stores piped music to each other, this innovation giving birth to commercial radio.

Leon L. Bean earned his first money at age nine, selling steel traps. He was an avid hunter and fisherman and in 1911 invented the waterproof boot. He prepared a mail-order circular, and by 1917 had enough money to build a boot factory. By 1834, the catalog grew to 52 pages. By 1937, sales surpassed $1 million.

Herbert Marcus, his sister Carrie and her husband A.L. Neiman founded a department store with women's clothing in Dallas, TX, Neiman-Marcus, in 1907. The store premiered the first annual fashion show in the U.S. in 1927. Men's clothing was added in 1929. Stanley Marcus joined the store in 1927 and became the CEO in 1950. He was responsible for massive expansion and innovations such as the Distinguished Service in Fashion Award, the first haute couture boutique to introduce weekly fashion shows, the first to host concurrent art exhibitions, the International Fortnight celebrations, his and hers gifts, holiday catalog and more. Stanley Marcus stood as a beacon for women's fashions globally.

Ward Melville created the Thom McAn brand of shoes, opening the first retail store in New York in 1922. The name was inspired by a Scottish golfer, Thomas McCann. By the late 1960's, Thom McAn was the largest shoe retailer, with 1,400 stores. The chain closed stores and began providing the shoes to other chains, notable K-Mart and Wal-Mart.

Ronald M. Popeil went to work in 1952 at his family's manufacturing company in Chicago. He sold his father's inventions to department stores, including the Chop-O-Matic and Veg-O-Matic. Since he could not carry enough demonstration equipment to all stores, young Ron filmed demonstrations. The next leap was to television, and the infomercial was born. He was known for using the phrases "slice and dice," "set it and forget it"," "slice a tomato so thin it only has one side" and "but wait there's more." In 1964, he formed his own company Ronco, to market his father's products and those of others. Ronco got into the production of record albums, compilations of hits from other labels. In 1993, Ron Popeil was awarded the Nobel Prize in Consumer Engineering for redefining the industrial revolution with his devices.

After Markets

Army-Navy surplus stores evolved into large retail chains. Max Gotchman opened a chain of Army surplus stores in 1937 in San Antonio, TX, and Austin, TX. It evolved into Academy Super Surplus and later Academy Sports & Outdoors. It is the fourth largest chain of retail sporting goods stores.

The market for used clothing and home goods grew into retail chains. Retail stores are operated by Goodwill Industries, Salvation Army and Disabled American Veterans.

Goodwill was founded in 1902 in Boston, MA, by Reverend Edgar J. Helms. The focus is on vocational rehabilitation for disabled persons. The Goodwill thrift stores in 17 countries (now known as Select stores) provide employment and community outreach. Customers get great bargains, make donations and further the outreach.

The Salvation Army was founded in 1865 by William Booth in England to respond to conditions stemming from the industrial society. In 1880, the U.S. branch was formed by George Railton. The Army has worked to serve those most in need, combatting forces of evil.

DAV was founded by Robert Marx in Cincinnati, OH, in 1921. Marx had been injured during his World War I service. A women's auxiliary was formed in 1922. Disabled American Veterans was given a federal charter in 1932. DAV provides benefits assistance, outreach, research and advocacy.

Many other thrift stores are operated by local non-profit organizations, churches, schools, hospital guilds and volunteer coalitions. With these popular retail concepts, along came auto superstores, furniture resale centers, clearance home goods locations, used record stores and used bookstores.

Founding of the Internet

On March 12, 1989, the World Wide Web was founded. Scientist Tim Berners-Lee invented the internet while working at the European Organization for Nuclear Research. The Web was developed to meet the demand for automated information sharing between scientists in universities and institutes around the world. The 21st Century is dominated by technology, from cell phones to wi-fi, from the internet to social media and modern adaptations of technologies of earlier centuries to commercial utilization. In 2004, Berners-Lee was knighted by Queen Elizabeth II for his pioneering work. There are now 4 billion Internet users worldwide.

The popularity of thrift stores spawned on-line variations. Ebay was founded in 1995 by Pierre Omidyarin as the Echo Bay Trading Group. The Ebay website facilitates consumer and business ecommerce via online auctions of goods. PayPal is a subsidiary. Peter Thiel founded PayPal, an online funds transfer system, with Max Levchin in 1996. He was the first outside investor in Facebook in 2004. He launched Clarium Capital, a global macro hedge fund, in 2005.

Amazon started as a used book outlet, as well as resource for independent publishers, authors and resellers. Jeff Bezos was born in Albuquerque, NM, and raised in Houston, TX, where he attended River Oaks Elementary School. As a child, Bezos spent summers at his grandfather's South Texas ranch, where he developed talents in scientific pursuits. He graduated from Princeton University and founded Amazon.com in 1994. Bezos was named Time Magazine's Person of the Year in 1999. He founded Blue Origin, a human spaceflight company, in 2000.

Technologies that Brought Us E-Commerce

Bill Gates was in the eighth grade when he bought a computer terminal and a block of time for use by the school's students. He wrote his first computer program on a GE system. He wrote the school's computer system to schedule classes. While studying at Harvard, he and Paul Allen established their own computer software company, Microsoft, with its first office in Albuquerque, NM. The company moved to Bellevue, WA, in 1979. Microsoft launch its retail version of Windows in 1985. He topped the Forbes list of wealthiest people several times. The Gates Foundation has brought philanthropy, compassion and vision to countless global initiatives.

Steve Jobs was 13 when he called on Bill Hewlett of Hewlett-Packard, asking for parts for an electronics school project. Hewlett gave him a job, working on the assembly line. While at Homestead High School, he met Steve Wozniak, a fellow electronics aficionado. Jobs worked at Atari and began attending meetings of the Homebrew Computer Club with Wozniak in 1975. Wozniak invented the Apple I computer in 1976. Jobs, Wozniak and Ronald Wayne formed Apple Computer Corporation in the garage of Jobs' home in Los Altos, CA. Apple II was introduced in 1977. Jobs became one of the youngest people to reach the Forbes list of America's richest people. The Macintosh was introduced in 1984. Jobs left Apple and founded NeXT Inc. in 1985. Jobs funded a company in 1986 that later became Pixar. In 1997, Apple bought NeXT, and Jobs came back as CEO. He shepherded company innovations, such as iTunes, the iPhone, Mac OS X and the Apple Stores.

Larry Page and Sergey Brin were Ph.D. students and teamed on a research project at Stanford University in 1996. They studied search engines and how they ranked websites. They created Page Rank and incorporated their company Google in 1998. By 2011, the number of visitors to Google surpassed one billion per month.

Michael Dell bought his first calculator at age seven and his first computer at age 15, an Apple II, which he disassembled to see how it worked. He sold newspaper subscriptions, thus amassing an understanding of demographic data. While a student at the University of Texas at Austin, Dell started rebuilding computers and selling upgrade kits. In 1984, he opened a company to sell personal computers directly. In 1996, he started selling computers over the Internet. The Michael and Susan Dell Foundation support children's issues, medical education and family economic stability.

Steve Chen, Chad Hurley and Jawed Karin founded YouTube, a video sharing website, in San Bruno, CA, in 2005. The original office was above a restaurant, and the first video posted was Karin at the San Diego Zoo. More than 100 million views per day have been realized, with videos uploaded by individuals and companies.

Mark Zuckerberg wrote a program called Facemash, while a student at Harvard University in 2003. Facemash attracted 450 viewers during its first hours online, as a website for students to communicate with each other. It evolved into Facebook, opened to public access in 2006. By 2010, it had 500 million users, making it the largest social network site.

Eric Yuan founded Zoom in 2011, having been a lead engineer with Cisco Systems and its business unit WebEx. The service started in 2013 and became a resource for teleconferencing, meetings, webinars and conferences. Consumers utilized Zoom during the coronavirus crisis, utilizing the service for school lessons, interactive concerts, religious services and family gatherings.

Search engines have included Google, Yahoo, DuckDuck Go and Netscape.

Transportation applications connect to companies who dispatch to independent drivers. These ride share services include Uber, Lyft, Cabify, Citymapper, Curb, Easy Way, Moovit, One Bus Away, Transit and local taxicab and mass transit providers.

Home care resource websites, including Bright Star, Care.com, Right at Home, Home Helpers, Synergy, LivHome, Home Health Resources, Evergreen Private Care, In Home Care, Family and Nursing Care, Kindred at Home, KC Home Care Senior Services, Hampton Home Care, National Care Planning Council.

Food delivery and restaurant takeout websites, including Door Dash, Uber Eats, Grub Hub, Postmates, Instacart, Chow Now, Go Puff, Delivery.com, Eat Street and Favor.

Grocery store and supermarket delivery websites, including Amazon Fresh, Google Express, Peapod, Publix Delivery and Curbside, Shipt Same Day Delivery, Amazon's Prime Pantry, Go Puff, InstaShop, Walmart Grocery, Dunzo, Instrcart and Beelivery.

Travel bookings websites including Expedia, Hotel.com, Priceline, Orbitz, Momondo, Hotwire, Agoda, Skyscanner, Travelocity, Google Flights, Kayak, Cheapo Air, Hopper, Flight Network, Vayama and booking directly through the airlines' websites. Travel websites for students include STA Travel, Generation Fly, Student Universe and One Travel Student Fares. Travel package websites for seniors include CIE Tours, Butterfield & Robinson, GeoEx, Globus, Tauck, Classic Journeys, Artisans of Leisure and Uniworld.

Business management, bookkeeping, payroll and tracking tools, websites including Paycom, Quick Books, Google Analytics, Bitly, Onpay, Gusto, Paychex, Xendoo, Bookkeeper.com, InDinero, Pilot, Xoom.

Social news and communities of interest, task and vocation: Facebook, Twitter, YouTube, Reddit, Instagram, Linkedin, Tumblr, WhatsApp, Messenger, WeChat, QQ, Tik Tok, Q Zone, Sina Weibo, Baidu Tieba, Snapchat, Viber, Pinterest, Line, Medium, Telegram.

Other popular websites and apps on the Internet include music resale, clothing online retailers, furniture retailers, online counseling, resume posting and dating websites.

Education Websites

Educational websites for kids include Sesame Street, Scholastic, PBS Kids, Cool Math, National Geographic Kids, How Stuff Works, Time for Kids, Starfall, Fun Brain, The KIDZ Page, Learning Games for Kids, Exploratorium, Nick Jr., BBC History for Kids, Highlights for Kids, Disney Jr., Old Almanac for Kids. Home schooling websites and learning resources include Share My Lessons, Simple homeschool, Ted-Ed, Khan Academy, Reading Eggs, NASA for Students, Exploratorium, Duolingo, Home School.com, Xtra Math, Steve Spangler Science, How to Smile, The Learning Network, The Activity Mom, Discovery Education, Power My Learning, Coursera/edX, Brain POP, K-12.com, Special Needs Home Schooling.

Homeschooling membership sites include Productive Homeschooling, Education.com and Enchanted Learning. Teacher share websites include Teachers Pay Teachers.

Sources of free homeschooling printable websites include Teaching Mama, The Chaos and the Cluster, Home Preschool Made Easy, Steam Powered Family, Math Geek Mama, Left Brain Craft Brain, Growing Hands-on Kids, Donna Young, Free Homeschooling Deals, Frugal Homeschool Family, 123Homeschool4Me, Blessed Beyond a Doubt, 1+1+1=1, Confessions of a Homeschooler, 3 Dinosaurs, This Reading Mama, Homeschool Share, Picklebums, Home Grown Learners, Kids Activities Blog, Living Montessori Now, Homeschool Creations, Every Star is Different, Teach Beside Me, Simply Vicki, Royal Baloo, Handwriting Worksheets, Montessori Print Shop, File Folder Fun, It's All You Do, Free Printable.com, Gift of Curiosity, Homeschool Encouragement, Making Learning Fun, The Crafty Classroom, Pinterest, It's All You Do.

Price Comparison Websites

Comparison and price quote websites are where you can view rates from participating companies. Some have real quotes, and others have estimated quotes. Many are lead generation based, and you will be contacted directly by companies selected to receive quotes.

Comparison shopping engines are channels containing product information from participating retailers, displaying the listings in response to customer search queries. This allows viewers to compare product listings, prices, shipping, availability and service from multiple retailers.

For merchants, these sites are for marketing, advertising and sometimes for placing orders. Comparison shoppers are ideal target audiences, as the websites look like virtual marketplaces. Customers have already made the decision to buy and are visiting these sites to gather information in order to make the most informed decisions.

For consumers, these sites work like site engines. For ecommerce businesses, the pricing strategies differ, and these sites are good ways for the sellers to test what the markets will bear. Mega-websites for price comparison include Rakuten, Google Shopping, Price Grabber, Shopzilla, Buy Via, Shop Savvy, Amazon Sponsored Products, Camel, Shopping.com, Idealo, Price Pirates, Bizrate, My Shopping Data Feed, Become, Bing Shopping Campaigns, Shop Mania, Yahoo Shopping, Pronto.

Specific industries have price comparison websites. Popular niche super-sites include online grocery shopping, pharmacies, insurance, hotels, travel, real estate, apartment rental, senior living, electricity and gas utilities, home services, car buying, medical informational sites and legal informational sites.

Online grocery shopping websites including Amazon Fresh, Walmart Grocery, Safeway Grovery Delivery, Kroger Click List, Jet.com, Vitacost, Peapod, Instacart, Fresh Direct, Shipt, Shop Food Ex. On-line pharmaceutical websites include Good RX, Single Care,

Comparison quote websites for insurance include Insurify, Gabi, Nerdwallet, The Zebra, DMV.org, Insurance Quotes, Smart Financial, Net Quote, Esurance, Value Penguin, Compare.com.

Comparison websites for hotels are where you can actually book hotel rooms at great savings. Those sites include Trivago, Kayak, Booking.com, Agoda, Hotels.com, Priceline, Hotels Combined, Expedia, Travelocity, Orbitz, Trip Advisor, Google, Hotwire and the sites of hotel chains. Booking websites for travel include Momondo, Expedia, Skyscanner, Hotwire, Expedia, Priceline, Orbitz, Agoda, Travelocity, Kayak, Cheapo Air, Google Flights, Hopper, Vayama and Flight Network.

Real Estate websites include Zillow, Realtor.com, Trulia, Redfin, MLS, HomeFinder, Craigslist, Homes.com, PropertyRecord.com, Movato, Open Listing and the sites of each real estate broker.

Apartment booking websites include Apartments.com, Vrbo, Air BNB, Sonder, Top Villas, Booking.com, Home Away, Flip Key, Hotels Combined, Homestay, RentaVilla, Agoda Homes, Quest Apartments, Trip Advisor Vacation Rentals, Blueground, One Fine Stay, Navasol, Interhome, Outdoorsy, Couch Surfing, Luxury Rentals and local booking websites.

Senior Living marketing, advertising and booking websites include A Place for Mom, ASBICO, Seniors Blue Book, Senior Living.org, Positive Aging Source Book, Air BNB of Senior Living, Aging in Place and websites of the companies operating senior living complexes.

Electricity and gas utility comparison websites include Simply Switch, Vault Energy Solutions, Choose Energy, Money Saving Expert, Bulb, Energybot, Save on Energy.

Home services marketing, advertising and booking websites and directories include Angie's List, Home Advisor, Google My Business, Yelp, Yahoo Local Listings, Facebook Ratings and Reviews, the Better Business Bureau, Houzz, Porch.

Online car buying sites include Carmax, Auto Nation, Carvana, Car Gurus, True Car, Auto Trader.com, Carfax, Tred, Ebay Motors, Cars.com, Vroom. Their features include prices, geographical location, time availability, user reviews, warranty information, insurance, financing, ratings, affordability calculator and vehicle history reports.

Medical and healthcare informational websites include Web MD, Kids Health, Net Doctor, Yahoo Health, Drugs.com, NHS Direct, National Institutes of Health.

Legal informational websites include LegalZoom, Public Resource.org, Responsive Law.org, Justia.com, Oyez.org, Timeshare Termination Team, Bensguide.gpo.gov.

Acronyms Used in the Internet Era

ATM Automated Teller Machine, Asynchronous Transfer Mode

BCR Bar Code Reader

BLOB Binary Large Object

B2B Business to Business

BVD Bradley, Voorhies and Day

CAD Computer Aided Design

CAT (scan) Computerized Axial Tomography

CD Compact Disc

COBOL Common Business-Oriented Language

CRM Customer Relationship Management

DES Data Encryption Standard

DSL Digital Subscriber Line

DVD Digital Versatile Disc

EBAY Echo Bay Trading Group

4GFourth Generation Mobile Telephone System

GIGO Garbage In, Garbage Out

HTML Hyper Text Mark-up Language

HTTP Hyper Text Transfer Protocol

IBM International Business Machines

INTEL Integrated Electronics

IP Internet Protocol

ISO International Standards Organization

ISP Internet Service Provider

JPEG Joint Photographic Experts Group

KPI Key Performance Indicators

LASER Light Amplification by Stimulated Emission of Radiation

MRI Magnetic Resonance Imaging

PDF Portable Document Format

POP Point of Presence
R&D Research and Development
SCSI Small Computer Serial Interface
SEO Search Engine Optimization
TIFF Tagged Image File Format
USB Universal Serial Bus
VHS Video Home System
VLAS Virtual Local Area Network
WPA Wi-Fi Protected Access
WWW World Wide Web

Realities of the Internet, Opportunities to Grow

1. Newness. As with fax machines and telecommunications, the uniqueness commands current attention. As the novelty wears off, higher standards will be set. New generations of usage for this medium will spend efforts and knowledge toward upgrading it.

2. Limited Audiences. People now on the net have the equipment, time and interest. Vast audiences who truly need the net's capabilities still need to be recruited. A word of caution: make recruitment customer-friendly. Too much pseudo-technology snobbery exists toward non-users, many of whom resist because they feel spurned.

3. There are many selling on the net. As time passes, fast-buck artists will move on. It is the responsibility of consumers to patronize reputable websites with solid products.

4. Customer Assertiveness. Shuffling customers off to websites only aggravates the situation and causes more confusion. Poor customer service should not be blamed on the Internet. Consumers must learn to demand their rights, stand their ground, insist upon personal service and utilize the Internet for informational support. Customers who do not assert their rights and continue to accept impersonal service deserve what they get or do not get.

5. Collaborations and Alliances. This communications medium can foster consortiums of individuals and organizations...for purposes of doing business and much more. This technology is a tool of the trade, not an end

in itself. How human beings interact with each other depends upon their abilities, willingness and attentiveness to do so.

6. Educational Advantage. They say that the internet is "the world's largest library." To date, it's more of a catalog. Educational institutions must open their contents, realizing their obligations to public education and community outreach.

7. Responsibilities. Those who make money, court public favor and must benchmark their progress in responsible use of this medium. Their right to stay in business is based upon how the public's only true "free speech medium" is upheld and upgraded.

Chapter 8

REPACKAGING, REPURPOSING, REISSUES AND COMPILATIONS OF MUSIC
History of Greatest Hits Records, Sets and Marketplaces.

F orty two percent of all records sold each year are reissues of originals and repackaged compilations. They are some kind of reissue, be they oldies, re-released albums, anthologies, greatest hits compilations, Christmas music, spoken word reissues and novelties.

The first recordings were on 78RPM records. They were bulky, breakable and limited the amount of music on each side. Record companies put multiple discs into sleeves and began calling them "albums," the terminology still existing today. Those albums started as collections of "sides" but became thematic. Further packaging enabled various-artist albums and collections of "greatest hits."

The two major labels went into research and development on non-breakable records that would play at slower speeds, with thinner grooves and more music on each side, producing a cleaner sound (without pops and scratches). The results were Columbia (owned by CBS) introducing the 33-1/3RPM long playing vinyl record in 1948 and RCA Victor (owned by NBC) introducing the 45RPM vinyl record in 1949. Why those speeds? They were combined derivatives of 78RPM, known by engineers as "the mother speed." Not surprisingly, today's CDs play at 78RPM, a technological updating of Emile Berliner's 1888 invention of the phonograph record.

The 1930s and 1940s were growth periods for the recording and broadcast industries. Along came other record labels: Brunswick, Decca, Capitol, Coral and jazz imprints. Movie studios got into the record business. Entrepreneurs brought Atlantic, King and other labels to showcase black artists and country music (two major growth industries attributable to the interrelationship of radio and records). Then came the international recording industries.

The 1950s saw exponential growth. There were more retail outlets for the music than ever before or ever since. One could buy music at every grocery store, department store and many unexpected locations. There was an industry of sound-alike records, sold at reduced prices. The result was that all families had phonographs, and music was going into cars via radio, thus stimulating record sales and thus encouraging other technologies to bring music into cars (emerging as homes in our mobile society).

The emergence of teens as the primary record buyers was fed by TV shows, increased disposable income and recording artists catering to younger audience. Due to broad radio playlists, there was ample airplay for every musical taste, and the record industry continued to grow. Independent record labels proliferated, as did recordings by local artists.

With the British Invasion of the 1960s came the reality of the international nature of entertainment. To package and market emerging modern music, media were implemented to make the best possible sounds and reflect the plastic portability of youth traffic. Along came music available on cassette tapes, then 8-track tapes. The music industry experimented with Quadraphonic Sound, and that experiment fell flat after one year.

At every juncture, there were transition periods in the adoption and acceptance of new media. For the first 11 years of 45RPM records and LPs being manufactured, there were still 78RPM discs on the market. Throughout the tape formats, there were still records. With the advent of Compact Discs, there were still records and cassette tapes on the market. To now rush to conversion of all music to digital downloads is short-sighted and stands to kill markets and after-markets for CDs that still have another 20 years to run.

Repackaging the Golden Oldies

With every technological shift in the presentation and distribution of recorded music came the opportunities to repackage past recordings into variations of the old packages and into repurposed variations.

Repackaging of recordings by popular artists put the hits into context. They adapted to the next technologies, allowing new listeners to hear great tunes. Often the albums included alternate tracks, B-sides of singles and other archival material. They sustained careers, drawing younger fans to the body of work.

Revival shows by vintage acts tour the country. TV reunions, fair/rodeo circuits, casinos and other venues have convinced entertainers to continue into longer careers than their initial chart hits. Golden oldies are ever-present on TV commercials, YouTube, Itunes and other file sharing media.

Melodies and hooks from classic tunes are integrated into contemporary music, no matter what the era. Familiarization with such sounds propels music fans to seek out the older recordings. Re-packagers know that money, nostalgia and music content inspire frequent visits to the vaults of sounds. Oldies keep on, as cash registers jingle at record rates.

In the 1960s, 1970s and 1980s, every major label put out its own reissue series, most of them back-to-back hits, re-enhanced for stereo, digitally re-mastered for better quality sound. Those include Columbia's "Hall of Fame," RCA Victor's "Gold Standard Series," Epic's "Memory Lane," Capitol's "Starline Series," Mercury's "Celebrity Series," Warner Bros. Records' "Back to Back Hits," United Artists' "Silver Spotlight," Musicor's "Startime," A&M "Forget Me Not," Arista "Flashback," Brunswick "Gold Series," Buddah "Radioactive Gold," Motown "Yesteryear Series," MGM "Golden Circle Series," Roulette "Golden Goodies Series," Philips "Double-Hit Series," King/Federal "Golden Treasures, Gusto and Old Gold" series, Polydor "Band of Gold," Stax "Double-Hitter Series" and others. For three decades, these catalogs were prominent in record stores and in mail-order catalogs.

ABC-Dunhill acquired masters from the vaults of Veejay, Duke, Swan, Del-Fi, Fraternity and many other independent record labels that came and went.

They were reissued on ABC's "Goldies 45" and "Treasure Chest" collectors series.

New York's Abkco Corporation bought the Cameo-Parkway stock, including the recordings of Chubby Checker, Bobby Rydell, Deedee Sharp, The Orlons. Abkco also reissued MGM recordings by Herman's Hermits and other groups.

Eric Records put out quality releases from small independent labels. Eric added stereo versions of the 45's, as home jukeboxes became a market for oldies reissues. In the 1990s and beyond, Eric produced "First Time on Stereo" CDs and "Hard to Find Records in Stereo" releases. Bootleg companies got into the act, including Trip Records. In the CD era, countries around the world copied tracks from other sources, thus making up mega-compilations releases.

In the 1960s and 1970s, several record companies put together compilations and sold them via TV advertisements. Such sets got customers collections of 45RPM hits in LP sets. They were advertised as comprehensive sets, at economic prices far less than buying all the singles from retail stores.

Record Label Custom Pressings

The first record label was Columbia, founded in 1898. To serve oldies after-markets, the label established Columbia House Special Products, whose compilations included "Swinging the Classics," "Italian Love Songs," "The World's Most Beautiful Music," "Remember How Great," "Best of the Hit Parade," "Good Times in Country Music," "Million Dollar Country."

It was Columbia who introduced the Greatest Hits LP record series. In 1958, Johnny Mathis was at his peak, and there was not enough material yet for a new album. Mitch Miller, head of Artists and Repertoire for Columbia, decided to put together Johnny's first few singles with B-sides and issued "Johnny's Greatest Hits." That album holds the record for longest stay on Billboard's Top Albums chart, nine and one-half years. After that Greatest Hits by other Columbia artists ensued, followed by second and third volumes still later. Columbia also launched its Harmony series for reissuing recordings at budget costs. This set the precedent for other record labels to follow suit with Greatest Hits albums and budget record series.

The second record label was RCA Victor, founded in 1901. RCA Victor had the largest inventory of Big Band era recordings, which spawned an endless supply of reissues in the LP, cassette tape and CD eras. Victor's budget record series was named RCA Camden, after the location of the record production plant, in Camden, New Jersey.

The third record label was Brunswick, founded in 1916 by Brunswick-Balke-Collender, a company based in Dubuque, Iowa since 1845, which manufactured farming and sporting equipment. Brunswick was sold to Warner Bros. Pictures in 1930, to Decca UK in 1932, to Columbia Records in 1939, with Vocalion established as the imprint label to press reissues.

The fourth record label was Decca Records, founded in the U.K. in 1932 and the U.S. in 1934. The first superstar was Bing Crosby, initially recorded by Brunswick and from 1934-1957 by Decca. In 1943, Brunswick and Vocalion were both sold to Decca, which then added the Coral, Kapp and Uni labels. All Decca labels were combined as MCA Records in 1973. Vocalion became the reissue label in the UK, and MCA began reissuing everything from the catalog in 1973, the same year that Elton John and Neil Diamond were turning out new hit records.

The fifth record label was Capitol. It was founded in 1942 by songwriters Johnny Mercer and Buddy DeSylva with record store owner Glenn Wallichs. Mercer supervised the early recording sessions, wrote hit songs and recorded many of his own. Capitol was the first major West Coast label to compete with the others based on the East Coast. Capitol had a strong country music division, produced children's records and streamlined distribution mechanisms. Capitol created a Library Production Music division, with the Capitol Hi-Q series being recognizable soundtracks and themes songs on 1950s and 1960s TV shows and movies.

In 1955, British music empire EMI acquired Capitol records and built the famous Capitol Tower in Hollywood to compliment its famous Abbey Road studios in London. Capitol released many international recordings plus EMI's Angel label, thus paving the way to Capitol's dominance in the 1960s British invasion recordings by The Beatles, Peter & Gordon and other groups.

Capitol-EMI released such hit compilations as "Do You Wanna Dance," "The Way We Were," "Death, Glory & Retribution," "Rock N' Roll at the Capitol Tower," "Only in America," "Unforgettable," "Happy Trails, Songs of the Great Singing Cowboys," "Great Country Stars Singing Their Biggest Hits," "Hillbilly Heaven."

CEMA was a record label distribution branch of Capitol-EMI. The name CEMA stood for the four EMI-owned labels it originally distributed: Capitol Records, EMI Records, Manhattan Records and Angel Records. Subsequently, several other labels were distributed, including Chrysalis Records, Virgin Records and Blue Note Records. CEMA was one of the largest record distribution branches. After a restructuring, CEMA was renamed EMI Music Distribution. CEMA Special Markets handled licensing of recordings by Capitol-EMI artists and also distributed jukebox singles throughout the 1990s.

Mercury Records was founded in Chicago in 1945. It aimed primarily at jukeboxes, had plants to issue recordings within 24 hours and rose the pop charts throughout the 1950s and 1960s. Mercury signed Patti Page as a top talent on the rose. Patti recorded many of her hits with her own voice on second, third and fourth harmonies. This followed the recording process of Les Paul and Mary Ford on Capitol, who sang all the voices ands overdubbed all the instruments. Andy Williams later recorded many multi-part harmony hits on the Cadence and Columbia labels.

Mercury began putting out greatest hits LPs in the 1950s, with titles like "Vocal Group Collection," "Original Golden Hits of the Great Groups." Mercury's budget label was Wing, and its jazz label was Emarcy. It had country, classical and children's divisions.

In the 1960s and 1970s, Mercury was a major lanel, with pop stars such as Brook Benton, Dinah Washington, Ray Stevens and Sarah Vaughn. In the rock era, recording artists included Manfred Mann, Spanky & Our Gang and John Cougar Mellencamp. R&B stars on Mercury included Kool & the Gang. After 2000, Elton John's albums and reissues were on Mercury.

Warner Bros. Pictures established a record label in 1957, as one of their top stars Tab Hunter was having hits on the Dot label. Warner Bros. actively recorded actors in their stable as singers with a teen pop bent. Warner Bros. also recorded soundtracks. In the 1960s, the label became a major source of hit recordings for the Top 40 and rock markets. Warner Special Products released many compilation sets in the 1970s, 1980s and 1990s.

Randy Wood owned radio station WHIN in Gallatin, TN. In the early 1950s, he founded Dot Records, doing the recording in the station's production studio in the evenings, with early artists including The Hilltoppers, Johnny Mattox and Billy Vaughn. In 1955, Dot moved to Hollywood, CA. Its recordings by Pat Boone, The Fontane Sisters, Gale Storm and others were backed by Billy Vaughn's orchestra. Vaughn also had a 20-year string of hit 45RPM singles and LP albums. Its subsidiary was Hamilton Records.

Labels Created Exclusively for Oldies Re-Packaging

Reader's Digest began in 1922 by gathering articles of interest and book excerpts, disseminating them in magazine format. At its peak, Reader's Digest had more than 30 million subscribers and had 30 international editions.

In the 1950s, with the advent of LP records, Reader's Digest started compiling great music and began releasing LP box sets. The first releases featured Big Band Era recordings, known for their high fidelity and greater sound quality than the previous scratchy 78RPM records from which they were re-mastered. Next came classical music box sets, easy listening compilations and Christmas collections.

With the advent of CDs, Reader's Digest became a prime supplier of re-released material in sets. Biggest selling titles included "Big Band Era," "Till the End of Time," "Original Hits of the Big Bands," "The War Years," "A String of Pearls," "Beautiful Melodies of Our Time," "Nature's Music," "Songs of Joy & Devotion," "The Gershwin Years," "Great Melodies From Great Musicals," "Melodies and Memories," "Music for Listening and Relaxation," "Tchaikovsky's Greatest Hits." Pop and rock sets published by Reader's Digest covered sets by prominent stars, plus such compilations as "Moments to Remember," "Legendary Singers of the 20th Century," "Country Sweet N' Sentimental."

Longines Symphonette was a pre-recorded classical music program broadcast nightly on many Mutual Broadcasting System stations from 1943-1949 and the CBS Radio Network from 1949 to 1957. The conductor was Macklin Marrow, followed by Mishel Piastro, concertmaster of the New York Philharmonic Orchestra. The Longines Symphonette Society was formed to re-issue recordings from the radio series. Longines records covered the gamut of classical music, opera, show tunes and easy listening pop music.

K-tel was founded in Canada in 1962 by Philip Kives. He named the company K-tel, as his record reissues were sold via television commercials, with viewers directed to phone numbers and mailing addresses to buy. In addition to records,

Kives sold the Veg-O-Matic, Miracle Brush and Feather Touch Knife, with the tagline "Wait there's more." K-tel record offers were compilations of the latest hits, with titles such as "Summer Cruisin," "20 Power Hits," "Disco Rocket," "Goofy Greats," "Night Moves," "Super Bad."

Bear Family Records was founded by Richard Weize in 1975. Bear Family specialized in extensive box sets covering major artists. Compilations included "Precious Years," "Bakersfield Sound," "Rootin' Tootin' Santa," "She's Selling What She Used to Give Away," "Plug It It, Turn It Up, Electric Blues," "Banana Split For My Baby," "Autumn Leaves," "Blues Kings of Baton Rouge" and the 52-disc set, "History of Pop Music."

Rhino was founded in 1978 by Harold Bronson and Richard Foos. It started in Foos' record shop, where customers requested rare novelty titles. Rhino started to compile the novelty records into LP records. Then, Rhino acquired catalogs of records, getting into oldies compilations at the dawn of the CD age in 1984. Rhino partnered with major labels to reissue Greatest hits and specialty compilations, ultimately taken over by Time Warner in 1998.

Tele House was a telemarketing label owned by Roulette Records in the 1970s. Its releases included "Greatest Hits of the Century," "Love Italian Style," "Country Style," "Country-Pop," "Polka Party," "Greatest Musical Masterpieces," "Love Continental Style," "Greatest Hits of the War Years," "No. 1 Hits of the 60s," "Dance, Dance, Dance," "Treasury of Golden Classics," "Greatest Hits of the 50s and 60s" and "Treasury of the World's Greatest Waltzes." It was sold to Adam VIII, Ltd., another reissue company. Adam VIII releases included "Heavy Hits," "Every Artist Has a Song," "Soul Train Super Tracks," "Rock On," "Easy Listening," "Feelings," "Disco Party," "Rock is Here to Stay," "Disco Hustle."

Sessions was the record label arm of Audio Research, located in Chicago. Their multiple-record sets were pressed by the major labels. Sessions compilations included "Freedom Rock," "Solid Gold," "Senior Prom," "Cruisin," "Freedom," "Secret Love," "Hot Rod Classics," "Memory Lane," "Rock Revival," "Cosmic Dreams."

Tee Vee Records was founded in 1978. Its compilations included "Midnight Fire," "Disco Kings and Queens," "Candlelight and Wine Album," "Greased Lightning," "Cutting Loose," "Hit Action," "Got a Feeling," "Superstar Country," "Disco Heat," "Just For Laughs."

Continental House released "Greatest Love Songs of the Century." Jeitco Concepts Incorporated released "Lovin' Fifties" and "Fathers and Sons." Candlelite Music produced "Bright Lights and Country Music."

Charly Records issued such compilations as "One Hit Wonders." Rare Bird Records released its "Memories of the Past" series. Savoy Records released "The Roots of Rock N' Roll." Dynamic House released "Country Love" and "Great American Songbook, Ladies of Song."

Heartland Music released such popular sets as "Magic Moments," "Always," "The Fabulous Fifties, The Wonderful Years," "Country Love," "Slow Dancing," "Back to the 50s," "They're Playing Our Song," "Easy Listening Gold," "Love Songs."

Starland Music released such record sets as "Lost in Love," "Last Kiss," "42 Original Hits," "Forever Young," "Love Beat," "One Hit Wonders of the 70s," "Rockin' USA," "40 Summer Fun Hits," "Good Times Rock & Roll."

Good Music Record Company releases included "White Cliffs of Dover," "Sioux City Sue," "Rare Gold," "Over There," "A 1950s Christmas," "Great Instrumental Hits."

Brookville Records released such sets as "Turn Back the Hands of Time," "Sentimental Journey," "100 Great Hits of the 30s and 40s," "At the Hop," "32 Sound Alike Hits," "English Cats & Others," "Leaders of the Pack," "Treasures of Great Faith," "Rock and Roll Heaven," "Elvis in Hollywood," "The Sound of Philadelphia," "The Great Groups."

Time Life got into music compilations in the rock era. Their compilation sets included "Singers & Songwriters," "The Rock N' Roll Era," "Smooth Soul," "Instrumental Favorites," "Sounds of the Seventies," "Legends Do It Again."

Sony-BMG Music Group issued the "16 Most Requested Songs" series for major artists. Other releases included "Silence is Golden," "Legacy Recordings." Direct Source released such archival CDs as "Soul Fever." Sony-BMG released popular material from Columbia and RCA Victor on CDs from the 1990s forward.

Cover record labels included Value, Tops, Broadway, 18 Big Hits, Bravo, Hit, Gateway, Gilmar, Promenade, Waldorf. Tops Records was a Los Angeles-based record label owned by Tops Music Enterprises, both founded in 1947 by Carl L. Doshay and Sam Dickerman. After a prolific and profitable run, Tops merged with PRI Records in 1958, which in turn, sold to a group of investors in 1960, then went bankrupt in about 1962. Its assets were sold to Pickwick Records, a label that had been its main competitor throughout the 1950s Pickwick's assets were purchased by PolyGram Records in the late 1970s. In 1990, Combined Artists acquired the Tops catalog.

Reissue record labels included Eric, Collectables, Underground. Discount record labels included Royale, Hallmark, Silvertone, Vocalion, RCA Camden, Columbia Harmony, Metro. The appetite for re-released music on CDs spawned marketers in other countries. Coming along during the internet age were labels such as Marginal, Not Now, Regency, Master Piece, Stomper Time, Reel to Reel, Gone Beat, Sparkletone, Golden Lion, Crypt.

Hank Moore with sets of repurposed music collections. 42% of all records sold each year are reissues and repackaged compilations of golden oldies, greatest hits and retrospectives.

Chapter 9

NAMING COMPANIES, PRODUCTS AND NICKNAMES

N aming applies to companies, brands and products. There are company legal names and monikers for the products, services and marketplaces served.

Companies are named for the simplest of purposes, often for ease and recognition factor. Companies should create monikers that let customers clearly know what they do, or at least make the public curious to learn more.

These steps are recommended on how to name a product:

1. Accurately describe what the product is.
2. Make it easy to spell and pronounce.
3. Combine words to create a compound word.
4. Make it short and memorable.
5. Utilize metaphoric logic to include symbols.
6. Acronyms of terms create unique names.
7. Use nouns and verbs.

8. Chose terms that inspire emotional responses.
9. Embrace your target markets.
10. Contextualize the name.
11. Test the name, its usage and adaptations.

Everything we are in business stems from what we've been taught or not taught to date. A career is all about devoting resources to amplifying talents and abilities, with relevancy toward a viable end result. Failure to prepare for the future spells certain death for businesses and industries in which they function.

These are the marks of building upon early business activity and moving forward to the next plateaus:

- Personal abilities, talents and working style.
- Resources being developed.
- Relationships and interaction with other people
- Ability to rise above circumstances beyond your control.
- Timing.

A rich and sustaining Body of Work results from a greater business commitment and heightened self-awareness. None of us can escape those pervasive influences that have affected our lives, including music and the messages contained in songs. Like sponges, we absorbed the information, giving us views of life that have helped mold our business and personal relationships.

Good company names ring true to company values, offer something for the marketplace to aspire and differentiate each company from the others.

The best company names are clear and direct, without trite jargon. Business is a mirror of life and offers opportunities to free enterprise. Many of the most respected corporate names have clarity and long shelf lives. Often, the great names ring new meanings into old words, phrases and ideas.

Here are the characteristics of good company names and, thus, company philosophy:

- Focus upon the customer.
- Honor the employees.

- Show business as a process, not a quick fix.
- Portray their company as a contributor, not a savior.
- Clearly defines their niche.
- Say things that inspire you to think.
- Compatible with other communications.
- Remain consistent with their products, services and track record.

How Companies Got Their Names

Here are examples of how memorable company names (and strategies) evolved:

3M stems from the company's original name, Minnesota Mining and Manufacturing Company.

7-Eleven. Convenience stores, originally called U-Totem, renamed in 1946 to reflect their newly extended hours, 7:00 a.m.-11:00 p.m.

Adobe was named after the Creek that ran behind co-founder John Warnock's house.

Amazon symbolizes a larger volume of potential sales than with a single bookstore.

Arby's stands for the initials of its founders, the Raffel brothers.

Arm and Hammer represents the strength of the Vulcan, the Roman god of fire and metal working, adopted from the Vulcan Spice Mills.

Atari was adapted from a Japanese word when the player's pieces are in danger of being captured in the game Go.

Audi was adapted from the Latin for the last name of its founder, August Horch.

Bridgestone was named after founder Sojiro Ishibashi. His last names translates to "bridge of stone."

Canon was named after Kwanon, the first camera produced by Precision Optimal Instruments Laboratories.

Coca-Cola was named for the cola leaves and kola nuts, which were originally used in the flavoring of the soft drink.

Comcast comes from the words "commercial" and "broadcast."

ConocoPhillips is shortened from the merger of the Continental Oil Company and Phillips Petroleum Company.

CVS originally stood for Customer Value Stores.

Ebay was originally part of the Echo Bay Technology Group. EchoBay.com was taken by a mining company. Thus, the shortened designation to Ebay.

Hasbro is short for the name of its founders, brothers Henry and Halel Hassenfeld.

H&R Block was founded by Henry W. Bloch and Richard Bloch, who changed the spelling in order to avoid mispronunciation.

IBM stems from the company's original name, International Business Machines.

Ikea a composite of the first letters in the Swedish founder's name plus the first letters of names of the property and village in which he grew up: Ingvar Kamprad Elmtaryd Agunnaryd.

Intel. Robert Noyce and Gordon Moore initially incorporated their company as NM Electronics. Intel came by using the initial syllables from INTegrated Electronics.

JVC stands for the Japan Victor Corporation.

Kia translates as "rising from Asia" in Hanji.

Lego comes from the Danish "leg godt," which means "play well."

Mattel comes from the names of its founders, Harold Matson and Elliot Handler. Mattel's Barbie Doll was named after Handler's daughter.

Nabisco is shortened from the original name, National Biscuit Company.

Nikon was shortened from the original Japanese name Nippon Kogaku, which means Japanese Optical.

Nintendo comes from the Japanese name Nintendou, which translates to "entrusted heavens."

Nissan was abbreviated from the original name Nippon Sangyo, which translates as "Japan Industries."

Nokia was founded as a wood pulp mill that later produced rubber products in the city of Nokia, Finland.

QVC stands for quality, value and convenience.

Pepsi Cola was named from the digestive enzyme pepsin.

Reebock is named after an African antelope, the rhebock.

SEGA started as Service Games of Japan, which began by importing pinball machines to American military bases in Japan.

Sharp was named for the company's first product, the ever-sharp pencil.

Skype was originally Sky-Peer-to-Peer, shortened to Skyper, then to Skype.

Sony came from the Latin word "sonus," meaning sound. It was chosen in order to be pronounced in multiple languages.

Sprint was an acronym for the Southern Pacific Railroad Internal Communications.

Starbuck's was inspired by a character in "Moby Dick," the book written by Herman Melville.

Taco Bell was named in honor of founder Glen Bell.

Verizon is a combination of the Latin word veritas (truth) and horizon.

Virgin Records was the name suggested to founder Richard Branson because they were new at the record business.

Volkswagen. Ferdinand Porsche wanted to produce a car that was affordable, the Kraft-Durch-Freude-Wagen (German phrase for people's car).

Walmart was a modification of the name for Sam Walton's Five and Dime stores, expanded into supercenters.

Wendy's was named Dave Thomas after his daughter Melinda, who used Wendy as a nickname.

How Some Cities Got Their Names

Azusa, CA was a made-up name for the town in California, symbolizing that it has everything from A to Z, in the USA.

Charlotte, North Carolina's largest city, gets its name from German Princess Charlotte-Mecklenburg-Sterlitz, best remembered as Queen consort of British King George III. Early settlers named the city in her honor, which is why Charlotte still has the nickname "the Queen City."

Chicago, IL came from the French pronunciation for shikaakwa, which means "wild garlic" in the Miami-Illinois language.

Minneapolis, MN: In 1852, a schoolteacher combined the Sioux word mni for "water" with the Greek word polis for "city," paying tribute to the town's lakes.

San Antonio, TX: Spanish missionaries and explorers came to what is now San Antonio on June 13, 1691, feast day of Saint Anthony of Padua, naming their settlement in his honor.

Seattle, WA gets its name from an English version of the name of Si'ahl, a Duwamish chief who was a valuable ally to the area's early white settlers.

Truth or Consequences, NM was named for a popular radio quiz show, hosted by Ralph Edwards.

Topeka, KS, the capitol city, has a tasty name. The word "Topeka" comes from the local Kansa and Iowa term for "to dig good potatoes." The potatoes in question were prairie potatoes, a staple of Native American diets that is said to taste a bit like turnips. According to city founder Fry W. Giles, early white settlers picked the name for the city because it was "novel, of Indian origin, and euphonious of sound."

Waco, TX was named after the Waco Indian tribe, as was radio station WACO.

Nicknames

Nicknames are warm, light-hearted or endearing. Some are humorous. They note and respect people. They add to the image of the people who are noted. They celebrate accomplishments, character and personality.

Some nicknames are easy to remember. Others call attention to qualities and recognize creative attributes. Some nicknames are extensions of the given name.

Other comparable terms are moniker, pseudonym, epithet, byword, sobriquet, pet name, nom de plume, stage name, assumed name, label and tag.

Some product names, many of them trademarked, have become generics. These include jacuzzi, teflon, crock-pot, Kleenex, chapstick, Styrofoam, q-tips, popsicle, Google, windbreaker, hoodie, dumpster, GED, scotch tape and Sharpie.

Mac is a nickname for Macintosh computers. Kleenex is a line Kimberly-Clark facial tissues. Chevy is a nickname for the automobile Chevrolet. Coke is the abbreviation for Coca-Cola. Alexa and Siri are voice activated devices.

Nicknames for institutions:

The House That Ruth Built, Yankee Stadium.
Wally World, Walmart.
The Pentagon, U.S. Department of Defense.
The Magic Kingdom, Disneyland.
Tinseltown and La-La Land for Hollywood, CA.
The Great Wen and The Smoke for London, England.
City of Lights and City of Love for Paris, France.

Big Apple, City That Never Sleeps. Gotham and City of Dreams for New York City.

City of Angels, Double Dubuque and L.A. for Los Angeles, CA.

The Windy City, Chi-Town and Chicagoland for Chicago, IL.

Bayou City, H-Town, Clutch City and Magnolia City for Houston, TX.

City of Brotherly Love and Sisterly Affection for Philadelphia, PA.

The Big Easy for New Orleans, LA.

Sin City, What Happens Here Stays Here, City of Lost Wages for Las Vegas, NV.

The Motor City and Motown for Detroit, MI.

Athens of the South, Smashville and Music City for Nashville, TN.

Bluff City and Home of the Blues for Memphis, TN.

City by the Bay, Frisco, Paris of the West, Golden Gate City for San Francisco, CA.

The Magic City for Miami, FL.

Biggest Little City in the World and Neon Babylon for Reno, NV.

The Big Pineapple and Pacific Diamond for Honolulu, HI.

Crossroads of America, Indy, Circle City, Naptown and Railroad City for Indianapolis, IN.

Dogwood City, The Big Peach and Badstreet USA, for Atlanta, GA.

The Golden Door, The Sixth Borough and Wall Street West for Jersey City, NJ.

Camp David is the presidential retreat in Maryland, named by President Dwight D. Eisenhower in honor of his grandson David. It was previously named Shagri-La by President Franklin D. Roosevelt.

30 Rock is an office complex located at 30 Rockefeller Plaza in New York City.

The Empire State Building in New York stood for 40 years as the world's tallest building.

Generic nicknames for business leaders include top banana, boss, big kahuna, kingpin, top dog, bigwig, kingfish and big shot.

Nicknames for prominent business leaders include:

Uncle Walt and Retlaw Elias Yensid, Walt Disney

Trey Gates, William Henry Gates III

Sage of Omaha, Warren Buffett

Crazy Henry, Henry Ford

Hustler Walton, Sam Walton

Doc Rockefeller, John D. Rockefeller

Sonny and World's Greatest Womanizer, Howard Hughes

Colonel Sanders, Harland David Sanders

Patron Saint of Libraries and Star-Spangled Scotsman, Andrew Carnegie

Aleck, Alexander Graham Bell

The Wizard of Menlo Park, Thomas Edison

Nicknames for prominent public figures include:

First Lady of the World, Eleanor Roosevelt

Lady Bird, Claudia Taylor Johnson

Jackie O, Jacqueline Bouvier Kennedy Onassis

The Squire of Hyde Park and Houdini in the White House, Franklin D. Roosevelt

Give 'Em The Haberdasher, Harry Turman

Ike, Dwight D. Eisenhower

Crash Kennedy and J.F.K., John F. Kennedy

Landslide Lyndon and L.B.J., Lyndon B. Johnson

Slick Rick, Red Hunter and Tricky Dick, Richard Nixon

The Gipper, Jelly Bean Man and Dutch, Ronald Reagan

Dubya, George W. Bush

The British Bulldog, Winston Churchill

America's poet laureate, Robert Frost

M.L.K., Dr. Martin Luther King Jr.

Nicknames for celebrities include:

King of Hollywood, Clark Gable

Queen of Comedy, Queen of the B Movies and First Lady of Television, Lucille Ball

First Lady of Film, Bette Davis

The Little Tramp, Charlie Chaplin

Missy, The Queen and Best Actress Who Never Won an Oscar, Barbara Stanwyck

Old Ski Nose, Bob Hope

The Duke, John Wayne

Redd Foxx, John Elroy Sanford

The most trusted man in America, Walter Cronkite

America's oldest teenager, Dick Clark

Mr. Radio, Casey Kasem

J-Lo, Jennifer Lopez

Bogey and Baby, Humphrey Bogart and Lauren Bacall

King of Late-Night, Johnny Carson

Nicknames for sports figures include:

The Sultan of Swat and The Great Bambino, Babe Ruth

The Greatest, Muhammad Ali

Broadway Joe, Joe Namath

Joltin' Joe and The Yankee Clipper, Joe Dimmagio

The Baltimore Bullet, Michael Phelps

The Dream, Hakeem Olajuwon

The Commerce Comet and The Mick, Mickey Mantle

Tiger Woods, Eldrick Woods

Pistol Pete, Pete Maravich

Recap on Names, Labels

From experience, I learned the value of:

- Using specific, imaginative language to express ideas.
- Saying what you mean and meaning what you say.
- Calling the elephant what it really is.
- Writing for the eye is different from writing for the ear.
- Not settling for trite expressions, slang jargon and other people's quotes.
- Taking the time to educate people on subtle nuances and meanings of words.
- Believing that listeners and readers are more intelligent than others might believe.
- Using vocabulary that expresses thoughts and rises to higher levels.
- Challenging people to read new meanings into old words, phrases and ideas.
- Compelling people to discern ideas for themselves, based upon insights and ideas.

In business (a mirror of everyday life), terms are used interchangeably and out of context. The public doesn't discern differences. With the passage of time, as people and companies "market the hype," they begin to believe the blurred usages of expressions they use.

Thus, improper semantics perpetuate in the mass culture. Constituents accept what they hear. If they hear it enough times, it must be true. They believe what they are familiar with. Getting them to modify familiar patterns is difficult but still must be done. Here are some cases in point:

- Retailers offer "service" as an enticer to close sales of products. Sales support and follow-p customer service are light years away. Whereas, they'll say anything to make a sale, true-quality customer service is presently at an all-time low. There are many tiers of service, with service to make the sale the lowest rung on the ladder.

- Business "consultants" often misrepresent what they do. Accounting firms believe themselves to be full-scope business advisors and sell themselves as such. Training companies tell clients that they also conduct strategic planning and consulting, believing all of those professional disciplines are the same thing.

- There are many differences in business. Sales and marketing are not the same thing. Advertising and public relations are different services. Financial projections do not constitute business planning. Sales quotas do not produce an empowered staff. Edicts by management do not directly lead to behavioral modification. Selling more products does not solve the manufacturing and distribution problems. Career workers and seasoned professionals are different breeds. Grumbling by workers does not constitute discontent and mutiny.

- People place labels on everything and everybody, without distinguishing the subtle differences. People and companies believe the labels, without looking into the subtle nuances. All differences become opportunities to educate each other about the subtle nuances of labels, terms, phrases and categories.

Chapter 10

CODES, CATEGORIES AND STANDARDS

C odes and labels are terminology or characteristic idioms of a special activity or group. Most terms have particular meaning within specific industries. A driving force in the creation of codes is precision and efficiency of communication, when a discussion must easily range from general themes to specific topics.

Codes enrich everyday vocabulary with meaningful content and can potentially become catchwords themselves. They allow greater efficiency in communication among those familiar with it, a benefit in that it raises the threshold of comprehensibility for outsiders. Jargon usually means the specialized language used by people in the same work or profession. Internet advertising jargon includes terms such as "click through" and "page view." This can also refer to language that uses long sentences and hard words.

Codes encompass professional language, professional linguistic culture, professional jargon, formal speech style and functional styles. They are enriched in their usage by vocabulary, grammar and phonetics. Formal business style is characterized by conciseness and economical use of language means.

Most codes are symbolic of standards. There are seven levels of standards:

1. No Standards. Either too young to know better or do not choose to develop further value systems. This is the crossroads…those who advance further will experience success in life.

2. Standards Held by Those with Whom We Interface. When we do business with them, we observe their values, which is one of the tenets of total quality management. These standards include values of people in positions of authority, caretakers of activities (such as public officials) and those with whom we must presently associate for business reasons. We may not agree with their values but understand how to work within them.

3. Basic Teachings. These are lessons that we learned or have assimilated from parents, teachers, friends and community resources. Periodically, these lessons need to be re-examined, updated and reapplied to current life circumstances.

4. Learning by Example, Trial, Error and Life Skills. There is no substitution for experience.

5. Community Standards, Etiquette, Common Decency. When in Rome, we behave as the Romans do. Etiquette is sophisticated and must be mastered over time. If it's not the right thing to do, then a person has some real ethical considerations. By this stage, one is committed only to doing the right thing, doing it with class and inspiring others by example.

6. Standards Learned by Living, Learning, Earning. We learn what worked and what failed..

7. Deeper Lessons from Mentorship, Risk Taking and a Balanced Life. Career and life Bodies of Work sprout from many roots. Must be viewed as a whole, the sum of the parts and the lessons learned to make each branch-limb-twig-leaf remain healthy.

Specialty codes describe the kind of medicine physicians, non-physician practitioners or other healthcare providers/suppliers practice. Appropriate use of specialty codes helps reduce inappropriate suspensions and improves the quality of utilization data.

A security code, or CVV2, is a 3-digit or 4-digit number printed on either the back or front of a credit or debit card.

A fire warning (FRW) is issued through the Emergency Alert System (EAS) in the United States by civil authorities to inform the public of major, uncontrolled fires (usually wildfires) threatening populated areas and major roadways.

Nautical flags are an international code system used for two ships to signal to each other or for a ship to signal to shore. They are also called signaling nautical flags. Three-flag signals are for points of the compass, relative bearings, standard times, verbs, punctuation and also general code and decode signals.

Medical Codes

Code blue alerts staff that someone is experiencing a life threatening medical emergency. Usually, this means cardiac arrest (when the heart stops) or respiratory arrest (when breathing stops). Staff members near the location of the code may need to go to the patient.

Code white refers to medical emergencies in children and babies. Some hospitals may still use code white to alert staff that a child or baby is in respiratory or cardiac arrest, or to signal that they are experiencing another serious medical emergency. Other hospitals use code white to indicate a mandatory evacuation, involving the entire hospital or limited areas.

Code red alerts staff to a fire or probable fire. To respond to this code, staff must follow the hospital's fire protocols, which typically require evacuation. Patients near the fire who cannot move on their own will need assistance to escape the fire. The code will often come with information about the fire's location.

Code purple alerts hospital staff to a missing child or child abduction. Some hospitals use code pink, to denote an infant abduction. The code should include clear details about the child, what they were wearing, where they were last seen and, details of with whom they were last seen. Sometimes, the hospital will go on lockdown during the search for the child, to ensure that nobody leaves the building with the child.

Code gray is a call for security personnel. It might indicate there is a dangerous person in a public area, that a person is missing or that there is criminal activity somewhere in the hospital. A hospital may use code gray if someone, including a patient, is being aggressive, abusive, violent or displaying threatening behavior. Security personal can assist other hospital staff to resolve the situation or remove the person from the premise. Code gray may include a description of the dangerous person and their current location.

Code green may indicate the arrival of patients from a mass casualty event. Hospitals use code green along with other codes, as it indicates that the hospital is activating an emergency operations plan. The code may include a description of the mass casualty scenario, as well as information about which emergency operations plan that code activates.

Code orange is a call for medical decontamination, usually due to a hazardous fluids spill. A hospital may call a code orange if toxic chemicals spill in an emergency room, or if a bag of patient blood spills on the floor. Some hospitals use code orange to call for help with a violent or combative patient.

Code silver alerts hospital staff to an active shooter in the hospital. The code alert includes information about the appearance and location of the shooter. Personnel should follow the hospital's active shooter protocols, which may include locking doors or evacuating to a specific location. Some hospitals use code silver and code gray interchangeably.

ISO and Quality Standards

Quality Management, ISO 9000 and ISO 9001
Medical, ISO 13485
Environmental Management, ISO 14000 and ISO 14001
Auditing, ISO 19011
Social Responsibility, ISO 26000
Risk Management, ISO 31011
Sampling by Attributes, 21.4
Sampling by Variables, 21.9
Food Safety, ISO 22000
Health and Safety, OHSAS 18001
Aerospace, AS9100C
Oil and Gas, API Spec Q1/Q2

Manufacturing Codes

The product code is assigned to each finished/manufactured product which is ready, to be marketed or for sale. Product codes include:

- Universal Product Code, common barcode used to identify packaged products.
- Electronic Product Code, an RFID code mainly applied as a packaging code for packaged products.
- Motion Picture Production Code.
- Product key, verifying the authenticity of a software as a license code.
- Serial number, identifying an item per instance.

Key codes used by manufacturers include:

1. Use-by or best-before, as packaged foods with a shelf-life under two years must have a use-by date on the primary packaging and a best-before date in most other cases.
2. Batch numbers or lot numbers are critical for traceability. Traceability is the ability to track any food through all stages of production, processing and distribution (including importation and at retail).
3. Identification codes are also used to trace a product through the supply chain. Identification codes may be in the form of barcodes or alphanumeric codes. They can be printed on labels that are affixed to the product, or printed or engraved directly onto it.
4. Barcodes can be used to identify trade items/products, locations, logistic units/cartons or pallets, and assets in a wide range of industry sectors, from retail to healthcare. A barcode (also often written as "bar code") is a machine-readable image used to represent data. Applications include product, carton and pallet.
5. QR codes and promotional codes are two-dimensional computer-generated images that can be scanned by smartphones or tablets to generate an action.

The Standard Industrial Classification (SIC) is a system for classifying industries by a four-digit code, used by government agencies to classify industry areas: Agriculture, Forestry and Fishing, 0100-0999. Mining, 1000-1499. Construction, 1500-1799. Manufacturing, 2000-3999. Transportation, Communications, Electric, Gas, 4000-4999. Wholesale Trade, 5000-5199. Retail Trade, 5200-5999.

Finance, Insurance and Real Estate, 6000-6799. Services, 7000-8999. Public Administration, 9100-9729. *Non-classifiable, 9900-9999.

Acronyms for Technology

AQS, Advanced Quality Systems

BCR, Bar Code Reader

CAD, Computer Aided Design

COBOL, Common Business Oriented Language

DVD, Digital Versatile Disc

Ebay, Echo Bay Trading Group

4G, Fourth Generation Mobile Telephone System

HTML, Hyper Text Mark-up Language

HTTP, Hyper Text Transfer Protocol

Intel, Integrated Electronics

IP, Internet Protocol

ISO, International Standards Organization

JPEG, Joint Photographic Experts Group

LASER, Light Amplification by Stimulated Emission of Radiation

MRI, Magnetic Resonance Imaging

PDF, Portable Document Format

RFD. Rural Free Delivery

ROM, Read Only Memory

SCSI, Small Computer Serial Interface

SEO, Service Engine Optimization

TIFF, Tagged Image File Format

USB, Universal Serial Bus

VHS, Video Home System

VLAS, Virtual Local Area Network

WD-40, Water Displacement, Formula 40

WWW, World Wide Web

Zip Code, Zone Improvement Plan

Government Forms

IRS-1040—income tax

DD-214—discharge from military duty

TTB F 5110.74—Application for alcohol fuel producer

DD-1351-2—travel voucher

SS-5—application for Social Security card

SSA-3820-BK—disability report for a child

DS-0011—application for U.S. passport

SF-424—application for federal assistance

OSHA-300—log of work related injuries and illnesses

SF-LLL—disclosure of lobbying activities

10-0246—Veterans Administration patient statement

CBP-4457—registration for personal effects taken abroad

I-9—employment eligibility verification

I-94—arrival-departure record form

IRS-941—employer's quarterly federal tax form

PHS-416-5—research fellowship activation notice

FEMA-81-65—flood proofing certificate

DD-220—military active duty report

BOEM-0329—permit to conduct geological exploration for mineral resources

BOEM-1919—insurance certificate

CMS-10055—Medicare skilled nursing facility advanced beneficiary notice

G-639—Freedom of Information Act

PS-1093—application for postal office box service

PS-2976—customs declaration form

OWCP-44—rehabilitation action report, Office of Workers' Compensation Programs

8-2.100—civil rights statutes, Department of Justice

SF-1094—U.S. tax exemption form

I-246—application for a stay of deportation or removal

FHS-3276—master deed issues by the Federal Housing Administration

SBA-750—lender's loan guaranty agreement

OGE-202—notice of conflict of interest, U.S. Office of Government Ethics

OMB-0181-0055—hemp cannabis objective description of variety, USDA

2000-222—self rescuer inventory and report, Mine Safety and Health Administration

DS-0160—electronic non-immigrant visa application

SSS-1—registration form for Selected Service System

Categories of Hurricanes

Category 1 hurricane: Very dangerous winds will produce some damage. Winds range from 74-95 mph.

Category 2 hurricane: Extremely dangerous winds will cause extensive damage. Winds range from 96-110 mph.

Category 3 hurricane: Devastating damage will occur. Winds range from 111-129 mph.

Category 4 hurricane: Catastrophic damage will occur. Winds range from 130-156 mph.

Category 5 hurricane: Catastrophic damage will occur. In this highest category hurricane, winds are 157 mph or higher.

Bankruptcy Chapters

Chapter 7 is available to both businesses and individual consumers. It involves the liquidation of qualifying assets to help repay the debt involved. In order to qualify for a Chapter 7 bankruptcy, the debtor's income level must not exceed a certain amount, as set by individual states.

Chapter 9 deals specifically with municipal entities, such as utility companies, school districts and cities. This form of bankruptcy was designed to allow the restructuring of debts by municipalities without having to resort to the liquidation of their assets.

Chapter 11 allows an individual or a business to reorganize debt, allowing debtors to repay part or all of their debt according to a repayment plan.

Chapter 12 deals with family farmers and fishermen, enabling them to repay all or part of the debt while still remaining in operation.

Chapter 13 enables individual wage earners to repay all or part of their debt as part of a repayment plan.

Chapter 15 bankruptcy deals specifically with debt incurred in a country other than the U.S., by which such cross-border cases are handled in the U.S. court system.

Police Codes

Many departments use a variety of different radio calls. These are the basic codes:

Code 1: Answer your radio, acknowledge call.

Code 2: Routine call, non-emergency response.

Code 2-High: Priority call, use your lights and siren only if necessary to get through traffic.

Code 3: Emergency, get here now, lights, sirens, speed is essential.

Code 4: No additional units required.

Code 5: Stakeout, all marked units stay out of the vicinity.

Code 6: Out of car for investigation.

Code 7: Lunch.

Code 9: Responding to medical emergencies occurring in and around a hospital.

Code 10: Clear Frequency for Broadcast.

Code 99: Emergency.

Code 100: In position for intercept (used during pursuits).

Codes of Ethics

Standards allow for clarity and continuity. With standards come codes of ethics. There are seven levels of ethics.

1. Base Level. Just needing and attempting to get by. Basics of food, clothing and shelter. Knowing right from wrong. Trying to pursue a good life and aspire to something higher.

2. Society's Lowest Common Denominators. Although knowing better, subscribing to prevailing philosophies and behaviors of others. This leads some to take advantage of the system, want more than one's share and fail to be accountable. Sadly, the common denominators are below what they used to be, and society continues to lower them. The mission of a successful person or organization is not to succumb quite that low.

3. Lessons from the School of Hard Knocks. Learning by experiences, trial and error, successes and life skills. Becoming more familiar with one's

strengths, weaknesses, opportunities and threats. Understanding what an organization can and cannot accomplish, represent and become. Maximizing one's resources to the most practical advantage.

4. Launching a Quest. Striving to learn more and go further. Includes intellectual pursuits, professional realities, nurturing of people skills and executive abilities. At this point, people change careers, and organizations revisit their goals and crystalize new visions.

5. Standards. Set and respect boundaries. Many times, people and organizations will attempt to violate those standards or fail to acknowledge their existence. The test is how consistently one sets, modifies and observes one's own standards.

6. Values and Vision. No person or organization stands still. It is not enough to accept change but more importantly to benefit from it. See yourself on a higher plateau, and quest for more. Success comes from charting a course, encompassing value systems and methodically reaching goals.

7. Codes of Ethics. These include fundamental canons, rules of practice, professional obligations, accountability-measurability, professional development, integrity, objectivity and independence. Maintain a commitment to uphold and enforce codes of ethics (yours and those of others) and the ethical responsibilities of members in business.

Quotes on Codes, Standards, Values, Ideals

"You get what you pay for." Proverb

"If you believe in an ideal, you don't own it. It owns you." Raymond Chandler

"A cynic is a man who knows the price of everything and the value of nothing." Oscar Wilde"

"There ain't a wrong man in the world who can stand up against a right man who knows he is right and keeps on a-comin'." Western movie cowboy star Lash Larue

"Good merchandise, even when hidden, soon finds buyers." Plautus

"Things are only worth what you make them worth." Moliere

"A radical is a man with both feet firmly planted in the air." President Franklin D. Roosevelt

"Failure comes only when we forget our ideals and objectives and principles."
Jawaharal Nehru

"Ideals are like stars; you will not succeed in touching them with your hands.
But like the seafaring man on the desert of waters, you choose them as your guides,
and following them you will reach your destiny." Carl Schurz

"Some have half-baked ideas because their ideals are not heated up enough."
Anonymous

"People love high ideals, but they have got to be about 33% plausible." Will
Rogers

"Let us have faith that right makes might. And in that faith, let us do our duty
to the end, as we understand it." President Abraham Lincoln

"You cannot hold a man down without staying down with him." Booker T.
Washington

"The whole history of the American Revolutionary War is one of false hopes
and temporary devices. We must champion more lasting solutions." President
George Washington

Chapter 11

BEST PRACTICES

B est practices are methods and techniques that have been generally accepted as superior to any alternatives. They produce results that are above those achieved by other means and have become a standard way of doing things.

The EOA Clearinghouse defines Best Education Practices as the wide range of individual activities, policies, and programmatic approaches to achieve positive changes in student attitudes or academic behaviors. A similar term used to describe this type of practice is evidence-based education practice.

These are best practices in education, the top qualities of an effective teacher:

- Positive. Keep your students engaged with a positive attitude.
- Prepared. You should know the course material.
- Organized. Have a plan for what you want to teach.
- Clear. Effective teachers can explain complex ideas in simple ways.
- Active. Keep your students thinking.
- Patient.
- Fair.

These are the most effective teaching strategies:

- Focus upon young people's real interests; all across the curriculum, investigating students' own questions. This is juxtaposed with required lessons, blending a balanced curriculum.
- Active, hands-on experience is the most powerful and natural form of learning. Students should be immersed in the most direct experience of the content of every subject.
- Children learn best when they encounter whole ideas, events, and materials in purposeful contexts, not by studying subparts isolated from actual use.
- Rich ideas and materials are at the heart of the curriculum. Lessons or textbooks that water down, control, or oversimplify content tend to disempower students.
- Students learn best when faced with challenges, choices and responsibility in their own learning.
- Children grow through a series of stages, and schooling should fit its activities to the developmental level of students.
- Learning is always socially constructed and often interactive; teachers need to create classroom interactions that "scaffold" learning.
- The classroom is a model community where students learn what they live as citizens of the school.
- These are best practices in the classrooms:
- The only acceptable label is a student's name.
- We should "normalize difference" by incorporating students into classroom life instead of sending them away.
- Kids should not have to "earn" their way into a regular education classroom; instead, it should be the home of all students, whenever possible.
- All kids can meet the same educational standards, but not in the same way or at the same time.
- Classrooms should support effort-based learning.
- Community building is key; successful learning requires strong relationships.

- Caring is OK, but pity is not.
- All students deserve the dignity of taking risks and doing challenging work.
- When you set up a decentralized classroom with high individualization, plenty of hands-on activity, genuine choices for students, and a strongly supportive social climate, then a much broader range of learners can not only feel at home, but thrive and excel.

Best Practices in Training and Professional Development:

1. Teaching and Training. Conveying information, insights and intelligence from various sources. Categorized by subject, grade level and methods of delivery. Expert teachers are fountains of learning material. Teachers are the building block in the educational process. The student must be an active participant, rather than be a non-involved or combative roadblock.

2. Studying. One cannot learn just by listening to a teacher. Review the material, taking notes, seeking supplementary materials to learn additionally.

3. Learning. The teacher instructs, informs and attempts to enlighten. The student accepts, interprets and catalogs the material taught. Periodically, the material is reviewed.

4. Information. As one amasses years of learning, one builds a repository of information, augmented by experiences of putting this learning into practice.

5. Analysis. One sorts through all that has been learned, matched with daily life. One determines what additional learning is necessary and desired. Education goes beyond formal schooling. If committed, one turns the quest for knowledge into a life priority.

6. Knowledge. A Body of Knowledge is derived from years of living, learning, working, caring, sharing, failing and succeeding.

7. Wisdom. This requires many years of commitment to learning, compounded by the continuous development of knowledge. Few people attempt to get this far in the educational process. Those who do so have encompassed profound wisdom.

8. Levels of training: Mandated. Basic education. Informational. Technical, niche skills. Procedural. Optional. Insightful, deep and meaningful.

Best Practices in Leadership

1. Evolving from manager to executive to leader.
2. How top professionals evolve.
3. Plateaus of professional accomplishment.
4. Developing a winning work ethic.
5. Characteristics of those who make it long-term.
6. Characteristics of those who fall by the wayside.
7. Executive mentoring means mining what we've learned.

Best Practices in Community Stewardship

1. Creating something necessary that did not exist before.
2. Eliminating something that poses a problem.
3. Developing the means for self-determination.
4. Including citizens who are in need.
5. Sharing professional and technical expertise.
6. Tutoring, counseling and training.
7. Repairing, upgrading or restoring.
8. Promotion of the community to outside constituencies.
9. Moving others toward action.

Best Practices in Business

A best practice strategy can help your business to become more competitive, increase sales and develop new markets. Best practices reduce costs, increase efficiencies, improve the skills of your workforce, use technology more effectively, reduce waste, improve quality and respond more quickly to innovations in your sector.

Best practices in running companies:

1. The business you're in (core business). Protection of intellectual property, materials, business continuity and core business production information.

Prevention of theft, leaks in proprietary information and delays in deliverables.

2. Running the business. Protection of physical plants, equipment, office files and other supplies. Prevention of unnecessary downtimes, spoilage, stoppage in processes and theft.

3. Financial. Protection of fiduciary responsibilities and financial assets. Prevention of theft, embezzlement, accounting fraud and overpayments.

4. People. Protection of human capital, knowledge bases of workers, executives, company safety and the work environment. Prevention of unnecessary employee burnout.

5. Business development. Protection of company reputation, partnerships and alliances, marketplace intelligence and customer interests and relationships. Prevention of leaks in customer information and losses in company market position.

6. Body of Knowledge. Protection of status and utilization of organizational working knowledge, management's activities and relationships with regulators. Prevention of strains in company relationships with others and attacks from outside the organization.

7. The Big Picture. Protection of the overall organization, compliance standards in the organization. Prevention of loss in quality, purpose or vision.

Best practices in managing employees:

1. Know the organization's mission, goals, tactics and methods to achieve results.

2. Know job responsibilities, performance standards and contributions toward total effort.

3. Procedures, regulations, scope of work and ramifications are communicated.

4. Support for actions. Accountability for mistakes. Fair and consistent supervision.

5. Training is provided. Latitude is given to exercise judgment. Support by management.

6. Everyone expresses ideas and suggestions. People mentor others, learning from experiences.

7. Empowerment to do something worthwhile.

Best Practices in Change Management and Making Progress

Vision + caring + commitment + implementation + follow-through = a successful company. If any of the elements are missing, the equation does not add up. An incomplete equation means that a company which will falter and fail.

Perspective is the most changeable part of doing business. Understand from where you came, and it will indicate where you may be headed. Spend more time analyzing it. That is where solutions for problems present themselves. Through deep insight into your perspective comes the route toward success. Without perspective, you never make the journey. No quick fix on earth will make the journey for you.

Good companies sandbag themselves by doing nothing. Doing anything—even making a few mistakes—is better than doing nothing. I've spent more than 40 years of my career in trying to explain that concept to otherwise reasonable people who simply stick their heads in the sand.

Read and learn from case studies of failure and success. Understand why decisions were made, conditions affecting them and the ramifications of actions and non-actions. Think like the boss and the workers. Learn to see company activities from every possible perspective.

Stay current on front burner issues affecting the climate and opportunities in which key corporate executives function. Have a mentor to keep your company on track. Stimulate "outside-the-box" thinking. Build customer coalitions. Distinguish your company from the pack.

Collaborations with other people create success. One cannot be successful alone or working in a vacuum. One is always dependent upon other people, and other people are dependent upon you. Commitments must be made to other people. By establishing new ways of working together, we paint new horizons for organizational success, individually and collectively. When we take creative approaches toward problem solving, dealing with business realities and strategic planning, we assure that organizations will truly succeed.

Expected results of an Institutional Review:

- Your service is efficient and excellent, by your standards and by the publics. You are sensitive to the public's needs, and you are flexible and human in meeting them.
- Your staff is likeable and competent. They demonstrate initiative and use their best judgment, with authority to make the decisions they should make.
- You have a good reputation and are awake to community obligations. You contribute much to the economy. You provide leadership for progress, rather than following along.
- You give your customers their money's worth. Your charges are fair and reasonable.
- You are in the vanguard of your industry.
- You provide a good place to work. You offer a promising career and future for people with ideas and initiative. Your people do a day's work for a day's pay.
- The size of your organization is necessary to do the job demanded. Your integrity and dependability make the public confident that you will use your size and influence rightly.

Best Practices in Industry

The real value of Manufacturing Operations Management (MOM) can be seen in the success of best-in-class manufacturers who have experienced 5% increases in on-time delivery to a total of 97%, an 11% increase in equipment effectiveness for a total of 89%, and an 11% increase in raw material usage for a total of 97%.

These improvements are quite significant and can lead to a much better bottom line as well as improved customer service and cost effectiveness across your company.

Best practices can be established by examining the most common characteristics shared by some of these best-in-class manufacturers. These companies are:

- Twice as likely to combine automated data collection with traditional methods, such as analytics and data historians.

- Up to four times more likely to standardize their procedures enterprise-wide including KPI measurement, optimization, and exception handling.
- 2.5 times more likely to make decisions based on operational metrics and financial information examined in real-time.
- 114% more likely to utilize Manufacturing Intelligence.
- 56% more likely to try Lean manufacturing.
- 55% more likely to make use of Advanced Planning and Scheduling.
- 50% more likely to use Plant Floor Automation.
- 17% more likely to use Quality Management Systems.

Best Practices in Healthcare

1. Using collaboration to cut readmission rates: Hospitals that have forged collaborations among providers and community-based organizations and that encourage self-management have rapidly reduced readmissions.
2. Adopting telemedicine platforms that engage patients before and after surgery produce better results than traditional approaches.
3. Thwarting the spread of deadly bacteria: To stop the spread of hard-to-treat infections, hospitals are sending weekly emails to hospital leaders that include an update on the number of cases and a ranking of unit performance as well as an action plan.
4. Providers' use of medical scribes has been shown to reduce wait times for patients and encourage more patient-centered care.
5. Using software to avoid misdiagnoses. Computer-assisted diagnosis technology is underutilized, but studies suggest it can help by boosting physicians' diagnostic confidence, reducing costs and improving patient outcomes.
6. To increase transparency, insurers are creating searchable databases that allow the general public to see how much it pays particular providers for services.
7. Hospitals are implementing processes—including starting discharge planning on the date of admission and using checklists—to reduce bottlenecks and ease patient flow.
8. The Patient Activation Measure, developed by a team at the University of Oregon and introduced in 2004, helps health systems predict which

patients are best equipped to engage in their care and which ones will be overwhelmed and in need of additional support.

9.   Leadership development for future administrators. Hospitals are creating formal programs to identify and retain promising leaders and to give them the skills to move up within the organization.

10. Nursing residency-type programs can help meet demand for trained nurses while cutting costs for hospitals.

Medical guidelines aim to guide decisions and criteria regarding diagnosis, management and treatment. Such documents have been in use for thousands of years during the entire history of medicine. Modern medical guidelines are based on an examination of current evidence within the paradigm of evidence-based medicine. A healthcare provider is obliged to know the medical guidelines of his or her profession and has to decide whether to follow the recommendations of a guideline for an individual treatment.

Nursing best practices are crucial to excellence in healthcare. Examples of Nursing Best Practices include nurse-to-nurse communication of patient status at shift change, prevention of infection, patient care and discharge.

Best Practices in Networking

Questions to ask about networking include:

- Is the person making the request a true friend, a business associate or just an acquaintance? Who are they to you, and what would you like for them to be?
- Will there be outcomes or paybacks for the other person? Will there be outcomes or paybacks for you? If there's a discrepancy in these answers, how do you feel about it?
- Are there networking situations that are beneficial for all parties? If so, analyze them, so that you can align with those situations, rather than the fruitless ones?
- What types of "wild goose chases" have you pursued in your networking career? Analyze them by category, to see patterns.

- Is the person requesting something of you willing to offer something first?
- Are the people truly communicating when they network? Or, are hidden agendas the reason for networking? Without communicating wants, it is tough to achieve outcomes.
- How much time away from business can you take? How does it compare with the business you can or will generate?
- Networking is a two-way proposition. Associate with those who feel similarly. Show and demonstrate respect for each other's time. See your time for networking and volunteering as a commodity. Budget it each year. Examine and benchmark the reasons and results. Set boundaries, and offer your time on an "a la carte" basis.

Best Practices in Diversity

- Seek and train multi-cultural professionals.
- Contribute to education in minority schools, assuring that the pipeline of promising talent can rise to challenges of the workforce.
- Design public relations programs that embrace multicultural constituencies, rather than secondarily appeal to them after the fact.
- Interface with community based groups, sharing in activities and civic service, to learn how communications will be received.
- Realize that minority groups are highly diverse. Not every Asian knows each other, nor speaks the same language. There are as many subtle differences in every ethnic group as the next. Thus, multicultural communicating is highly customized.
- Multi-cultural communications applies to all. Black professionals do not just participate in African American community events. Cultivate communicators toward cross-cultural process.
- As media does a good job of showcasing multicultural events, note it positively. If thanked enough, media will continue to shine the light on multicultural diversity.
- Sophistication in the gauging of public opinion will result in a higher caliber of communicating.

Best Practices in Sportsmanship

Being a good sport will reflect well on your child throughout their life. Talk to children about what sportsmanship is and why it matters. Teach a child to enjoy games for fun, not just for winning.

Some popular examples of good sportsmanship include shaking hands, help an opponent who may have fallen over, encourage everyone, cheer, clap or hi-five, and be respectful to everyone including teammates, the opposition, parents and officials.

Recommendations on teaching children good sportsmanship:

- If you lose, don't make up excuses.
- If you win, don't rub it in.
- Learn from mistakes and get back in the game.
- Always do your best.
- If someone makes a mistake, remain encouraging and avoid criticizing.
- Show respect for yourself, your team, and the officials of the game.

Sportsman spirit is the act of accepting one's success with humility. This type of policy helps us to cope with failures and disappointments that come our way and make renewed and challenging efforts to achieve success next time. Sportsman spirit tells to take things easily and amiably.

A good sportsman is the one who puts all his efforts, uses all his skills; pursue the goal with perseverance, work with the team. It doesn't matter after that whether he loses or wins.

Quotes About Sportsmanship by Sports Figures

"I never thought about losing, but now that it's happened, the only thing is to do it right." Boxer Muhammad Ali

"One man practicing sportsmanship is far better than a hundred teaching it." Football coach Knute Rockne

"You are never really playing an opponent. You are playing yourself, your own highest standards. When you reach your limits, that is real joy." Tennis player Arthur Ashe

"Champions keep playing until they get it right." Tennis player Billie Jean King

"It does not matter how many times you get knocked down, but how many times you get up. Winning isn't everything, but wanting to win is." Football coach Vince Lombardi

"I can accept failure. Everyone fails at something. But I can't accept not trying." Basketball player Michael Jordan

"The Great Scorer writes not that you won or lost but how you played the game." Sports writer Grantland Rice

"Winning is about heart, not just legs. It's got to be in the right place." Cyclist Lance Armstrong

"If you win through bad sportsmanship, that's no real victory." Track and golf legend Babe Didrikson Zaharias

Chapter 12

THE BEST ADVICE I EVER GOT
Lessons Learned Meeting and Working with the Legends

L ady Bird Johnson was my first mentor. She was Claudia Alta Taylor when she and my parents were students at UT-Austin in the 1930s. I started visiting with Mrs. Johnson when I was 10, discussing societal issues at her kitchen table in Austin, TX. At 10, I became a DJ at KTBC-KLBJ Radio. She mentored me: "You are a visionary and a humanitarian. Now grow into the roles."

Over the ensuing years, she introduced me to some phenomenal people, all of whom were generous with their wisdom and advice. She introduced me to Winston Churchill, Eleanor Roosevelt, Mamie Eisenhower, Ima Hogg, Walt Disney, George R. Brown, Bob Hope, Lucille Ball, Jackie Kennedy, Oveta Culp Hobby, George Mitchell, Sam Rayburn, Thurgood Marshall and dozens of other humanitarians. She endorsed my work. Her endorsement appears on the back of this very book.

On July 11, 1960, in Los Angeles, CA, Lady Bird Johnson introduced me to Winston Churchill and Eleanor Roosevelt. We discussed lifelong humanitarianism. Sir Winston Churchill was 85 at the time. Mrs. Roosevelt was 75. I was 12. Churchill advised: "Remain an intellectual, but don't act like it." Mrs. Roosevelt said: "We teach other people the things we've most recently learned and applied." One never forgets being in the presence of greatness and their shared wisdom. Another Churchill quote: "All great things are simple, and many can be expressed in single words: freedom, justice, honor, duty, mercy, hope." Lady Bird Johnson was First Lady of the U.S. from 1963-69.

From Bill Moyers, I learned these lessons:

- You cannot go through life as a carbon copy of someone else.
- You must establish your own identity, which is a long, exacting process.
- As you establish a unique identity, others will criticize. Being different, you become a moving target.
- If you cannot take the dirtiest job in any company and do it yourself, then you will never become "management."

On Jan. 19, 1965, I met Walt Disney and Howard Hughes. We sat together at a luncheon for LBJ's inauguration. Disney said to me: "Kid, don't forget this. A good idea has six creative extensions. If it does not have that many arms and legs, it's not a good idea." I was 17 at the time, a senior in high school. Hughes advised me: "Keep a pocketful of notecards, and write down what people like us say. You'll wind up with a series of books." I subsequently advised both Disney and Baker Hughes through corporate visioning. Walt Disney & Howard Hughes appeared on the cover of my 8th book, "Pop Icons and Business Legends," my first Pulitzer Prize nomination. These stemmed from a meeting at an inaugural event.

Lyndon B. Johnson taught me: "You always start at the top." Frank Sinatra told me: "Nobody is Number One forever."

Cactus Pryor was a radio personality and comedian. He said to me: "Nobody cares about you unless you're behind the microphone."

Sonny Bono told me: "There's nothing more permanent than change. History repeats itself. The beat goes on."

Texas Governor John Connally said to me: "Always put on the stamp straight. Everything we do portends to the way we handle everything else. Get used to wearing a tuxedo. You're in for a life of recognition."

Elvis Presley was the King of Rock n' Roll. I met Elvis in 1958. He came to visit me at KTBC Radio in Austin, TX, when he was a private in the U.S. Army.

The next time was in 1962 at the Seattle World's Fair, where he was making a movie. The last time was backstage at his 1975 concert at Hofheinz Pavilion in Houston. First question I asked Elvis was his favorite food. Answer: burnt bacon, because that's what they served to him in Army basic training at Fort Hood. He kept the affinity for burnt bacon the rest of his life. Second question was about the staying power of rock n' roll, then known as kids' music. Answer: "They won't always be kids."

Thurgood Marshall was the only Supreme Court justice that I knew, Thurgood Marshall (1908-1993). In 1961, President John F. Kennedy appointed Marshall to the United States Court of Appeals for the Second Circuit. In 1965, President Lyndon B. Johnson appointed Marshall as U.S. Solicitor General. In 1967, Johnson nominated Marshall to succeed retiring Associate Justice Tom C. Clark. Marshall retired during the administration of President George H.W. Bush, and was succeeded by Clarence Thomas.

Justice Thurgood Marshall said: "Where you see wrong or inequality or injustice, speak out, because this is your country. This is your democracy. Make it. Protect it. Pass it on. None of us got where we are solely by pulling ourselves up by our bootstraps. We got here because somebody—a parent, a teacher, an Ivy League crony or a few nuns—bent down and helped us pick up our boots."

Dick Clark was known as "America's oldest teenager," a seminal influence on music for 50 years. Pictured, Hank Moore with Dick Clark. I met him in 1971, appeared on an "American Bandstand" special and spoke at his final tribute dinner in 2011 in Los Angeles, CA. Sat at head table between Frankie Avalon & Burt Bacharach and introduced Beyoncé to give her tribute to Dick Clark. At the time of his death on April 18, 2012. Clark was worth $200 million. In 1972, he introduced "New Year's Rockin' Eve," in 1973 went into game shows with "$10,000 Pyramid" and created American Music Awards.

Dick Clark said: "Rock had a huge impact. Anything that the older generation hates is usually loved by kids. Nothing much changes, and that still continues today. Humor is always based on a modicum of truth. Have you ever heard a joke about a father-in-law?"

Hugh Downs served as announcer and sidekick for "Tonight Show Starring Jack Paar," 1957-1962. Co-host of "Today Show," 1962-1971. Host of "Concentration" game show, 1958-1969. Anchor of "20/20" ABC News magazine, 1978-1999.

Downs started his career in radio and live television in 1945 in Chicago. He moved to New York City in 1954 and was a perennial TV presence for the next 45 years. He wrote a column for "Science Digest" and served on the UNICEF board.

Hugh Downs once said to me: "I don't want to be anything. I want to do things. As soon as you be something, you're pegged there, and I think it's bad. I've worked to avoid labels."

Mary Tyler Moore was one of America's sweethearts. Mary began her career as a dancer, appearing in Hotpoint TV ads as a dancing cat. She then appeared as Sam, the telephone operator on "Richard Diamond, Private Detective," shown in profile only. Then came dramatic TV roles, followed by co-starring on "The Dick Van Dyke Show." Then came the beloved "Mary Tyler Moore Show," followed by movies and TV guest appearances.

Mary Tyler Moore said: "You can't be brave if you've only had wonderful things happen to you. Take chances, and make mistakes. That's how you grow. Pain nourishes your courage. You have to fail in order to practice being brave. Sometimes you have to get to know someone really well to realize you're really strangers."

Muhammad Ali, the three-time world heavyweight boxing champion, was presented the Presidential Medal of Freedom in 2005. I met him in 1968 in New York City. Second photo when we received awards at a charity gala in Houston in 1974. Fourth photo, Ali with Dr. Martin Luther King Jr. Ali devoted his life to promoting world peace, civil rights, cross-cultural understanding, humanitarianism, hunger relief and basic human values. His other causes include the Ali Care Program, Athletes for Hope, Ali Parkinson Center, Project A.L.S., and the non-profit Muhammad Ali Center in Louisville, KY. He invented the expressions "rope a dope" and "float like a butterfly, sting like a bee."

Muhammad Ali said: "Don't count the days, make the days count. I hated every minute of training, but I said, 'Don't quit. Suffer now, and live the rest of your life as a champion.'"

I met Burt Reynolds several times during his TV career, appearing as Quint Asper on "Gunsmoke," then starring on "Hawk" and "Dan August." When making the TV movie "Hunters Are For Killing," Burt told me that his acting role model was Spencer Tracy. Reynolds was working on the TV series "Riverboat" in 1960 when Tracy was filming "Judgment at Nuremberg" at the same studio (Universal).

Tracy advised Reynolds, "Don't let anybody catch you acting." He was the top movie box office draw 1978-1982.

In his dressing room on the "Dan August" set, Burt Reynolds said to me, "The only way you hurt anyone in this business is by succeeding and hurting their pocketbook or just smiling and not giving up."

I met Kenny Rogers in 1960 and introduced him in concert in 1976 and 1986. Photos from a 1985 public service shoot for the Houston Police Dept., with Dolly Parton, promoting seatbelt safety. During his 6-decade career, Kenny Rogers released 65 albums and sold more than 165 million records, one of the most successful recording artists of all time. He won 3 Grammy Awards, 13 American Music Awards, 6 Country Music Assn. Awards, CMA Lifetime Achievement Award, CMT Artist of a Lifetime Award.

Kenny Rogers said: "I have this theory about performers who last for a long time, and that is, if you break it down, music is not as big a part of it as personality and who you are. I think that we are all 3 people. I am who I think I am, I am who you think I am, and I am who I really am. The closer those 3 people are together, the longer your career's gonna last. 'Cause people don't like to be fooled. Don't be afraid to give up the good for the great. You gotta know when to hold 'em, know when to fold 'em, know when to walk away, know when to run."

Chuck Berry, who died this weekend at age 90. He was the premiere guitar hero of rock n' roll, bursting on the scene in the 1950s with hits like "Sweet Little Sixteen," "Roll Over Beethoven," "Johnny B. Goode," "Reelin' and Rockin'," "Maybelline," "Memphis," "Rock and Roll Music," "Back in the U.S.A.," "Nadine," "You Never Can Tell," etc. He inspired countless musicians since. I met him at the taping of "American Bandstand" in 1972 in Hollywood. I emceed a concert with Chuck Berry on Aug. 12, 1980, held at Hofheinz Pavilion in Houston. His influence on rock, R&B, country and pop music was strong.

Chuck Berry said: "It's amazing how much you can learn if your intentions are truly earnest. Don't let the same dog bite you twice. Of the five most important things in life, health is first, education or knowledge is second, and wealth is third. I forget the other two."

Lee Iacocca joined Ford Motor Co. in 1946 as engineer. In 1960, he became VP-GM of the Ford Division. He championed the design and introduction of the Ford Mustang, Ford Escort & models of Lincoln-Mercury. He left Ford in 1978 and went to Chrysler Corp. Iacocca worked with Congress to negotiate a bailout for Chrysler, working to turn the company around and repay the loan. New models released included the Dodge Aries & Plymouth Reliant. In 1987, he engineered acquisition of AMC, including Jeep lines. He retired as chairman-CEO of Chrysler in 1992. His endorsement appears in my "Big Picture of Business" book series. President Ronald Reagan appointed Iacocca to head the Statue of Liberty-Ellis Island Foundation.

Lee Iacocca said: "You can have brilliant ideas, but if you can't get them across, your ideas won't get you anywhere. In times of great stress or adversity, it's always best to keep busy, to plow your anger and your energy into something positive. Management is nothing more than motivating other people."

Dr. Denton Cooley, heart surgeon famous for performing the first implantation of a total artificial heart. In 1970, Dr. Cooley performed the first implantation of an artificial heart in a human when no heart replacement was immediately available. In 1984, he was awarded the Medal of Freedom by President Ronald Reagan. In 1998, he was awarded the National Medal of Technology by President Bill Clinton. Dr. Cooley authored more than 1,400 scientific articles and 12 books.

Dr. Denton Cooley said: "I still take failure very seriously, but I've found that the only way I could overcome the feeling is to keep on working, and trying to benefit from failures or disappointments. There are always some lessons to be learned. So I keep on working. So much goes into doing a transplant operation. All the way from preparing the patient to procuring the donor, it's like being an astronaut. The astronaut gets all the credit, he gets the trip to the moon, but he had nothing to do with the creation of the rocket, or navigating the ship. He's the privileged one who gets to drive to the moon. I feel that way in some of these more difficult operations, like the heart transplant."

I met 10 of Time Magazine's "100 Women of the Year": Jackie Kennedy, Lucille Ball, Margaret Thatcher, Eleanor Roosevelt, Beyoncé, Margaret Chase Smith, Rita Moreno, Oprah Winfrey, Irna Phillips and Gloria Steinem.

Eleanor Roosevelt said to me: "We teach other people the things we've most recently learned & applied."

I met British Prime Minister Margaret Thatcher when we were speakers at an Economic Summit, saying: "The spirit of envy destroys; it can never build."

Gloria Steinem said to me: "Logic is in the eye of the logician."

Oprah Winfrey shared what happens before the show & during breaks shapes a better show.

From Margaret Chase Smith, I learned: "The right way is not always the popular and easy way. Standing for right when it is unpopular is a true test of moral character."

I met Lucille Ball in 1962, had dinner at her home in 1970, when she talked about the serious business of comedy and maintaining high standards.

I met Beyoncé in 2011 at a Dick Clark tribute event in Hollywood, CA. She said: "I get nervous when I don't get nervous. If I'm nervous I know I'm going to have a good show."

I met Irna Phillips, queen of soap operas, in 1969 on the set of "Guiding Light." Phillips wrote & produced radio's first soap opera. In the next 43 years, she would create 18 radio and television serials, 4 still on the air when she died in 1973, including "Guiding Light" and "As the World Turns."

Rita Moreno said: "My middle name really is perseverance. I've always believed that I had talent, even when I felt like a very inferior sort of person, which I spent a lot of time living my life feeling that I wasn't worthy. But even then I knew that I had something special, and maybe that's what it takes. Maybe people need to have that kind of particular core driving them. But I felt I had talent."

One never forgets being in the presence of greatness and their shared wisdom.

Chapter 13

GREATEST LESSONS LEARNED FROM HISTORY

Putting past activities and events into perspective
Learning from the past, to plan for the future

P eople are interesting combinations of the old, the new, the tried and the true. Individuals and organizations are more resilient than they tend to believe. They've changed more than they wish to acknowledge. They embrace innovations, while keeping the best traditions. When one reflects at changes, he-she sees directions for the future. Change is innovative.

From history, I've learned that there's nothing more permanent than change. For everything that changes, many things remain the same. The art of living well is to meld the changeable dynamics with the constants and the traditions. The periodic reshuffling of priorities, opportunities and potential outcomes represents business planning at its best. One learns three times more from failure than from success. By studying and reflecting upon the events of the past and the shortcomings of others, then we create strategies for meeting the challenges of the future.

The past is an excellent barometer for the future. I call that "Yesterdayism." One can always learn from the past, dust it off and reapply it. I call that "Lessons

Learned but Not Soon Forgotten." Living in the past is not good, nor is living in the present without benefiting from the wisdom of the past.

Trends come and go, the latest not necessarily the best. Some of the old ways really work better and should not be dismissed just because they are old or some fashionable trend of the moment looks better.

When we see how far we have come, it gives further direction for the future. Ideas make the future happen. Technology is but one tool of the trade. Futurism is about people, ideas and societal evolution, not fads and gimmicks. The marketplace tells us what they want, if we listen carefully. We have an obligation to give them what they need.

In olden times, people learned to improvise and "make do." In modern times of instantaneous disposability, we must remember the practicalities and flexibilities of the simple things and concepts. In business and society, we must learn lessons from the corporate crises, the also-rans and the conditions that controlled the history. Some of those lessons that we could well learn came from these watershed events:

- The Civil War. This is a classic and tragic case of two sides fighting for causes and not fully understanding the other side's motivations. The South saw slavery as an economic factor and the only system of labor management they had ever known. The North saw opportunities to champion humanity issues, underlying the threat of insurgence within our own nation. Neither side fully articulated its issues, nor sought to negotiate before hostilities broke out. This war caused severe rifts in U.S. society for another 100 years.
- America's shift from an agricultural to an industrial economy.
- Prohibition. Take something away from consumers, and say that the action is in their best interest. They'll want the commodity even more. The great lengths that people went to getting their liquor fixes enabled organized crime to gain major footholds in America. The legislation that created Prohibition was wrong, and that action by a few spawned the gangster era, which became big business in America. Congress finally recounted after untellable damage was done.
- The Great Depression. Economics are a series of ebbs and flows. Failure to anticipate and to prepare for the next drop and to expect that the good

times will never cease is foolhardy. Failure to exercise crisis management after the crash and to restore stability in judicious ways caused the Depression to drag on. It was a World War that finally pulled America out of its greatest economic slump. Lessons from the Great Depression should have been applied during the high-riding days of technology stocks and a stock market that over-hyped so much. The dot.com bust and corporate debacles could have been avoided if lessons from the Great Depression had been learned, updated and utilized.

- Diversity in the workplace.
- Shift from an industrial to an information economy.
- Watergate, bringing about more accountability by the public sector.
- The Dot.Com Bust. Analogies from the Great Depression to the dot.com crash were many. Too many tech companies did not feel as though corporate protocols of the older companies applied to them. Shortcuts were taken. The media unfairly crowned superficial darlings, such as Enron. Regulators had relaxed standards. Common practice in investment communities was to over-hype stock potential, without seeing who was truly at the switches of these companies. Had the scandals not triggered public outcry when they did, this chain of events could have led to another Great Depression.
- Corporate scandals, bringing about reforms, ethics and higher corporate accountability.
- COVID-19 and the resulting economic crisis. This is covered in Chapter 4 of this book.

Fond Remembrances of the Past

Drugstore soda fountains.

Driving into the gas station and saying, "Fill her up." Response: "Regular or ethyl?"

Gas station attendants, in uniform, cleaning windshields.

One phone book that encompassed all listings.

Chinese laundries (local family operated).

Black and white movies and TV shows.

Newscasts that contained actual news.

Cream on top of milk delivered to your door in bottles.

Schools broadcasting radio coverage of space launches over PA system.

Quilting bees.

Homemade bread.

Ice cream socials.

4-poster bedposts.

Laundry was hung out to dry on clotheslines in the backyard.

Aluminum foil was called "tin foil."

An umbrella was called a "parasol."

Trash and garbage were called "debris, refuse, rubbish."

A bathroom was called a "water closet."

Records were played to hear music.

One filled out business forms in triplicate, with carbon paper.

Ironing boards were built into the wall of the kitchen (accessed by a door).

Salt, pepper, sugar and other spices kept in a cupboard in the kitchen.

The primary source of home or office building cooling was a ceiling fan.

All office buildings had ledges.

Milk came in glass bottles, delivered to your door.

All hotels were located downtown.

Suburban and rural hotels were called tourist courts, later motels.

One opened beer or soft drink cans with a "church key."

All movies and novels had happy endings.

Do you remember when:
- The entire family would take Sunday drives and hold picnics on the weekends.
- The entire family would gather around the 78-RPM record changer (a new invention) to enjoy new releases by such contemporary artists as Bing Crosby, Glenn Miller, Rudy Vallee, Tommy Dorsey, Duke Ellington, Gene Austin, Paul Whiteman, Benny Goodman, Guy Lombardo, Enrico Caruso, Artie Shaw, Russ Columbo, The Andrews Sisters, The Mills Brothers, Kate Smith, Vaughn Monroe, Harry James, Count Basie, Al Jolson.

- The entire family would gather around the radio to enjoy family-oriented programs such as "Fibber McGee and Molly," "The Shadow," "Edgar Bergen and Charlie McCarthy," "H.V. Kaltenborn With the News," "Suspense," "The Great Gildersleeve," "The March of Time," "Lux Radio Theatre" and "Bing Crosby's Kraft Music Hall."
- The entire family would gather around the three-speed record changer (a new invention) to enjoy new releases by such contemporary artists as Perry Como, Doris Day, Frankie Laine, Teresa Brewer, Nat "King" Cole, Rosemary Clooney, Eddie Fisher, Dinah Shore, Tony Bennett, Jo Stafford, Dean Martin, Patti Page, Frank Sinatra, Eartha Kitt, Vic Damone, The McGuire Sisters, Kay Starr, The Four Aces, Joni James and Peggy Lee.
- The entire family would gather around the TV set to enjoy family-oriented programs such as "The Ed Sullivan Show," "What's My Line," "Wagon Train," "George Burns and Gracie Allen Show," "The Life and Times of Wyatt Earp," "Dragnet," "The Milton Berle Show," "Four Star Playhouse," "Disneyland" and "Gunsmoke."
- The entire family would gather around the Atari video machine (a new invention) to enjoy family-oriented games such as Pac Man and Donkey Kong.

Signs, Trends and Fads of Their Times

Judges wearing powdered wigs and robes

Car hops at drive-in restaurants

Pizza parlors (in-store dining only)

Jousting contests

Dances: the Charleston, twist, etc.

Married couples shown on TV sleeping in twin beds

Short wave radios

CB radios

Mega Super Bowl parties

Polio vaccinations

Catholic church services entirely in Latin

Pens and inkwells in schools and offices

Slide rules as standard part of school supplies

Choice of either a 2-ring or 3-ring binder

Political messages printed on cardboard fans

Advertising messages printed on schoolbook covers

Automobiles: Trends, Fads and Technologies

Hood ornaments and tail fins on cars

All cars on the road being of the nation in which they were made

Rumple seats and running boards on cars

Regular gasoline

Crank shafts

Music via AM-only radio

Spare tire mounted on the rear

Running boards

Visor over the windshield

Small, framed front and back windshields

Tail pipes

Spark plugs

Things Which Made Comebacks

Ceiling fans

The jitterbug and swing music

Hardwood floors

Stained glass

Things the Economy Has Exempted

Penny arcades

Five-and-dime stores

Full-service gas stations

Free car washes at gas stations

Towels in boxes of detergent

Mom-and-pop stores

S&H Green Stamps and other redemption programs

Things Technology Has Eclipsed

Telegraphs (including operators, poles and stations to support them)

The process of changing spark plugs in cars

Eye patches

Stagecoaches

Monocles

Horse-driven buggies

Shooting horses when they go lame

Muskets

Blacksmiths

Cobblestone streets

Cows being milked by hand

Fountain pen refills

Cotton being picked by hand

Wall-crank telephones

Rotary dial telephones

Telephone poles with glass conductors atop

Placing long distance calls through a live operator sitting at a switchboard

Fire places…which gave way to floor furnaces…which gave way to wall heaters…which gave way to space heaters…which gave way to central air and heat.

Open-air vents above doors in office buildings, hotels and apartments (the oldest ones containing stained glass).

Attic fans…which gave way to window fans…which gave way to water coolers…which gave way to window air conditioning units…which gave way to central air and heat.

Ledges on high-rise office buildings

Windows that open in high-rise office buildings

Baseball games played outside in the sunlight

Megaphones

Wagon trains taking settlers westward as a group

Steel coiled radiators

Ledges on office buildings

Check writing machines.

Typewriters

Typewriter paraphernalia (dust covers, pads, stands, carbon paper, ribbons, liquid paper)

Mimeograph machines while printed purple documents

Office buildings with elevator operators and crank-turning mechanisms

Things the Marketplace Has Eclipsed

Ice delivered in blocks via a horse-driven carriage by the ice man

Milk delivered in bottles via a horse-driven carriage by the milk man

Going downtown to do all of your shopping

Drive-in movies

Stores closed on Sundays

Things that Ceased but Should Have Remained

Locally produced children's TV shows

Saturday matinees at the movies for children

Neighborhoods coordinating Christmas decorations at the holiday season

Community ice cream socials

Frosted mugs of root beer

Signs on public facilities stating, "inspected by Duncan Hines" (or some other objective third-party resource)

Civil defense and community safety drills

Getting dressed up to go to dignified places (church, theatre, business offices, etc.)

Bookmobiles in the neighborhoods (i.e. formalized youth reading programs)

Movie newsreels, cartoons and short subjects

Regular immunizations against diseases in the schools, churches and community centers

Charm schools

Teaching formal ballroom dancing to children (and other social amenities that accompany it)

Printed Top 40 music surveys

Radio listeners being able to actually pick the songs that are played

Reading books, magazines and newspapers on a regular basis. (37% of all high school graduates will never read a book the rest of their lives.)

The Old Became the New Again

The original speed for phonograph records, as invented in 1888, was 78-RPM, which engineers have determined to be the most ideal for sound quality. In the 1940s, technology brought us the 45-RPM and 33-1/3-RPM records...adding up to the "mother speed" of 78-RPM. The 1980s brought us compact discs, which play at a speed of 78-RPM.

Station wagons of the 1950s went out of style. They came back in the 1980s as sport utility vehicles.

Midwives were widely utilized in previous centuries. In modern times, alternative health care concepts and practitioners have been embraced by all sectors of society. Herbal ingredients and home remedies have gained popularity, and cottage industries support them.

Telephone party lines went out in the 1920s. They came back in the 1990s as internet chat rooms.

Corporations have become extended families, embracing changes, modifications and learning curves.

Schools started out as full-scope community centers. As the years passed, academic programs grew and became more specialized, covering many vital subject areas. Today, with parents and communities severely neglecting children and their life-skills education, schools have evolved back to being full-scope community centers.

Major Inventions that Impacted Our Lives

Books, newspapers and magazines
Frozen, packaged and instantly prepared foods
Air conditioning, climate control
Health care medication, aids, procedures and equipment
Radio and television
Computers
Microwave ovens

Practical Extras that Impacted Our Lives

Swizzle sticks
Plastic spindles (couldn't play a 45-RPM record without one)

Straws

Sugar substitute

Creamer in granules

Progressions of the Times

Rabbit ears atop the TV set...to get better reception.

TV antennas on the rooftops of our homes...to get better reception.

Community television cable systems...to get better reception.

Cable TV...to get more choices.

Cutting off football games to begin the regularly scheduled show. (That was done for the last time in 1969, when NBC telecast "Heidi," and action in the untelevised last seconds altered the game's outcome. Through public outcry, games hence went their course and primetime programming ran in its entirety...just later.)

Brand Names that stuck as generic labels

Xerox, for making photocopies

Kleenex, for any kind of tissue

Coke, for enjoying a soft drink

Crime Waves of the Past

Cattle rustling

Bootlegging whiskey

Horse theft

Punishment for Crimes in the Past

Branded by a scarlet letter

Execution by a firing squad

Hanging

Being put in the stockades

Public thrashing

Being fed only bread and water

Debtors' prisons

Blacklisting

Internment camps for suspected aliens

Having your name posted in the town square

Behaviors and Social Customs of Times Past

Offering social conversations by offering the other person a cigarette.

Alcohol consumed at business lunches.

Serving guests water directly from the tap.

Opening school with both benedictions and the Pledge of Allegiance.

Condoms only being available via machines in gas stations or under the counter at pharmacies.

TV stations signing on and off with test patterns.

The Solid South (predictable voting patterns).

Behaviors that Have Evolved

Tossing soft drink cans out of the car. Through behavior modification and sensitivity to the environment, we now crush them and put them in recyclable containers.

Mellowing out and absorbing culture on Sunday mornings, varying forms and habits.

One set of water fountains and rest rooms for all. (It wasn't always that way.)

Expressions Not Heard Anymore

The bee's knees

The cat's meow

Well, I'll be pickled in brine

The cat's pajamas

Well, dog my cat

Heavens to Betsy

If that doesn't take the cake

Cock and bull

Mum's the word

Holy smokes

Well, Doggie

Snitch

Golly gee

Swell

Fiddlesticks

Well, I'll swannee

Jeepers creepers

Sunday go to meeting

A month of Sundays

Bust my britches

Fad Expressions, Hot at the Time

Would you believe (from TV series "Get Smart")

A silly millimeter longer (from a cigarette commercial)

Let me make this perfectly clear (from Richard Nixon)

Get while the gettin's good

Putting on the dog

Heavens to Mergatroid

See you later, alligator

All dolled up

That's the most

Steppin' out

What a drag

Hot rod

Gun moll

Ain't that a groove

What a bummer

Heavens to Mergatroid

Tell it like it is

Groovy

Rat fink

Bitchin'

Peace, Brother

Right on

Black is Beautiful

Far out

Have a nice day

Time to rock and roll

Keep on keepin' on

Sooky (have mercy, baby)

Tubular

Make my day

Shop till you drop

Doofus (acting silly)

Geek

Biker babe

Groupie

Talk to the hand

Good to go

Don't go there

Nicknames for People

Girlie

Bucko

Silly willy

Little lady

Buster

Buckeroo

Missy

Sweet pea

Negative Labels for People

Polecat

Skunk

Redneck

You old buzzard

Perspectives, Depending on Your Vantage Point

For most of us, the milkman brought products to your door. To farmers, the milkman was the delivery person who picked up the product.

When dining, Europeans and Americans hold knives and forks in different patterns.

Cherry coke in a drugstore soda fountain has a special meaning for consumers. It cannot be duplicated in consumable containers.

Hot dogs in a ballpark have their own unique flavor, appeal and ambience. So do hot dogs bought from a street cart. So do those grilled over an open fire at a youth campout.

The same commodity is seen differently, depending upon the circumstance.

The Winds of Change

It takes many years to raise a person but only a few minutes to arrange for their burial. Society spends three times more on prisons than on public education.

Kinder Notions that We Need Now

Heroes, role models.

Fighting for the honor of a lady.

Helping senior citizens across the street.

Smiling at other people whom you pass on the street or in public places.

Accountability by each person in their job.

Humane treatment of people, as we confer upon animals.

Voting for the man or woman, not the party.

Saying "yes sir" and "yes ma'am" to our elders…or as in general to show respect to other adults.

Applications for Yesterdayism, Shaping the Past into the Future

1. Re-reading, reviewing and finding new nuggets in old files.
2. Applying pop culture to today.
3. Review case studies and their patterns for repeating themselves.
4. Discern the differences between trends and fads.
5. Learn from successes and failures.
6. Transition your organization from information down the branches to knowledge.
7. Apply thinking processes to be truly innovative. The past repeats itself. History is not something boring that you once studied in school. History can be a wise mentor and help you to avoid making critical mistakes.

7 Kinds of Reunions

1. Pleasurable. Seeing an old friend who has done well, moved in a new direction and is genuinely happy to see you too. These include chance meetings, reasons to reconnect and a concerted effort by one party to stay in the loop.

2. Painful. Talking to someone who has not moved forward. It's like the conversation you had with them 15 years ago simply resumed. They talk only about past matters and don't want to hear what you're doing now.

3. Mandated. Meetings, receptions, etc. Sometimes, they're pleasurable, such as retirement parties, open houses, community service functions. Other times, they're painful, such as funerals or attending a bankruptcy creditors' meeting.

4. Instructional. See what has progressed and who have changed. Hear the success stories. High school reunions fit into this category, their value depending upon the mindset you take with you to the occasion.

5. Reflect Upon the Past. Reconnecting with old friends, former colleagues and citizens for whom you have great respect. This is an excellent way to share each other's progress and give understanding for courses of choice.

6. Benchmarking. Good opportunities to compare successes, case studies, methodologies, learning curves and insights. When "the best" connects with "the best," this is highly energizing.

7. Goal Inspiring. The synergy of your present and theirs inspires the future. Good thinkers are rare. Stay in contact with those whom you know, admire and respect. It will benefit all involved.

Chapter 14

FAMILY OPERATED BUSINESSES

F amily operated businesses are commercial organizations in which decision-making is influenced by multiple generations of a family, related by blood, marriage or adoption, who influence the vision of the business. The four ways in which a business may be set up are: Sole Proprietorship, Partnership, Corporation, and Limited Liability Company.

Here are statistics related to family run businesses:

- 30% of family owned companies transition from the first to a second generation.
- 12% transition from the second generation to the third.
- 13% of family businesses remain within the family for more than 60 years.
- 94% of family-owned companies are controlled by a board.
- 31% of board membership was comprised of family. Perspective from outside the family contributes to good governance.

- 40% of the companies include less-experienced family members on committees and boards, with the goal of nurturing the younger generation's management and business skills.
- 74% of family owned companies report stronger values and culture, which can be leveraged as strengths in areas like customer care, recruitment and employee retention.
- Family owned businesses account for over 30% of companies with sales over $1 billion.
- 90% of firms are out of business by year 10.
- The 4-year survival rate in the information sector is 38%.
- The 4-year survival rate in education and health services sector is 55%.
- The average start-up in education and health sector is 50% more likely than the average start-up in the information sector to live four years.
- 40% of all start-up restaurants fail. The elements of a strong family business are growth, risk, governance, profitability, productivity, transition and people.

Categories of family run businesses include:

- Started from scratch.
- Took over someone else's company, adding dimensions to make it their own.
- Freelance services.
- Part of lifestyle choices.
- Spinoff from corporate positions.
- Operating a franchise.
- Caretaker until a merger or rollup.
- Serial entrepreneur, operation several family businesses.
- Spinoff of corporation that evolves into a niche business.

The kinds of family run businesses include:

- Home services.
- Building, carpentry and repair.

- Plumbing, air conditioner servicing and electrical services.
- Restaurants.
- Repair and restoration services.
- Accounting, bookkeeping, legal and marketing services.
- Operating a franchise.
- Farming and agriculture.
- Niche websites.
- Personal shopping, party planning and event services.
- Home healthcare services.
- Technology reseller or provider.
- Sales and marketing of product lines.
- Artisans.
- Lawn care and landscaping.
- Retail shops and stores.
- Cleaning services.
- Catering.
- Photography and video shooting.
- Graphic design.
- Sampling, serving and trade show representation.
- Pet and animal services.
- Child care and elder care services.
- Writing and publishing.
- Florists and nurseries.
- Subcontracting to corporations.
- Business-to-business services.
- Vendors at markets, shows and events.
- Ecommerce resellers.
- Internet subcontract services.
- Tutorial and training services.
- Running errands, home shopping and delivery services.
- Home decorating, staging and remodeling.
- Pool design, installation, repair, refurbishing and maintenance.
- House flipping.

- Investments and financial services consultation.
- Antiques buying, selling, consignments, repair and repurposing.
- Moving, transportation and delivery services.
- Musical repair, sales, bands and venue services.
- Gift baskets, corporate gifts and acquisition of products for larger companies.
- Jewelry, glassware, designer clothing and luxury items.
- Security services.
- Developers and real estate.
- Entertainment, sports and recreation.

The types of family members that you really need in the business include:

- The innovator, who has created the widget or refined someone else's niche.
- The risk taker.
- The mediator, arbiter or team builder.
- Pragmatists, who bring order, structure and rules to the company.
- Fiduciary management.
- Leaders who can build teams and inspire performance.
- Technical, logistical and operational expertise.
- Creative resources.
- Family champions who work with stakeholders and outside resources.

Conflicts that plague family run businesses include:

- Parent-child rivalries.
- Feelings of guilt.
- Sibling rivalries and family feuds.
- Friction within the family.
- Relationships of family members with non-family members.
- False sense of "traditions."

The key success traits of family run businesses include:

- Understanding the family's strengths, weaknesses.
- Assessing the marketplace for challenges and opportunities:
- Knowing where to obtain financing and key business resources.
- Marketing and promotion of the company and its products-services.
- Ability to weather crises, planning to achieve after adversity.
- Unlocking potential, grooming managers and nurturing staff.
- Juxtaposing what the business started out to be with where it is headed.
- Go from positions of entitlement to contributing.
- Surviving when the principal is not there.
- Succession planning is in place.
- Bringing in outside leadership to take the company to next levels.
- Employment fairness that includes non-family members.
- Weeding out naysayers, toxic people and distractions to the mission.
- Consider customers in decision making and company strategies.
- Nurture customer relationships for company survival and future.
- Recognize loyalty, confidentiality and ethical conduct.
- Celebrate diversity as a business strategy.

Growth Curves Along the Route

These are the opportunities to grow and sustain the company:

- Roles and responsibilities are delineated.
- A sense of fraternal spirit is sustained.
- Conflicts can be mediated toward successful outcomes.
- There must exist an emotional dimension.

These are the stages of family business growth:

1. Want to Get Business. Seeking rub-off effect, success by association. Sounds good to the marketplace. Nothing ventured, nothing gained. Why not try!

2. Want to Garner Ideas. Learn how others work. Intend to package what the other does as your capabilities later. Each is scared of the other stealing business or scooping a client.

3. First Attempts. Conduct programs that get results, praise and requests for more.

4. Mistakes, Successes and Lessons. Crisis or urgent need led the consortium to be formed. Project required a cohesive team approach and multiple talents.

5. Continued Collaborations. Family members had prior successful experiences in joint venturing. The sophisticated ones are skilled at building-utilizing collaborations of experts.

6. Want and advocate teamwork. Members want to learn from each other. All are prepared to share risks equally. Early successes spurred future collaborations. Joint-venturing is considered an ongoing process, not a "once in awhile" action.

7. Commitment to the concept and each other. Each team member realized something of value. The client recommended the consortium to others. Members freely refer business to team members, without jealousies or the fear of not getting something in return. What benefits one partner benefits all.

This is where successful family-run businesses achieve long-term success:

1. Being Your Best Self. It is not acceptable to be a clone of what you perceive someone else to be. Those organizations and managers who use terms like "world class" are aspirants who won't ever quite make the measuring stick.

2. Being Consistently Excellence and Upholding Standards. There is no such thing as perfection. Yet, excellence is a definitive process of achievement, dedication and expeditious use of resources. Exponential improvement each year is the objective.

3. The Ability to Change and Adapt.

4. Learning from Experiences, Successes and the Shortcomings of All.

5. Thinking, Planning, Reflecting and Benchmarking.

6. Committing to the Next Great Challenge. Do not fall into the trap of some false commitment to "tradition," an excuse used by many to avoid change and accountability.

7. Ability to Communicate and Share with Others.

Chapter 15

IT'S ABOUT THEM, NOT THE CUSTOMERS

People That Sabotage Business Success.
How Leaders Can Learn from It.

T here was this person whom I met. He was the purchasing director for a large government entity. I was asked to put together a team of top professionals to pursue a large-scale performance review of several agencies. Previously, they had commissioned traditional accounting firm audits. It was said that they wanted something all-encompassing, and they called me to recommend the best approach.

The first hurdle was meeting with the potential client. He had fixed in his mind and schedule that he would go to lunch at the same time everyday, at 11:15 a.m. Therefore, his entire work schedule revolved around that rigid desire to go to lunch. My experience with bureaucrats was that the earlier their lunch hour, the more staid they were as managers, least of all as leaders. This bureaucrat was notorious for not scheduling morning meetings and cutting others short. He offended other agencies by not being available for their morning meetings.

I put together a top team, including accountants, technology gurus, law enforcement professionals, a former county commissioner, public relations experts, supply chain management experts and myself as the Big Picture overview expert to coordinate the entire contract (as I had done for decades). For our presentation. I commissioned a giant 16-inch cookie, with eight pieces inscribed as representing the eight parts of the process. It was thorough and comprehensive.

This guy jerked us around for meetings that satisfied his lunch hour obsession. When we brought in other public officials and showed the importance of this project's promise, he shut it down. After all, it interfered with his lunch hour. Then he admitted being threatened by people smarter than him.

Where I came from, you always exit as a gracious contestant. You never complain about the process being rigged. You expressed appreciation for being called in to fix a flawed agency review process.

This guy could not understand why people were so gracious. He kept contacting us, picking at us and trying to get us to lash out. After all, it was all about his lunch hour and maintaining his limited view of life. He wanted to preserve that he was in charge. People like this bring their poor behaviors into the workforce. They make so many bad judgments, based upon their own preferences. Examples:

- The medical office staff who advise you to go to the ER because they don't want to keep their office open later to see you.
- The service personnel who try to feather their own nest. They take the premium parking spots for themselves, believing it is a perk of the job. They tell you things that are not true because it is convenient for them.
- Telephone solicitors that will say anything to make a sale.
- The mid-managers who claim that they have the ear of top management.
- The vendors that pretend they are business experts.
- The employees who ask customers to step out of the way so they can pass.
- The networkers who constantly fester you to favor them.
- Clerks who say something had been sold out so they don't have to go back and check the stock.
- People who concentrate on their cell phones rather than serve customers.

- People who ask you to fill out the forms again because they are too lazy to go through your file.
- They expect you to wait for them.

Clues for the Clueless

Some people just don't get it until circumstances force them to acquire knowledge and use it in a positive flow. None of us are born with sophisticated, finely tuned senses and viewpoints for life. We muddle through life, try our best and get hit in the gut several times. Thus, we learn, amass knowledge and turn most experiences into an enlightened life-like perspective that moves us "to the next tier." Such a perspective is what makes seasoned executives valuable in the business marketplace.

Some people, however, stay in the "muddling through" mode and don't acquire seasoning. They "get by" with limited knowledge-scope and remain complacent-happy in some kind of security-state. As their clueless increases, they sink through the following seven numbers, like they would fall into a well.

These are the stages of cluelessness:

1. Youth. Haven't formulated clues yet.
2. Naivete. Limited life experiences. Don't know any better.
3. Ignorance is bliss. Feel they know all they need to get by. See no further need to learn.
4. Not going to get it. Confused by diversified life choices. Stick with the known.
5. Hardened, cynical. Different viewpoints are bad and to be criticized.
6. Fight change. Don't tolerate differences.
7. Surround with like-minded people. Ostracize those who are different.

Life forces the human condition to change. Due to circumstances, people start "cluing in." By that point, substantial career potential has been lost. Much damage cannot be recovered. Therefore, many people likely will stay on safe tracks that rarely ride the engine to glory.

At some point, each of us must take ownership for our lives, careers and accomplishments. Events necessitating or inspiring this to happen include:

- A recognition that old methods are not working.
- Successive failures via the old ways of doing things.
- Financial failures or the monetary incentive to rapidly create or change plans of action.
- Loss of one or more loved ones (by death) causes one to grow up exponentially.
- Loss of valued relationships, because they were not properly nurtured or were neglected.
- One realizes a pattern of attempting to scapegoat others for one's own problems-issues. *There is no choice but to change the modus operandi.
- Loss of substantial numbers of opportunities, customers, employees and market share.
- A "wake up call" of any type.

Questions for all of us to ask ourselves include:

- Who is really holding you back?
- Who did you pick to scapegoat? Why? What do they really represent?
- What will the world look like if you were totally in control of your destiny?
- Can you name anyone who is actually in complete control?
- What losses have you sustained? Have you analyzed why?
- By being successful in one area of life, what other facet has suffered?
- By failing to take full control of your own life, what have been the costs? How do you now achieve balance?
- By not rising to challenges, what have been your opportunity costs?
- Why keep pursuing the same defeating course (business as usual) if it's not working?
- If changes are not made now, when will they be completed?

Nobody sets out to become angry, negative, lonely, embittered or a failure. Nobody sets out to become mediocre. Such eventualities involve life experiences seen through rose-colored glasses. People do not set out to hurt us. Most could care less. It's our tinted viewpoint of transactions or communications that colors our perspective, not what has actually happened.

Many people are hard pressed to recall how their value systems emerged. Many become and remain clueless as a safeguard against taking risks, which they equate to getting hurt. Our society wants to push buttons to get quick fixes. Many embrace technology as a means to avoid addressing other issues (notably human communication).

When people just don't get it, they tend to:

- Stick to the past, adhering to the old ways of doing things.
- Support others who are like-minded to themselves.
- Scapegoat people who are the messengers of change.
- Blame others who cannot or will not defend themselves.
- Find public and vocal ways of placing blame upon others.
- Shame those people who make them accountable.
- Fight those who care the most about them.
- Relate best to strangers, hangers-on, business stooges, networking acquaintances or others who cannot or will not reciprocate.
- Waste time on the small things.
- Neither attends to details nor to pursue a Big Picture.
- Perpetuate co-dependencies.
- Selectively forget the good that occurs.
- Do little or nothing.
- At all costs, fight change in every shape, form or concept.
- Continue living but don't live well.

The clueless person, in the workplace, exhibits such syndromes as:

- Doesn't understand what has to be don and cannot figure out how to do things.
- Won't see beyond today's duties.

- Cannot fathom a career body of work. Just sees it as jobs.
- Never gives back to the community.
- Feels no ownership of company Vision.
- Is focused only to the next vacation day.
- Takes unfair advantage of health insurance and sick days.
- Never volunteers for anything and never asks questions.
- Doesn't want to be noticed, let alone praised.
- Hasn't a clue why training, quality improvement and other approaches should relate to him-her.
- Never thinks aloud with colleagues (brainstorming).

The clueless person, in management, exhibits such syndromes as:

- Is not fully sure what business the company is in.
- Doesn't subscribe to any organizational Vision. Simply reacts to busy-work steps.
- Doesn't rock the boat.
- Is nebulous about anything that is not in the policies and procedures.
- Is dis-inclined toward crediting new and creative ideas.
- Is vested toward maintaining the status quo.
- Feels compelled to root out "bad apples" who do not fully abide by the "company way."
- Considers employee requests for clarity of instructions as mutinous.
- Doesn't set tough standards for his-her own achievement.
- Avoids measurability or comparison to others.

The clueless person, in an entrepreneurial mode exhibits such syndromes as:

- Barks, "Do it my way, no questions about it."
- Shrugs off new approaches. "If it was good enough for me, then it's good enough for you."
- Low self-esteem translates into co-dependent relationships with employees.
- Thinks being good at his-her chosen trade is enough to succeed.

- Doesn't want to pay for training, least of all leadership development for the principal.
- Doesn't invest in effective marketing, notably doing the lead share.
- Hasn't learned to delegate.
- Blames others, never themself.
- Runs the business just like a family, remaining in denial over it.
- Over-punishes and condemns for failures.

The clueless organization, comprised of many clueless people and few of vision, exhibits these syndromes, in rank order:

1. Failure to change.
2. Undercapitalization.
3. Diversifying beyond the scope of company expertise.
4. Poor controls.
5. Overdependence upon one product.
6. Failure to understand what business you're really in.
7. Inability to read the warning signs or understand external influences.
8. Poor location.
9. Lack of marketing.
10. Unprofitable pricing.
11. Misuse of company resources, notably its people.
12. Regulatory red tape.
13. Excess overhead.
14. Inability to plan.

The fatal flaws of social upbringing include:

- People who say they are sorry when it is too late. Usually, they're sorry they were caught or that things didn't go their way.
- People who do not return your calls in as timely a manner as you return theirs.
- People who ask favors of you but do not offer anything in return.
- People who borrow things but are in no hurry to return them.

- People who think they're right all the time, and dissenting opinions are wrong.
- People who call you to review a document. You call them back with a prompt response. They're not there to take your call and take their time calling you back.
- People for whom you make or produce something, especially when it is a favor. They're never in a hurry to come pick it up.
- People who met you once. When you least expect, they're calling and wanting something from you. When does the statute of limitations on free use of your time, based on a chance meeting, run out?
- People who look at you and say they know all about you.

Corporate Blurs and Blunders

- Retail chains advertising items but do not stock in sufficient quantities on store shelves. They may have allocated a small number of items to go on sale, or employees are too lazy to restock the displays. Or, perhaps they indulged in "bait and switch" advertising.
- Service people who miss appointments, are overly late or arbitrarily change the time of service without asking your permission or at least letting you know why. Further, these people have no remorse about your inconveniences or wasted time.
- People who do anything "in your best interest" without consulting you first. Their convenience is all that matters.
- Companies to whom you complain about their poor customer service who simply apologize but do not offer to do anything to make amends. Very few know what true customer service is.
- Retailers are using the promise of discount coupons to sell items at full price, rather than discounting them. Consumers are paying for fulfillment houses to operate and do not realize as much discount as in a regular discount. Why couldn't they just discount it at the register? It's a sales gimmick, not a service to customers.
- People who refer your name to networkers but never to paying sources of business. People who refer your name as one of a group but never in your own right.

- People who take their lunch at the precisely same hour everyday and schedule all business so as not to interfere are equally myopic about most other aspects of their job.

Reflecting and Moving Forward Positively

The process of rethinking one's attitude and strategy toward life is hardly a simple process. Its implementation and ultimate success depends upon:

- Recognizing that change is 90% positive, resolving to stop fighting change so vehemently.
- Finding reasons and rationale to embrace change.
- See how change relates to ourselves.
- You never hear entrepreneurs talking about paid vacations, perks and sick days they took off.
- Starting to "let go" of the past and the excess baggage that it carries.
- Realizing that the process of mastering change and turning transactions into a series of win-win propositions constitutes the real meaning of life.
- Commitment toward a program of change.
- Documentation of steps made, celebrating the victories.
- Commitment to change being a long-term and never-ending process.
- Committing and celebrating others in your process of pro-active change.
- Practicing Continuous Quality Improvement in every aspect of your life.

Clues are learned and synthesized daily. Knowledge is usually amassed through unexpected sources. Any person's commitment toward leadership development and continuing education must include honest examination of his-her life skills. Training, reading and pro-activity are prescribed. The first way to start self-enhancement is to examine the vast numbers of people who are doing nothing to progress and, thus, remain clueless. From this study will emerge our own clues for overcoming challenges.

Chapter 16

CAREER EVOLUTION
Why People Work. Building Blocks of Careers.

T he average person has held 12 jobs between ages 18 and 48. Workers stay at each of his/her jobs for 4.4 years, according to the Bureau of Labor Statistics. Some devote more time and energy toward transitioning from one job to another.

Job-hopping is defined as spending less than two years in a position, often going across the street for a few more dollars. Some job-hopping can be beneficial and builds strong resumes. Experts caution that bouncing from one position to another can be a red flag to prospective employers.

Because of changes in business and the aspirations of employees, workers will have seven careers in his/her lifetime. Single careers are no longer realistic, as individuals need to adapt to the needs of the job market and competencies.

Careers that one can resume after years out of the workforce including nursing, lawyer, teacher, transportation provider, sales, customer service, food preparation, repairs, non-profit management and logistics coordination.

Why People Work

There are 26 reasons why people seek, keep and excel at jobs. Money is only one of the reasons. Here they are, per each category of The Business Tree™:

1. The Business You're In

Doing good work, with standards of professionalism.

Producing products/services that make a difference.

2. Running the Business

Maintaining high productivity.

Having the ability to control and influence.

Making correct decisions.

3. Financial

Receiving adequate compensation.

Maintain standards of accountability.

4. People

Being accepted and acknowledged.

Being part of a motivated team.

Receiving praise, recognition and advancement.

Having a certain amount of freedom on the job.

Learning new things.

Enjoying work and having fun with the job.

Working with good managers and leaders.

Being perceived as a role model.

5. Business Development

Having direct involvement in important projects.

Doing work that empowers customers.

Maintaining integrity, with customers and themselves.

6. Body of Knowledge

Exemplifying standards of quality.

Remaining confident about work.

Exemplifying value and excellence.

Achieving balance in life, thus becoming a more valuable employee.

Need for personal and professional growth.

7. The Big Picture

Feeling like you've made a positive contribution.

Accomplishing worthwhile things.

Being in an organization that makes a difference.

Differences Between a Career and a Job:

- 20 hours a week.
- Not knowing what a coffee break is.
- Working smarter hours, not necessarily longer.
- Possession and nurturing of a dream.
- An interest in pursuing and achieving, versus just doing something.
- A career is not something that one retires from or puts on the shelf temporarily.
- Thinking like the boss, whether or not you are it at this present position.
- Money is not the dominant driving influence.
- Training and professional development are rewards.
- The more you know, you realize what you don't know and proceed to learn.

Biggest Career Killers in the Early Years:

1. Insufficient Life Preparation. Home environment, parenting, school experiences, social interactions and life experiences influence the direction of a career. All of us are under-prepared, and the way in which we overcome and grow is what spawns success.

2. Not Wanting or Seeking a Niche. Waiting too long to establish a marketable niche causes the young person to ramble and search. Society tends to place labels, and the aimlessly searching young professional will get saddled with one that is not likely appropriate.

3. Waiting to Make Professional Commitments. One must do work that is satisfying, but opting for fun and thrills over a professional commitment sets life patterns. Holding a job is not the same thing as building a career foundation. Those who hold jobs are forever restless. Those who steadily build careers are more rewarded, in every sense of the word.

4. Underdeveloped People Skills. Saying irretrievable things, championing the wrong causes and holding grudges does damage to workers. One catches more flies with honey...oh, if only people had told us about this sooner! Continuing patterns of underdeveloped social skills hold one back. Those who really succeed cultivate and nourish people first, work product secondarily and processes thirdly.

5. Reality Based Education. Early preparation and formal schooling are valuable first steps. One must fulfill a plan of professional and leadership enhancement to be successful in the long-term. Corporations value you in relation to their objectives, not yours.

6. The Corporate Culture. You're only as valuable as the marketplace judges that you are. Job performance and exhibited professionalism make the difference. The successful professional must communicate with others. Doing great work matters little unless it collaborates with corporate cultures in which it exists. Document your worth and activities.

7. The Long Distance. Life and business test us constantly. Within the unfairness, inequities and confusion lie opportunities for the young professional to develop a niche, conceptualize a dream and pursue success professionally.

Characteristics of a Top Professional

- Understands that careers evolve.
- Prepares for the unexpected turns and benefit from them, rather than becoming the victim of them.
- Realizes there are no quick fixes.
- Finds a truthful blend of perception and reality, with sturdy emphasis upon substance, rather than style.
- Has grown as a person and as a professional...and quests for more enlightenment.
- Has succeeded and failed and has learned from both.
- Was a good "will be," taking enough time in early career years to steadily blossom, realizing that advanced status wouldn't come quickly.
- Has paid dues and knows that, as the years go by, one's dues paying accelerates, rather than decreases.

Rising Stars Who Will Go the Distance

Here are some characteristics of young people (rising stars) who will make it as professionals and business leaders:

- Act as though they will one day be management.
- Think as a manager, not as a worker.
- Learn and do the things it will take to assume management responsibility.
- Be mentored by others.
- Act as a mentor to still others.
- Don't expect status overnight.
- Measure their output and expect to be measured as a profit center to the company.
- Learn to pace and be in the chosen career for the long-term.
- Don't expect that someone else will be the rescuer or enable you to cut corners in the path toward artificial success.
- Learn from failures, reframing them as opportunities.
- Learn to expect, predict, understand and relish success.
- Behave as a gracious winner.
- Acquire visionary perception.
- Study and utilize marketing and business development techniques.
- Contribute to the bottom line, directly and indirectly.
- Offer value-added service.
- Never stop paying dues, and see this continuum as "continuous quality improvement."
- Study and comprehend the subtleties of life.
- Never stop learning, growing and doing. In short, never stop!

Qualities to Master in Career Evolution

1. Know Where You Are Going. Develop, update and maintain a career growth document. Keep a diary of lessons learned but not soon forgotten. Learn the reasons for success and, more importantly, from failure.
2. Truth and Ethics. If you do not "walk the talk," who will? Realize that very little of what happens to you in business is personal. Find common

meeting grounds with colleagues. The only workable solution is a win-win (or as close to it as can be negotiated).

3. Professional Enrichment. Early formal education is but a starting point. Study trends in business, in your industry and, more importantly, in the industries of your customers. There is no professional who does not have one or more "customers." The person who believes otherwise is not a real professional.

4. People Skills Mastery. There is no profession that does not have to educate others about what it does. The process of communicating must be developed. It is the only way to address conflicts, facilitate win-win solutions and further organizational goals.

5. Mentorship and Stewardship. We are products of those who believe in us. Find role models and set out to be one yourself. To get, you must give.

6. Going the Distance. Career and life are not a short stint. Do what it takes to run the decathlon. Set personal and professional goals, standards and accountability.

7. Standing for Something. Making money is not enough. You must do something worth leaving behind, mentoring to others and of recognizable substance. Your views of professionalism must be known.

Chapter 17

SUPPLY CHAIN MANAGEMENT

S uppliers are businesses that provide raw materials, equipment, supplies, tools and other goods or services that the dependent organization uses in the production of economic goods and services.

Suppliers have their own wants and needs that management must satisfy. The purchasing organization is a customer of the supplier, important to the supplier's business.

The satisfaction of suppliers is a function of competition. If the supplier is the only source, he may have a greater sense of satisfaction. If there is a high degree of competition is his field, then he may have to compromise more and parcel out the satisfaction factor. Most suppliers need to work effectively with customers and their marketplace.

Supply Chain Management is the coordination of activities to maximize customer value and achieve a sustainable competitive advantage. It represents a conscious effort by the supply chain firms to develop and run supply chains in the most effective & efficient ways possible. The term was introduced in 1982. In the late 1990s, Supply Chain Management rose to prominence, and operations managers began to use it in their titles with increasing regularity.

Other definitions of supply-chain management include:

- Management of upstream and downstream value-added flows of materials, final goods and information among suppliers, company, resellers and consumers.
- Strategic coordination of traditional business functions and tactics across all business functions within a particular company and across businesses within the supply chain, for the purposes of improving performance of the individual companies and the supply chain as a whole.
- Strategies requiring a total systems view of links in the chain that work together efficiently to create customer satisfaction at the end point of delivery. The supply-chain system must be responsive to customer requirements."
- The integration of key business processes across the supply chain for the purpose of creating value for customers and stakeholders.

Supply Chain Management encompasses planning and management of all activities involved in sourcing, procurement, conversion and logistics management. It includes coordination with channel partners, which may be suppliers, intermediaries, third-party service providers or customers.

SCM integrates management across companies. The loosely coupled, self-organizing network of businesses that cooperate to provide product and service offerings has been called the Extended Enterprise.

Key Aspects of Supply Chain Management Systems

Purchasing is a subset of procurement that generally refers to buying the materials or parts needed to manufacture a finished product. Purchasing requires teams to maintain knowledge of price and availability trends as well as supplier performance.

Plant operations is a range of activities, including quality control, inventory control, management, production planning and online changes in production plans.

Logistics is the organization of moving, housing and supplying troops and equipment. Inbound transportation. Its components include outbound transportation, fleet management, warehousing, materials handling, order fulfillment, inventory management and demand planning.

Supplier management, also known as procurement, describes the methods and processes of corporate or institutional buying.

Processes are a series of steps and actions taken to achieve a particular end.

Workflow is the way that a particular work is organized. It is the sequence of industrial, administrative and other processes through which a piece of work passes from initiation toward completion.

Inventory optimization is the practice of having the right inventory to meet target service levels while tying up a minimum amount of capital in inventory. Inventory optimization is the next level of inventory management for warehouse and supply chain managers and buyers.

Preparedness is a research-based set of actions that are taken as precautionary measures in the face of potential disasters. These actions can include both physical preparations and trainings for emergency action.

The physical flow of products is how they go from suppliers to e-retailers facilities and final delivery of products to end-customers usually done by a 3PL provider. The information flow represents different on-line services to customers and supply chain partners.

General strategies for supply chain management lead with customer driven planning, real-time demand insights and demand shaping. The ever-changing nature of customer demand is to build out a supply chain that is dynamic and responsive, where agility is a key capability. Changing market opportunities require that the entire team across the supply chain, from the frontline through to executives, have the ability to shift gears quickly from one set of requirements to another, in short order.

Product innovation, the starting point for all manufacturing, can occur with the development cycle in mind. Products built for sustainability can be easily reconfigured and meet changing demands as needs from customers change.

Quality is not something that managers assign others to achieve. It is a mindset that permeates organizations from top-down as well as bottom-up. Rather than assume all is wrong or right with an organization and take a defensive posture, management must view quality as essential to their economic survival or growth.

Quality entails these concepts:

- Success is determined by conformity to requirements.
- It is achieved through prevention, not appraisal. The quality audit by objective outside communications counsel is merely the beginning of a process.
- The quality performance standard is zero defects. That means doing things correctly the first time, without wasting counter-productive time in cleaning up mistakes.
- Nonconformance is costly. Make-good efforts cost more on the back end than doing things right on the front end.
- Next cycle supply chain is the sum of the longest lead-time for each stage in the cycle. It represents the total time taken to fulfill a customer's order at all inventory levels.
- Economics is the social science that studies production, distribution and consumption of goods and services. Economics focuses on the behavior and interactions of economic agents and how economies work.
- Ethics is a branch of philosophy that involves systematizing, defending and recommending concepts of right and wrong conduct.

Departments within Supply Chain Management include:

- Procurement and sourcing.
- Warehousing.
- Transportation and Logistics.
- Supplier Management.
- Returns Management. Costs must be lowered throughout the chain by driving out unnecessary expenses, movements and handling. The main focus is on efficiency and added value to the end users. Efficiency must be increased, with bottlenecks removed. The measurement of performance focuses on total system efficiency and an equitable monetary reward distribution to those within the supply chain.

Considerations for company Supply Chain Management programs:

- The next big trend in supply chain strategy and skills required for success.
- How to better structure a company's supply-chain strategy.

- Guidelines for making strategic sourcing and make-buy decisions.
- How to integrate e-business thinking into supply chain strategy and management.
- How to blend recent developments in information systems and communication technology with sophisticated decision support systems, creating comprehensive strategies for manufacturing and logistics.
- Clock-speed benchmarking is a tool for deriving critical business insights and management lessons from industries with the highest obsolescence rates of products, process technologies and organizational structures.
- How to assimilate sustainability into supply chain strategy.
- Why all advantages in fast environments are temporary.

Just-In-Time Inventory Control

Just-in-Time is a method in which materials arrive only as needed to meet actual customer demand and output. Receiving raw goods, products and parts right before they are needed reduces unnecessary inventory, with benefits including:

- Lower costs from excess inventory being shipped.
- Lower costs of storage.
- Less unnecessary inventory.
- More space for more productive uses.
- Less waste.

Just-in-Time applies to:

- Planning.
- Manufacturing.
- Production.
- Training.
- Logistics, including scheduling, trucking, freight, shipping, door-to-door services and delivery.
- Inventory System.
- Re-Ordering.
- Customer Services.

Features of JIT include:

- Continuous improvement in terms of quality, quantity and cost.
- Elimination of waste.
- Reduction in Inventory levels.
- Set-up time reduction increases flexibility and allows smaller batches.
- Mixed production to smooth the flow of products through the factory.
- Workplace cleanliness and organization. Characteristics of a just-in-time production process are:
- Daily or hourly deliveries of small quantities of parts from suppliers.
- Certification of supplier quality, so that no receiving inspections are needed.
- Arrangement of production areas into flexible work centers.
- Compression of production areas so that in-process goods can be directly handed off to the next work center in a production flow.
- On-site inspection of each in-process product from the preceding work center, so that flaws are discovered at once.
- Use of rapid machine setups, so that production runs can be as short as one unit.
- Production stops as soon as the immediate demand level has been fulfilled.
- Immediate shipment of completed goods to customers as soon as an order has been fulfilled.

The advantages of JIT inventory systems are that production runs are short, meaning that manufacturers can quickly move from one product to another. This method reduces costs by minimizing warehouse needs. Companies spend less money on raw materials because they buy just enough resources to make the ordered products and no more.

Disadvantages of JIT inventory systems involve potential disruptions in the supply chain. If a raw materials supplier has a breakdown and cannot deliver the goods in a timely manner, this could stall the entire production process. A sudden unexpected order for goods may delay the delivery of finished products to end clients.

In order to put a SCM program into place, the following steps must be taken:

- Study the activities of admired companies. Set meetings to review what works for them. Companies can and should be role models for each other.
- Retain outside experts. Good experts will tell you the hard facts and what needs to be done.
- Research drives SCM programs. It will provide comparisons between the realities and perceptions that are held.
- Assemble an internal SCM team, making sure that major departments are represented.
- Set realistic timelines for putting recommendations into place.
- Set schedules for routine review of the process. This includes repeating surveys to assure that you are making adequate progress.

Slogans only create adversarial relationships. Once the system owns up to its shortcomings and responsibilities, then a true quality process will occur. Failure to read the "handwriting on the wall" will thwart company growth and, thus, the overall economy.

Paying attention to relationships within the supply chain can realize:

- Lower operating costs. Research shows they can be cut in half.
- Premium pricing for preferred goods and services.
- Customer retention.
- Enhanced reputation.
- Access to global markets.
- Faster innovation.
- Higher sales.
- Higher return on investments.

Benefits of Supply Chain Management include:

- Expanded sourcing opportunities.
- Economies of scale.

- Reaching new customers in new markets.
- More room to grow.
- Impacting the bottom line.
- Standards of quality.
- Streamlined continuity of the processes.
- Transparency and reviews of accomplishments.

Chapter 18

SCREENS AND TOUCHSTONES OF INTEGRITY

Windows on the World and Business.
Valuing Differences to Establish Common Ground.

T he view of life by each person and each organization is like a screen. Each interprets different images, events, factors and outcomes based upon the perceptions they hold to be true and feel comfortable in recognizing.

Screens are our outlooks on the outside world. Depending upon one's focus, screens can open up perspectives or limit them. Screens can alter and illuminate through increasingly bright light shining through or filter it. Screens can amplify our viewpoints or can tint them. Screens can enlighten the truths revealed by others, or people can hide from these truths.

We look at various aspects of life through many different screens, including televisions, computer terminals, eyeglasses, clocks, microwave ovens, radar and the oscilloscope. Still other screens through which we establish cultural contexts include glass containers, movie projection screens, plastic containers, doors, windows and light. Our windows on the world may also take such forms as industrial control panels, arcade games, automobile windshields, picture frames, product packaging, microscopes and the looking glass.

In the conduct of normal daily business, organizations with different screens must intersect. Some see other people with different screens as being either wrong or contrary. Each is basing their scope of vision upon a limited screen. When considering perspectives of others, the answers change still further.

Research shows that people essentially agree on 95% of everything. It's that other 5% that starts wars and fans the fires of feuds. The sooner that both sides communicate their differences, this affords commonalties to flow in discussions. What defeats us is not the facts by which our screens differ from others. It is the second-guessing, projecting of values, failure to learn from past experiences, imagining wrongs, and so on.

A screen might be an eyeglass. It could be a series of icons and images. Some utilize screens to filter out truths and serve as barriers to new ideas (thus causing corporate tragedies as recent times).

When an individual or company opens its window on the world, they take on macroscopic, enlarged viewpoints. The following variables change our screens daily:

1. Focus. Type of screen. Viewpoints, depending upon information we have.
2. Clarity. Purpose for using. How the viewer affects how he or she watches the screen.
3. Channel Selection. Interface with others' screens. Experience with people and organizations of comparable characteristics, behaviors or values. If a certain personality type impacts us negatively, we will generalize about others of comparable types.
4. Fine Tuning. Prior experiences are the basis for future decisions. Definitions of success, failure and opportunities reflect how we perceive things that happen to us.
5. Off-the-Screen. Many mitigating factors create a ratio of correct perceptions to misperceptions. Some people stop trusting their gut instincts. Others have learned how to fine-tune their intuitions.
6. Viewing Conditions. These include the person's and organization's qualities and core values. One must view the overall energy level and

the company's motivations to look beyond the obvious or see things in different ways.

7. Type of Program. Factors include the person's cultural upbringing, education, training and intellectual stimulation. Their goals, objectives, motivations and rewards depend upon how all of these factors are reapplied.

Comparing Screens

There is a party game called Pictionary. In it, players are given instructions and cues and are asked to portray the descriptions into visual images. Given the same information, it is amazing how vastly different each of the finished drawings looks. Cues heard translate into drawings based upon each player's screen, what they believe the instructions to be, how they are trained to draw and what their perception of the image is.

Players marvel at the completed images, viewing based upon their own screens. "What's that," asks a partner. "How can I tell what you're trying to draw, based upon what you have put here on paper," inquires another. "It's awesome to see how many takes on life we all have," conclude the jovial team members at the end of the round.

In dating, they say that you must kiss a few frogs before finding a prince. The reason why people don't "click" has to do with many factors outside of the actual people involved. Criteria include physical preferences, emotional baggage, activity interests, educational-intellectual-spiritual preferences, existence of children, job demands and many more.

People and organizations are like ships passing in the night when searching for compatible partners. When several of the factors intersect, then they develop "chemistry." It doesn't mean that previous dates were bad people but that the screens just were not on the same channel, or at least on the same cable system.

The same holds true in business. "Do you know a good consultant" means the ability to get results for my type of project, based upon your results. Most referrals are made on the basis of chance meetings, one-time experiences, perceived "star value" of the purveyor or other surface criteria that do not always relate to credentials.

Ask business people to list the priorities of their jobs, and you get answers based upon their screens of what is needed, wanted and expected by them, not necessarily reflecting a common organizational Vision for the organization. Even in companies with written Policies and Procedures, views of norms and expectations vary. Sadly, most companies do not have viable job descriptions, policies and benchmark processes, which tends to create many other problems.

In a television interview, an astronaut stated that technology is the most important key to future success, progress and global understanding. No. Technology is one small key but not the most important key. It is superseded by people's developed abilities to think, change, grow, reason and work with others, none of which are created by technology. The speaker took the technology posture because that is his reference point, what he is selling for a living and what his screen believes to be true. His position was based upon personal background, agenda, training and bias.

Ask friends for recommendations of movies, restaurants, lines of clothing and other purchases based upon subjectivity. Their value judgments will reflect personal tastes, experiences, perceptions of quality and values received, theirs, not necessarily yours.

Ask a very poor person about the priorities in life, and you will hear about basic needs of food, water and shelter. Ask a wanna-be social climber about the vitalities of life, and you will be told about designer fashions, aligning with the "right charities" (few of which benefit the aforementioned very poor people) and the best social opportunities.

Ask business people about the concept of networking. People who are trying to sell something or use you to further their agendas love networking and use every trick to make it work for them. Top executives and global thinkers try our best to shy away from the hordes of networkers, feeling hit upon too often by the "dial and smile" types. We view networking quite differently from those who just want to "pick our brain."

Ask bureaucrats what they think of taxpayers, and you may hear grumbling about interchanges they have had with constituents. Ask call center people at large companies about customers, and they likewise grumble about all those upset people. These business screeners still have not gotten the fact that customers keep them in business.

Factors Creating Screens

The brain sees and senses things and then processes into screens. Every sense affects what images, ideas and ideologies appear on each of our screens. These include sight, hearing, emotions, perceptions, reactions and thought processes.

Other than the basic senses, each person's screens (views of life and each transaction) are affected by still other factors, such as family history, expectations, cultural background, physical characteristics and personality (of which there are 16 basic categories). Through schooling, we developed varying degrees of social skills, talents, aptitude, a body of education, life motivations, honor, integrity and values.

Generational differences factor in. There are six generations in the population: Greatest, persons born through 1926. Silent Generation, born 1927-1945. Baby Boomers, born 1946-1964. Generation X, born 1965-1983. Generation Y, aka Millennials, born 1984-2002. Generation Z, born 2003-2021. These are the correct figures.

Job, career and profession factors that shape the executive workforce include:

- Mentorship and encouragement by others.
- Opportunities created or available at various times.
- Training.
- Technical proficiency.
- Working-motivational style (of which there are seven basic categories).
- Management-behavioral style (of which there are four basic categories).
- Wrong turns, false starts and side trips along the way.
- Marketplace-industry factors outside your control but affecting your business.

Many managers never get past this point. This is the dividing point, after which executives emerge and continue their quest to become excellent leaders. Successful individuals will develop such additional self-regulated professional factors as:

- Ethical values, of which there are seven basic categories.
- Trial and error, the way that you handle, grow from and profit from mistakes.
- Creation and sustaining of a Body of Knowledge.

- Professional, personal and community interaction-stewardship.
- Adapting continuous quality improvement concepts to your company.

In order to succeed in the long-term, executives must develop these self-responsible life and professional factors:

- Ability to routinely face and master the realities of life, not to live in a dream world.
- Facing and breaking down defenses, procrastinations, self-sabotage and pain.
- Attitude.
- Perseverance.
- Self-esteem.
- Determination.
- Positive reinforcements.
- Success tracks.
- Creation of opportunities.
- Benchmarks of success.
- Creation and sustaining of a Body of Work.
- Giving something back to the profession and community.
- Achieving balance in life…self-fulfillment.
- Commitment toward excellence.

Touchstones of Integrity

Different perceptions of what is an ethical, honorable and successful business stem from the different screens from which executives emerge.

Different people can witness the same incident and come up with different accounts. Someone hears a story and passes it on. Hearsay has a way of getting distorted. The final version has no semblance to the truth. People believe a fabrication-distortion more quickly than the truth. A logical explanation for an event taken out of context is met with astonishment at first, then is believed.

One mannerism triggers reactions or reminds us of comparable events, circumstances or outcomes. Obsessive and compulsive behaviors blur one's screen. The media of communications affect and stylize every message.

Hearing and listening are not the same thing. Having good intentions and taking ethical actions are not the same thing. Expectations and accountabilities are not the same thing. Each person and organization has different standards, which must be reconciled and then met. Building commonalties is the best way to intersect standards and build ethical careers and solid-standing organizations.

Beware of over-standardization, which becomes unenforceable rigidity. Overly rigid people and organizations have problems backing down, adapting and changing.

Touchstones of Integrity mean dealing with different situations and teachings. Bad circumstances and successful times are what develop cohesion and solidarity. Touchstones are knowing the right thing, doing the right thing and choosing friends with integrity.

Certain expressions conjure different images, impressions and opinions, based upon one's screens. Imagine how different people and organizations could define the following:

- A well-run business.
- Customer service.
- Diversity in culture and the workplace.
- A good brand.
- A job. A career. A profession. A legacy.
- A friend. A colleague. A role model.
- Education.
- Networking.
- Quality. Excellence. Perfection.
- Empowered employees.
- Strategic Planning.
- Government services for communities.
- Collaborating, partnering and joint venturing.
- Investing in the future.
- Doing sufficient research.
- Company growth.
- Communicating with other people.
- Goals in life.

Some people and organizations go through life with one perspective, never updating or differentiating. There are others who are forced by circumstances to continually change. Most fall somewhere between, with a steady succession of adapting. The art of survival and growth is to create a happy medium.

Holding different answers, definitions and perceptions leads toward conflicting interests. Some imagine situations that simply are not accurate. Adhering to first impressions causes distortion of the real issues and perspectives. Multiple viewpoints create situations where something has to give.

When people want vastly different things and cannot agree upon the same definitions, then problems occur. When each party adheres steadfastly to their own screens, then trouble escalates. That's why people and organizations remain at odds, dysfunctional and complicated to administer.

Human beings agree upon things 95% of the time. It's that 5% where they disagree and are not willing to negotiate that gets them into trouble.

One of the hardest things to do is to accurately tune into someone else's or some company's wavelength. Human beings are unpredictable and, fortunately, changeable. People say things, and we interpret them out of context. We think that they should know what we know and, therefore, will tune into our screen. Wishing two-way communications to happen and seeing the process to fruition are polar points.

Time Changes and Passages

An interesting experiment is to take people who have interacted together in one time frame and reunite them years later.

In my earliest career, I was a radio disc jockey. A by-product and lucrative sideline was the opportunity to take the sound system, the records and air personality to play music for dances. In the early years, they were called "record hops." When they took place at shopping malls and grand openings, they were "personal appearances" (and talent fees included calling in live "remotes" back to the radio stations). In later years, the process was known as "mobile disco." Again, different screens look at the same basic concept.

I specialized in golden oldies and gravitated toward entertaining at high school reunions, doing about 150 of them over the years. I played reunions for classes who graduated between 1926 and 1990 (most of them being classes from the 1950s and

1960s). As an objective outsider, I played the music of their three-year high school eras and watched the attendees play out the screens of their lives, then and now.

Successful business people attending these events suddenly reverted back to their old high school roles, when at the party. Clique members re-associated, asking "Do you remember when?" and trying to recapture what once was. People showed up thinking that old loves were still carrying the torch, that old feuds were still remembered, or that some major revelation about the good old days might hit them during the evening.

By the third hour, they have the announcements, gag awards and recognition of special guests. It's like a magic wand has been waved over the crowd. I've been progressing the music toward this point, though the crowd is not supposed to know the method behind my art. After all, music is a form of psychology, and making memories can help put the past into clearer perspective.

One then begins seeing people talking with and dancing with people with whom they had little or nothing in common way back when. New screens about current realities begin to form.

The crowd now gives each other permission to move into the present. Having gone through the evening's metamorphosis, many put the past into clearer perspective. Reunions of all kinds can be cleansing events, or they can perpetuate old myths, egos and misperceptions.

There are seven reasons why one should review and take retrospective looks back at old screens. In the business vernacular, we make full-scope performance reviews, rethink core business strategies and evaluate where we have been, in order to chart where we are going. Sometimes we meet with old colleagues and partners, in order to gain reality checks.

Those seven reasons may include:

1. See things as they really were, not as we believe them to have been.
2. Periodically take snapshots of moments in time. Revisit old situations, contexts, resource bases and outcomes to get current perspective.
3. Put past perspectives into focus. Knowledge gleaned from the things you have accomplished gives the direction for the next plan.

4. See what you had to work with, as contrasted with today's knowledge and resources. Most deals and collaborations failed because resources at that time were not adequate to fulfill lofty projections.
5. Study how you reacted to situations, people and coping mechanisms.
6. Analyze external factors which were beyond your control and which adversely affected your previous courses of action.
7. Decide what you have accomplished as a result of those crossroads at which you made momentous decisions. Had it not been for those circumstances, could you have made it to this point?

Look at The Big Picture and See More

Different people view the world, business and their position in direct relation to their frame of reference, background and agenda. I've heard these definitions of business offered by niche experts:

- "The entire basis of business is to move products and services." (sales)
- "Business operates solely to interact people with other people." (human resources)
- "Business operates only for monetary reasons." (accountants)
- "We protect our turf and, thus, our people's future." (organized labor)
- "Processes that assure continuity in operations." (government bureaucracy)
- "Corporations need to be learning organizations." (trainers)

As the Big Picture overview proponent, I agree that all niches are important but cannot side with any one niche. My function is to be the overview mentor and uncle, endorsing all of the above as part of overall strategies. Most niche consultants are excellent at what they do, but they often do not sell the importance of their work beyond just their niche. As the cheerleader for the niches, I help top management to contextualize the specialty professionals as part of a bigger scope. Once put into broader perspective, then opportunities for the niche consultants and departmental service providers to be optimally successful are expanded.

While being the Big Picture catalyst for expanded horizon, I've heard several comments voiced by people in the niches (AKA, from one screen or another). These are sample remarks:

- "What you're talking about is 90% common sense. Why don't we get this broader perspective more often?" Yes, the tenets of this book are common sense. I phrase everything in such a way as they can be interpreted on several levels. Our society is so micro-niche focused because some of the niches (notably financial) have vested interests in keeping it micro-niche. We don't hear about the Big Picture again because we're so accustomed to hearing from limited niche perspectives. People can and do widen their scopes when events necessitate it or they realize themselves at an undeniable crossroads.

- "You're like an oasis in the desert." I feel the same way about the person who said it. I admire her as a professional, intellect and visionary. My goal is to inspire the hidden visionary qualities in most executives. Once acknowledged and nurtured, then they evolve to become effective and inspiring leaders.

- "This project was doomed to failure. Only your team could have pulled it off." The project was too much for my client's team. As objective outsiders, my team was willing to go the extra distance. We focused upon goals, rather than being bogged down by the client's internal politics, which included feelings of helplessness. The client should not have been so over-critical of the own operational abilities. The "can do it" attitude of the combined team really deserved the compliments.

- "I cannot say that I've implemented everything in your writings, but I read every word." Getting people's attention is the first step. Having them see validity in the content is the next. My ideas and strategies are a reflection of many past lessons that the audiences absorbed, simply refocused for contemporary business usage. The value of Futurism, change management and strategized growth is their willingness to read, learn and adapt to their own situations.

- "You're a lawyer's dream." The ability to consistently boil down facts, allegations and circumstances into succinct business briefing documents was praised. I believe that every true professional must develop the ability to put themselves into someone else's shoes and learn to communicate. The more that we learn about client industries and marketplace factors outside our own focus, we are better suited to meet the challenges of tomorrow.

• There is only one person who has our own set of life and business experiences. Put them all together, and we have corporate cultures that need to be nourished, rather than just evolving by happenstance. Nothing happens without a context. Screens go both ways.

Chapter 19

SLOGANS

The Big Picture of Business has been viewed in this book series through the prism of business, growth and entrepreneurial spirit. An appropriate Executive Summary of the contents is to recapitulate the history as a listing of slogans.

This takes marketing, cultural and historical approaches. In my own words, here is the emphasis upon a dynamic climate for commerce, entrepreneurship and opportunity. I summarize this book with slogans.

200 Years of Business History

Born out of revolution.

Grown on Independence.

Spirit of adventure.

Magnet of opportunities.

Celebrating the victories.

Built by immigrants, seeking better lives for themselves and children.

Modern companies, no matter the era.

Destination center.

Reasons for being here.

Celebrating our common culture.

Put together winning teams.

Let us do business all over the globe.

Forerunner of the 21st Century boom.

Gracious living on the frontier.

Impressed by the quality of life.

Not just for show.

Lively activity.

Exponential growth.

Business at every juncture.

Dreaming all the time.

We're all immigrants. We're all natives. Diversity personified.

Measured by the strength of each one's resolve.

Always ahead of the economy.

Beginning each decade optimistically.

Doors open for success.

Salad bowl of flavors.

Born out of revolution.

Maximizing the "good old days."

Business Now

The future is coming: past, present and future continuum.

The "good old days" are always here. The best is ahead of us.

Citizens of the world.

Businesses are families.

Each contributes, and all derive.

It's for the customer and their customer.

In the right direction.

Directions to take.

Answering the questions.

Do what you love through interlocking careers.

When the pieces fit together.

It only takes a moment.

Discover what you're best at.

Confluence of experiences, fusion, expressions, definitions and perspectives.

Know and highlight your strengths.

Understand yourself, and take action.

Find excellence after reflection.

When someone offers a quick fix, beware.

Professionalism, core values and success.

Really new perspectives via The Big Picture.

Ideas and dreams, backed with strategy, goals and tactics.

Coalescing dreams with ambitions.

The future brighter than imagined.

Keep refining your Business Success Checklist.

Windows of opportunity.

Big Think ideas.

Heart and Soul Reasons for Humanitarian Service

Being good citizens and helping others.

Volunteering, as time permits and worthy causes appear.

Business supporting communities.

Non-profit organizations operating more business-like.

Working together with others, exemplifying ethical behavior.

Sharing talents and skills.

Innovating programs, strategies and methodologies.

Recognizing and celebrating service.

Involving young people in the lifelong quest toward community service.

Diversity of society is reflected in service.

Building communities and interfacing with others.

Enlightening others and inspiring the next generation.

Creating new constituencies.

Re-involving those who have given, volunteered and participated in the past.

Understanding the relationship of causes to quality of life.

It's good for business, and it's the right thing to do.

Community events are fun and entertaining. Have fun while serving.

Knowledge is transferable from community service to family and business.

Injects heart and soul into yourself and your stakeholders.

Serving the under-served and predicting new community needs.

Benefiting humanity and fostering respect.

Putting ourselves in others' shoes.

Visioning the future of communities and the population.

Feeding, clothing, sheltering, educating and inspiring the needy.

Networking, beneficial for all concerned.

Growing as human beings and growing as a society.

Humanity is the basis for global peace and understanding.

Motivational Messages

Nice is the new cool.

It is nice to be important but more important to be nice.

Learn from the past without living in it.

The future has moved and left no forwarding address.

Advocate for others, discovering new frontiers, with opportunities to master.

Potlache means feeling happy and rewarded when serving others is appreciated.

Take good care of your future.

Go for the gold.

Satisfaction comes in a chain reaction.

Turn the world around.

The great mistake is thinking that tomorrow is the same as today.

Don't fight battles that don't matter.

The size of a problem is an indication of the size of your future.

You're only as good as the best thing you've ever done.

One learns to become their own best role model.

It is crucial to advance to higher tiers.

There is ALWAYS a next plateau, when we seek it.

You do your best work for free.

It's not if you change, it's how successfully you do it.

Life is a song sung well. Learn to appreciate the musical tastes of others.

Learn to pace and be in the chosen career for the long-run.

Behave as a gracious winner.

Find a truthful blend of perception and reality, with emphasis upon substance.

Shine, care, inspire and nurture.

Learn, mentor, lead, advance and actualize.

Leaders exemplify legendary behavior.

Communication is indicative of how you do business.

Don't interrupt the dream.

Chapter 20

STATISTICS AND RESEARCH ON THINGS
THAT AFFECT YOUR ABILITY TO DO BUSINESS

Business Realities
- 2% have a plan. 98% do not.
- Of the companies who continue to operate without a plan, 40% of them will be out of business in the next 10 years.
- 66.7% of all businesses cannot grow any further than they are.
- 44.1% of companies should not grow into large organizations.
- 36.2% of companies have limited life expectancies and are acquired by a larger organization.
- 2% of all consultants really are. The rest are vendors.
- 82% of all the companies that exist are small and emerging businesses.
- 98% of all new business starts are small and emerging businesses.
- 70% of all companies die in their first five years.
- 40% of those who do not plan will fail soon.
- 90% of firms are out of business by year 10.
- The 4-year survival rate in the information sector is 38%.

- The 4-year survival rate in education and health services sector is 55%.
- The average start-up in education and health sector is 50% more likely than the average start-up in the information sector to live four years.
- 40% of all start-up restaurants fail.
- 45% of small business owners are children of small business owners.
- 83% of all domestic companies have fewer than 20 employees.
- Only 7% of all companies have 100 or more employees.
- 69% of new companies with employees survive at least two years, and that 51% survive at least five years.
- 49% of new businesses survive for five years or more.
- 34% of new businesses survive ten years or more, and 26% are still in business at least 15 years after being started.

Distractions

The average person is bombarded by 1,200 messages everyday. More active people may encounter up to 3,000 messages per day. Messages come from other people, phone calls, e-mails, texts, billboards, publications, radio, television, the internet, phone apps, junk mail, website views, social media people you know and people who network. It has created a "too much information" environment.

The average attention span is 8 seconds. Most humans cannot stay focused on one thing for more than 20 minutes at a time. This is attributable to transient and selective attention. 11% of children have been diagnosed with Attention Deficit Hyperactivity Disorder. Males are three times more likely to be diagnosed with ADHD than females. 4% of adults now have ADHD.

Distracted driving accounts for 25% of all motor vehicle crash fatalities. Driver distraction is reported to be responsible for more than 58% of teen crashes. In 2018, 391,000 injuries were caused in distracted driving related accidents. Distracted driving was cited as a major factor in 3,477 traffic deaths.

Productivity on the Job

72% of employees admit to not giving it their all on the job, with 77% of managers agreeing. Employers dangle carrots to their staff in order to boost productivity. They include cash incentives, gift cards, family gifts, days off and lower insurance premiums for participating in a wellness program. Some offer to pay you tomorrow for extra work done today.

Consultants, with Percentages in the Marketplace

1. Wanna-be consultants. Vendors selling services. Subcontractors. Out-of-work people who hang out "consulting" shingles in between jobs. Freelancers and moonlighters, whose consultancy may or may not relate to their day jobs. (26%)
2. Entry-level consultants. Those who were downsized, out-placed, retired or changed careers, launching a consulting practice. Prior experience in company environment. (19.5%)
3. Grinders. Those who do the bulk of project work. Conduct programs designed by others. 1-10 years' consulting experience. (35.49%)
4. Minders. Mid-level consultants. Those with specific niche or industry expertise, starting to build a track record. 10-20 years' consulting experience. (13.5%)
5. Finders. Firms which package and market services. Most claim they have all expertise in-house. The more sophisticated ones are skilled at building and utilizing collaborations of outside experts and joint ventures. (3.5%)
6. Senior level. Veteran consultants (20 years+) who were trained for and have a track record in consulting. That's what they have done for most of their careers. (2%)
7. Beyond the strata of consultant. Senior advisor, routinely producing original knowledge. Strategic overview, vision expeditor. Creativity-insight not available elsewhere.

Customer Service

- 92% of customers will not return and simply won't come back.
- 89% of customers get frustrated repeating their issues to multiple representatives.
- 40% of consumers want to speak to a real person over the phone.
- 66% of customers will switch companies because of poor customer service.

- 77% of respondents believe a phone call is the most effective way to get an answer quickly.
- 62% have to repeatedly contact a company to resolve an issue.
- 86% of people are happy to pay up to 25% more if they get the right customer experience.
- 85% of people whose calls aren't answered will not call back.
- 51% of mobile searchers say they regularly call a business from a mobile search.
- 73% of marketers would more prominently feature phone numbers in their marketing emails if they could track data effectively.
- 65% of people prefer to contact a business by phone.
- 24% prefer to fill out an online form.
- 59% of customers prefer to call because they want a quick answer.
- 86% of telephone communication is tone of voice and just 14% the words we say.
- 70% of customers say agents' awareness of sales interactions is important to keeping their business.
- 80% of customers say the experience a company provides is just as important as its products or services.
- 59% of customers expect digital experiences to keep their business.
- 88% trust companies that vow not to share their personal information without permission.
- 79% of customers share relevant information about themselves in exchange for interactions.
- 27% report that ineffective customer service is their number one frustration.
- 72% say that explaining their problems to multiple people is poor customer service.
- 79% who used feedback to complain about poor customer experience online were ignored.
- 33% of recommend a brand that provides a quick but ineffective response.

- 17% of consumers would recommend a brand that provides a slow but effective solution.
- 88% of decision makers make significant investments in agent training.
- High-performing service teams are 3.2 times more likely to have a defined strategy.
- 82% of decision makers say their companies' customer service must transform to stay competitive.

Quality Improvement

- 36% of employees in companies with quality programs do not participate.
- Although 66% of employees are asked to be involved in decision-making processes, only 14% feel empowered to do so.

Percentages of Non-Profit Organizations

Arts and culture, 8%.

Education, 18%.

Foundations, 18%.

Human Services, 27%.

Religion, 9%.

All others, 11%.

Books

- 300,000 books out each year, most with information and opinion.
- 1 out of every 18,000 books started is ever finished.
- 1 out of every 12,000 completed manuscripts is published.
- 83% of books are self-published, vanity books for back-of-room sales. These include e-books.
- Of those published nationally, only 40% of the authors have follow-up titles.
- 4% of nationally published authors have book series.
- .2% of nationally published authors have more than one book series.

Employees and Their Work Behaviors

63% of survey respondents say they have witnessed behavior at work that was disruptive to culture, productivity and the business itself but didn't report it to management.

The success rate for organizational hires is 14%. If further research is put into looking at the total person and truly fitting the person to the job, then the success rate soars to 75%. That involves testing and more sophisticated hiring practices.

A disengaged employee can cost a company up to $3,400 per year for every $10,000 of salary. Every time that a business replaces a salaried employee, it costs 6-9 months' salary on average.

Retaining good employees, involving training, motivation and incentives, is yet another matter. According to research conducted by the Ethics Resource Center:

- Employees of organizations steal 10 times more than do shoplifters.
- Employee theft and shoplifting accounting for 15% of the retail cost of merchandise.
- 35% of employees steal from the company.
- 71% of employees are currently looking for another job.
- 28% of those who steal think that they deserve what they take.
- 21% of those who steal think that the boss can afford the losses.
- 56% of employees lie to supervisors.
- 41% of employees falsify records and reports.
- 31% of the workforce abuses substances.
- 61% of employees are burned out on the job.
- 89% of companies that support well-being initiatives are a good place to work.
- Highly engaged teams show 21% greater profitability
- 89% of HR leaders agree that peer feedback and check-ins are key for successful outcomes.
- Employees who feel their voice is heard are 4.6 times more likely to feel empowered to perform their best work
- 96% of employees believe showing empathy is an important way to advance retention.
- Disengaged employees cost U.S. companies up to $550 billion a year.

Behaviors of Parents Toward Their Children

- 76% reminded their adult children of deadlines they need to meet, including for schoolwork
- 74% made appointments for them, including doctor's appointments
- 15% of parents with children in college had texted or called them to wake them up, so they didn't sleep through a class or test.
- 8% of parents said they had contacted a college professor or administrator about their child's grades or a problem they were having.
- 11% helped write an essay or school assignment.
- 22% helped them study for a college test.
- 16% helped write all or part of a job or internship application.
- 14% told them which career to pursue.
- 14% helped them get jobs or internships through professional networks.
- 11% of parents with adult children call their child's employer if he or she had an issue at work.
- 12% gave $500+ per month for rent or daily expenses.

Use of the Phone

- Most of us spend 70% of waking hours in some form of communication: 9% writing, 16% reading, 30 percent speaking, and 45% listening. Studies also confirm that most of us are poor and inefficient listeners.
- Over 6 billion texts are sent everyday.
- Of the calls received on your phone, 58% are robo-call solicitations.
- 46% of e-mails are vendor solicitations from a list purchased by people trolling for business.
- 43% in your home mailbox is direct mail advertising.
- 97% of college students use their phones during class for non-educational purposes. Only 3% said they do not use a device during class for non-class-related activities on a typical day.

Social Media Addiction

- 3.1 billion people are social media users worldwide.
- 210 million people are known to suffer from internet and social media addiction.

- People who spend five hours a day on their phones are twice as likely to show depressive symptoms.
- Young single females are more addicted to social media than any other group.
- 71% of people sleep with or next to their mobile phone.
- 47 million people do not get enough sleep. 55% of teens are sleep deprived.
- 10% of teens check their phones 10 times or more per night.
- 45% of people check social media instead of sleeping.
- 50% of people driving are checking phones or using social media.

Robocalls

The telephone is a prime element in doing business. There are 50 billion robocalls per year, according to the robocall index operated by YouMail, a robocall blocking service.

Robocalls are phone calls using a computerized auto dialer to deliver a pre-recorded message, as if from a robot. Robocalls are often associated with telemarketing phone campaigns and can also be used for public service or emergency announcements.

Nearly half the calls made to US cell phones are spam, according to a study by First Orion. 90% of those calls will have familiar caller IDs, but there isn't a way of identifying a call as spam before answering.

SMS spam is illegal under common law in many jurisdictions as trespass to chattels. The Federal Trade Commission (FTC) has expanded Phone Spam regulations to cover also Voice Spam, mostly in the form of prerecorded telemarketing calls, commonly known as robocalls.

The FCC permits non-commercial robocalls to most residential (non-cellular) telephone lines. The federal Telephone Consumer Protection Act of 1991 (TCPA) regulates automated calls. All robocalls, irrespective of whether they are political in nature, must do two things to be considered legal.

Truecaller can automatically block unwanted calls based on known spammers, as well as numbers you manually add. You can look up specific names and phone numbers to get information on them. You can even make phone calls directly from the app to identify and call friends and other contacts.

When you answer the phone and hear a recorded message instead of a live person, it's a robocall. In addition to the phone calls being illegal, their pitch is a scam.

Most of us have gotten those annoying calls from telemarketers. If you have received the calls and tried all you can to make them stop, you can take legal action. One can sue telemarketers if proven they broke the law by constantly calling.

If you answer the phone and hear a recorded message instead of a live person, it's a robocall. If the recording is a sales message, and you haven't given your written permission to get calls from the company on the other end, the call is illegal.

A company that is a seller or telemarketer could be liable for placing any telemarketing calls (even to numbers NOT on the National Registry) unless the seller has paid the required fee for access to the Registry. Violators may be subject to fines up to $40,000 per violation.

Landlines have a function known as anonymous call rejection. To enable it, press "*77." Calls that come in as Anonymous, Private (a favorite of robocallers) or Blocked won't get through. You can turn the feature off by pressing "*87."

Caller ID spoofing is the practice of causing the telephone network to indicate to the receiver of a call that the originator of the call is a station other than the true originating station. The telecom industry plans to roll out new technology that would alert consumers when they are receiving a spoofed call, which is when criminals and others call you using numbers that look familiar but are fake.

Caller ID spoofing is the process of changing the caller ID to any number other than the calling number. When a phone receives a call, the caller ID is transmitted between the first and second ring of the phone. If you get calls from people saying your number is showing up on their caller ID, it's likely that your number has been spoofed. Scammers switch numbers frequently, and, within hours, they will no longer be using your number.

Scams trick victims into giving away precious information by calling them from what appears to be their own phone numbers. According to the WSPA, the "number spoofing" scam calls victims and displays the person's own phone number on caller ID.

Chapter 21

PUBLIC SERVICE ANNOUNCEMENTS

N on-profit organizations and the causes they promote are greatly served by enlightening the public. Public education is an important part of the charge for those organizations.

The earliest PSAs promoted the selling of war bonds and were shown in movie theatres during World War I and II. The campaigns included: "Loose lips sink ships" and "Keep 'em rolling." With the advent of radio in the 1920s and its popularity in the 1930s and 1940s, it was a natural sign-off for national shows to include public service messages. Local stations began airing PSAs during their programming to fill the holes when they had not sold all the commercial availabilities. Then, there were Community Calendar shows. Every disc jockey had their favorite causes, and talk shows often featured representatives of non-profit organizations to discuss their services.

When television hit in the late 1940s, public service advertising was institutionalized. PSAs were aired, just as had been done on radio. Local TV stations promoted non-profit organizations via recorded and live spots, ID slides and crawls of calendar items in local communities.

Some of the famous campaigns included annual United Way appeals, Smokey the Bear ("Only you can prevent forest fires"), McGruff, the dog ("Take a bite out of crime"), the United Negro College Fund ("A mind is a terrible thing to lose"), Just Say No to Drugs, the American Cancer Society ("Fight cancer with a check-up and a check"), anti-smoking campaigns, voter awareness, vaccinations, immunizations, educational programs, etc.

Many of the famous PSA campaigns were created by The Advertising Council. This was a consortium of advertising agencies who lent their creativity on a volunteer basis to a variety of causes. These ads won awards for creativity and spurred participating agencies to serve their clients and communities by their volunteer service. Other PSAs were devised by public relations agencies and the non-profit organizations themselves.

The Partnership for a Drug-Free America was founded in New York City in 1985. It was a consortium of advertising agencies who produced public service messages discouraging drug use. It coordinated campaigns with the federal government in its efforts to stem the spread of illegal drugs.

Entertainment shows got into the public service mode. Popular cop show "Highway Patrol" featured its star Broderick Crawford, at the end of each crime-fighting episode, delivering messages on public safety: "Reckless driving doesn't determine who's right, only who's left. If you care to drive, drive with care. It isn't the car that kills; it's the driver. Try to be as good a driver as you think you are. Leave your blood at the Red Cross or at your community blood bank, not on the highway. No matter how new, the safest device in your car is you. The laws of your community are enforced for your protection; obey them. The careless driver isn't driving his car; he's aiming it. It isn't what you drive, but how you drive that counts. The clowns at the circus, they're real funny, but on the highway, they're murder. We'll see you next week." That was the TV show that invented the sign-off "Ten Four," which was subsequently adopted by real police departments.

Another popular TV star of the 1950s and early 1960s was Ronald Reagan, host of "General Electric Theatre." He delivered public-spirited messages, which propelled his public persona enough to be elected Governor of California and President of the United States.

National PSAs tend to be image awareness for high-profile causes. Some highlight campaigns and fund-raising appeals. Local PSAs tend to be more specific, including:

- Image
- Campaign
- Cause awareness.
- Phone number to call.
- Special events.
- Cause to support.
- Fund raising.
- Collaboration with other groups.
- Prevention of disease.
- Support of the arts.
- Educational initiatives.
- Spread the word about social concerns.
- Inform and motivate the public.
- Volunteer recruitment.
- Appeals for help.
- Announcements of services, locations, times and delivery criteria.
- Take the cause to the next level.
- Cause related marketing by companies.
- Illuminate on humanitarianism and how citizens can get involved.

PSAs have had a massive impact on our culture. They steered many people into lives committed to community stewardship and leadership.

I have held a fondness and respect for public service announcements for many years. I began my career at age 10 at a radio station. I was a DJ and started writing PSAs, interfacing with people from the non-profit organizations.

Broadcasting used to be regulated. Stations had to reapply for licenses from the Federal Communications Commission every three years. We were required to keep Public Files of correspondence from listeners and community stakeholders. We were required to perform Community Ascertainment, a process by which we interviewed leaders on problems of the municipality and how our station might help to address them. Through all that, I became enamored with community service, developing trust relationships with stakeholders.

As the years progressed, I was asked to design public service campaigns, locally and nationally. Often, my work extended beyond the PSAs and to strategic planning the programs themselves. These included some memorable experiences:

- For the Houston Police Department were three campaigns: "The Badge Means You Care," "Reach For It" (seatbelt safety) and the Neighborhood Oriented Policing program.
- For UNICEF, I worked with celebrity spokespersons Audrey Hepburn, Roger Moore and Vincent Price. I got to direct both stars.
- For Neighborhood Centers, I wrote and produced the longest running TV PSA, for CHATTERS, a latchkey children's program, running a total of 12 years.
- I put together a food bank and literacy organizations, resulting in the campaign "Food for Thought," then got a corporate sponsor (Chevron) to support it.
- For United Way, I wrote two campaign themes: "The You in United Way" and "You're Doing So Much for So Many."

One night, I was dining at a restaurant and witnessed children acting out behavior at one table, while being noticed askance by other diners. That inspired me to write a series of PSAs. I got the idea from watching "As the World Turns," where tables at a restaurant play out dysfunctional behavior, with other tables watching in review.

Each of the five spots focused on one table, played out the dialog and ended with the tagline: "Even the best of families have the worst of times. With appropriate help, you can get through it. Houston Child Guidance Center, a United Way agency, phone number." We shot those mini-dramas in the style of soap operas. Thus, the TV stations ran our PSAs during daytime programming, in lieu of network promos.

The best compliment that I received was from the TV station public service directors: "We run everything that you send us. You know our needs and audiences." Once, I asked the directors if they had special time-slot needs beyond the traditional

30-second spots. They replied that they needed 10-second and 20-second spots. To meet that request, I produced a series of 16 different spots for the YWCA, shot in music video style, focusing on each program service area. The tagline was "YWCA: Always Here, Then + Now." We premiered those PSAs at a YWCA banquet, followed by a documentary on the agency. That campaign earned seven awards.

There were others:

- For Gulf Coast Legal Foundation, we dramatized issues related to poverty, with the tagline: "Nobody set out to be poor, and it's not fair. A compassionate and just legal system can help."
- Restaurateur Ninfa Laurenzo appearing as an advocate at a battered children's shelter.
- Athletes and entertainers celebrating the anniversary of NASA's landing on the moon, followed by a series for the Challenger Center.
- For Midtown Art Center, we projected the "Fabric of the Community."
- For the Texas General Land Office, we generated the "Buy Recycled" campaign.
- For the Association for Organ Procurement Organizations, the program built alliances in many communities.
- For the Texas Department of Human Services, the ESP program encouraged citizens to get off welfare and train for the job market.
- The Asian American Heritage Foundation fostered multi-cultural programs.

That work resulted in me serving on boards of non-profits and getting recognition for the pro-bono work (culminating in a Lifetime Achievement Award in 2015). That spawned my overall commitment to the work of non-profit organizations.

Newspapers began contributing space to non-profit causes back in the 1930s, plus writing stories on many of the programs. Community newspapers followed suit in the 1950s, 1960s and 1970s.

The billboard industry began offering free public service facings to non-profit organizations in the 1960s. As public opposition to billboards as environmental blockages increased, its industry made efforts to work with non-profit organizations to get their words out. In the 1990s, I testified to my city council on behalf of the billboard industry. I stated that they would never get rid of the signs, and their best strategy would be to work with the industry, assuring that local non-profits would be served through PSA boards.

Then came my next time to testify, and recalling this incident makes me sad. I testified before the U.S. Congress, begging them NOT to deregulate broadcasting. I was there in support of non-profit organizations and said that deregulation would be a death-knell to public service advertising on radio and TV. I said that unless the FCC requires PSA quotas to broadcasters, they would not deliver the time. I opined that a handful of mega-corporations would ultimately own broadcasting frequencies and would not have the same public service commitment as did the "mom and pop" broadcasters that they purchased. Sadly, history has proven me to be correct.

Because of deregulation, non-profit organizations were forced to buy time on radio and TV. Many got corporate sponsors to pay the freight. Others cut into programs and services in order to fund marketing. That is exhibited when you see every competing educational institution buying airtime to promote their services to the community. I performed a management study for my state comptroller's office. I reviewed the costs of public awareness campaigns on behalf of state agencies. I opined that agencies felt compelled to spend funds to compete with each other in the arena of marketing.

New forms of public service announcements have emerged to take the place of lost free time on radio and TV. In the 1980s, I started producing filler ads for community newspapers. They were laid out in the style of paid advertising and were furnished as camera-ready copy for newspapers, in the most-needed space fillers as the newspapers had. Thus, they were used.

In the 21st Century, I believe that the future for public service announcements lies on-line. Every non-profit has its own website, and most have blogs in order to disseminate public awareness messages. Many non-profit organizations are producing videos for YouTube.

I believe that corporate websites are the most untapped source for public service messages. I encourage corporations to have a Community Corner on their homepages. Highlight the causes that they support. Put filler ads for non-profit groups on their websites. Encourage their customers and stakeholders to support their designated causes. Non-profit organizations need the support of Cause Related Marketing.

Here are some final tips for non-profit organizations in constructing their public service campaigns:

- Carefully choose your topic. Create plausible narratives.
- Research the marketplace and your cause for support.
- Consider your audience. Get reactions from your audiences.
- Get the attention of stakeholders carefully and tastefully.

PSAs that I Wrote

These public service announcements were written for UNICEF. They were delivered by such celebrity ambassadors as Vincent Price, Roger Moore and Audrey Hepburn.

These represent UNICEF's Campaign for Child Survival.

Children are the world's future. How do you plan for the future when 15 million children die each year from frequent illness and malnutrition? Public education is the answer. That's why health agencies, spearheaded by the United States Committee for UNICEF, created the Campaign for Child Survival. Through growth monitoring, sufficient water, proper nutrition, and immunization, we can cut deaths of infants and young children in half. Let's all be aware of healthier conditions for our future, our children.

At least 15 million children under five die each year in the world's less-developed countries. More than 4 million of them die from diarrhea, which can be corrected through oral rehydration. This small packet is the cure. UNICEF has developed this solution of sugar, salt, and water to treat dehydration. It costs 10 cents and can help a dehydrated child's body absorb 25 times more water and salts than it could before. If widely distributed, it has the potential to cut the yearly child mortality rate in half.

Hear the cry of a child in the night. 40,000 children die each day in the world, from lack of food, clean water, and vaccines. At least half die from diseases that can be prevented by immunization. These include measles, diphtheria, tetanus, polio, whooping cough, and tuberculosis. Vaccines for all six threatening diseases can be obtained for only five dollars per child. The goal of UNICEF's Campaign for Child

Survival is to help parents understand the need for vaccination. By increasing the number of immunized children, we'll hear fewer cries of dying children.

More than 40% of children in the world's less-developed countries suffer growth failure. This does not have to be1 UNICEF's Campaign for Child Survival recommends that parents keep a monthly growth chart, to pinpoint poor growth before malnutrition sets in. Even the poorest of families can improve nutritional health. Oils and fats may be added to enrich weaning foods. Varied green vegetables compliment the diet. Breast-feeding for infants is vital and sets the tone for life. The more parents know about nutrition and growth monitoring, then thousands of lives can be saved each day.

In poor communities, illness and death have been found to be three times more common among babies who are bottle-fed. UNICEF's Campaign for Child Survival wants mothers to understand that breast-milk provides perfect nutrition and a degree of protection against common childhood infections. This is an alternative to over-diluting milk powders with unclean water in unsterile containers. Exclusive breast-feeding for the first six months and continued breast-feeding into the second year of life are recommended. This will protect the health of many millions of infants.

It's the silent emergency. Every day, the deaths of 40,000 children worldwide go unnoticed. That's 15 million per year. The tragedy is that they die from readily avoidable causes, from vaccine-preventable diseases, dehydration due to diarrhea, and malnutrition. I'm part of the Campaign for Child Survival, spearheaded by UNICEF and other world health agencies. We want to supply the technology and knowledge to less-developed nations. Opportunities exist to do so much to relieve the world of this intolerable silent emergency. Please join us by caring.

Of the world's 4.7 billion population, 37% are children. Approximately 80% of them live in the world's less-developed nations. Their quality of life is limited by many inadequacies: income, employment, education, sanitation, health care and diet. These inadequacies have an adverse effect on children. More than 40,000 children die each day from malnutrition. UNICEF1s Campaign for Child Survival says these deaths do not have to occur. By educating less-developed countries about care and feeding of children, we can begin making a positive impact on the world.

In well-developed nations like ours, average life expectancy is 73 years. In the world's less-developed countries, life expectancy is 57 years. Deaths early in life are the main cause of reduced life expectancy. At least 1S million children under five die each year in those nations. The Campaign for Child Survival wants to curb unnecessary deaths through growth monitoring, sufficient water, proper nutrition, and immunization. Healthier conditions will insure that our children—our future will stay with us.

Our Earth is called the "Water Planet." 75% of the Earth's surface is water. Yet, in developing countries, inhabitants of remote villages spend hours walking to distant sources of water, bringing back only what they can carry. And often, the water they find is unsuitable for human consumption. UNICEF is working with other health organizations to bring wells and clean water into remote areas. Otherwise, we would continue experiencing millions of deaths due to dehydration. First, we have to save lives. Then, the future is theirs.

Chapter 22

WHAT IT TAKES TO BE A LEGEND

**Leadership Advice from the Halls of Fame,
Beacon to Your Business Success.**

D o you admire people who went the distance? Have you celebrated organizations that succeeded? I hope that you are and will continue to be distinctive.

This chapter is to give insights into those who leave legacies. The secret to long-term success lies in mapping out the vision and building a body of work that supports it. The art with which we build our careers and our legacy is a journey that benefits many others along the way.

These are the ingredients that make a legend:

- Significant business contributions.
- Mature confidence and informed judgment.
- Courage and leadership.
- High performance standards.
- Professional innovation.

- Public responsibility.
- Ethics and integrity.
- Cultural contributions.
- Giving to community and charity.
- Visionary abilities.
- Commitment to persons affected (stakeholders).

I have been blessed by receiving several legend honors. What I remember the most are the ceremonies and the nuggets of wisdom that flowed. The commonality was the zest of giving back the honors to others.

The first was a Rising Star Award, presented to me in 1967 by Governor John Connally. That was the first time that I was called Visionary, and that experience told me to live up to the accolades later. The governor whispered to me, "Get used to wearing a tuxedo. Live up to the honor by saluting others."

That same year (1967), I met singers Sonny and Cher, little knowing that 25 years later, I would be inducted into the Rock N' Roll Hall of Fame and that they would hand me the award. I remarked to Sonny that I often quoted his song "The Beat Goes On" as analogous to change management, and he was pleased. Cher recalled the 1971 occasion where she and I visited at a jewelry store on Rodeo Drive in Beverly Hills, CA. I remembered that we drank champagne in a pewter cup. Her quote: "There are new ways to approach familiar experiences," and I have applied that to corporate turnarounds.

It was by being inducted into the U.S. Business Hall of Fame that I met Peter Drucker. We subsequently worked together, doing corporate retreats. You'll note his endorsement on the back cover of my books.

One year, I received several awards. I got a Savvy Award, for the top three community leaders. I was a Dewar's profile subject. I had gotten a standing ovation at the United Nations for volunteer work that was my honor to do (especially since it enabled me to work with my favorite actress, Audrey Hepburn).

Subsequently, I was judging a community stewardship awards program. I quizzed, "Why is it that the same old names keep popping up? There are great people to honor other that those of us from business, high society or other top-of-the-mind awareness. What this community needs is an awards program that people like us cannot win."

I was then challenged to come up with such a program, the result being the Leadership in Action Awards. At the banquet, the swell of pride from the winning organizations was heartening to see. These unsung heroes were finally getting their just recognition for community work well done.

One cannot seek awards just for glorification reasons. However, recognition programs are a balanced scorecard that involves the scrutiny of the company and its leaders by credible outside sources.

Awards inspire companies of all sizes to work harder and try more creative things. Good deeds in the community are not done for the awards; they just represent good business. Receiving recognition after the fact for works that were attempted for right and noble reasons is the icing on the cake that employees need. Good people aspire to higher goals. Every business leader needs to be groomed as a community leader.

Recognition for a track record of contributions represents more than "tooting one's own horn." It is indicative of the kind of organizations with whom you are honored to do business. The more that one is recognized and honored, the harder that one works to keep the luster and its integrity shiny. Always reframe the recognition back to the customers, as a recommitment toward serving them better and further.

Characteristics of a Legend
- Understands that careers evolve.
- Prepares for change, rather than becoming the victim of it.
- Realizes there are no quick fixes in life and business.
- Finds a blend of perception and reality, with heavy emphasis upon substance.
- Has grown as a person and professional and quests for more enlightenment.
- Has succeeded and failed and has learned from both.
- Was a good "will be" in the early years, steadily blossoming.
- Knows that one's dues paying accelerates, rather than decreases.

Best Advice to Future Legends

Fascinate yourself with the things you are passionate about. Be fascinated that you can still be fascinated. Be glad for people who mentored you. Be grateful for the opportunities that you have had. Be proud of yourself and your accomplishments. Do not let the fire burn out of your soul.

There comes a point when the pieces fit together. One becomes fully actualized and is able to approach their life's Body of Work. That moment comes after years of trial and error, experiences, insights, successes and failures.

As one matures, survives, life becomes a giant reflection. We appreciate the journey because we understand it much better. We know where we've gone because we know the twists and turns in the road there. Nobody could have predicted every curve along the way.

However, some basic tenets charted our course. To understand those tenets is to make full value out of the years ahead. The best is usually yet to come. Your output should be greater than the sum of your inputs.

This is accomplished by reviewing the lessons of life, their contexts, their significance, their accountabilities, their shortcomings and their path toward charting your future.

- Whatever measure you give will be the measure that you get back.
- There are no free lunches in life.
- The joy is in the journey, not in the final destination.
- The best destinations are not pre-determined in the beginning, but they evolve out of circumstances.
- You've got to give in order to get.
- Getting and having power are not the same thing.
- One cannot live entirely through work.
- One doesn't just work to live.
- As an integrated process of life skills, career has its place.
- A body of work doesn't just happen. It is the culmination of a thoughtful, dedicated process, carefully strategized from some point forward.

Chapter 23

SPEAKERS, MEETINGS AND CONVENTIONS

M eetings, seminars, conferences and retreats are mainstays of business. Many fail to achieve goals because they are not unique. Thus, folks are highly selective about those they will attend.

Here are some tips for organizing and executing successful seminars:

- Have a reasonable business goal for hosting a program. Someone's ego or a half-baked idea will not suffice as basis for a conference.
- Designate one company seminar coordinator, with outside demonstrated conference expertise.
- Select the date, time and topics that will most likely spur interest from potential attendees.
- Select a venue that is original and which will inspire creative thought and maximum participation.
- Have attendee prospects in mind, with a plan of how to obtain their addresses.

- Tailor the concept to make it memorable. Remember the most boring seminars that you have previously attended and the great ones. Learn from your past experiences.
- Pick speakers with flair, not those who will bury their heads in speech texts.
- Achieve a good mix of podium speakers and panels, depending upon the subject matter.
- Do not hold your seminar with expectations of media coverage. Your topic must be highly provocative to get the reporters out. However, your business mentor can often disseminate significant highlights of the program afterwards.
- Invitations should clearly state the benefits of attending. In your quest to be creative, do not blur the business goal.
- Always serve refreshments appropriate to the occasion.
- Thank attendees for coming. Publicly acknowledge members of your staff who did the legwork in orchestrating the meeting.
- Always provide handouts.
- Distribute evaluation forms, which yield ideas for subsequent programs.
- Offer additional information or some other reason for attendees to call you back later and to do business with you.

Whether you occasionally sponsor seminars for business development or lend your name to someone else's program, please pay attention that proper thought is applied. Make yourself that rare company that is credited with staging seminars the right way. People will remember your successes, as well as your mistakes.

7 Ways in Which Speakers Are Utilized by Organizations

1. Base-Level Education. Instruct about techniques, practices, procedures, technologies and methodologies to accomplish jobs, tasks and roles.
2. Resource. Convey cultivated expertise, skills, case studies, applications, procedures and knowledge to niche audiences. Localized toward job and subject area.

3. Convey Policies and Philosophies. Confirm what the organization already believes. Elaborate further and enlighten on aspects to get resources optimally utilized within the organization.

4. People to People. Help company members to develop abilities to work more effectively together. Includes team building, empowerment, time management, stress management and other training topics.

5. Introduce New Concepts. Elaborate on new trends, processes and techniques, especially those that the organization itself is developing and championing in the marketplace.

6. Raise the Bar. Encourage excellence, benchmarking and setting different standards.

7. Tackling the Future. Think Tanks, Visioning process, strategic planning and growth strategies that poise the organization to master change, nurture a corporate culture and evolve successfully to the next level.

Speakers

Most top professionals are called upon to speak at some occasion. Networking breakfasts, business clubs, media opportunities, company presentations, prospect meetings and professional development seminars offer opportunities to position your company.

Overcoming the fear of audiences and lack of formal speech training is a hurdle that most executives must accomplish. Some corporate officials make a priority out of seeking high-profile speaking platforms. Somewhere in between lies the ongoing need for public presentations.

These are pointers for speakers to keep in mind:

- Confirm all speaking engagements in writing.
- If the organization has a newsletter or other advance communications, be sure that your topic and bio are received in time for publication deadlines.
- Send the person who will introduce you a typed one-minute introduction. Don't send a vita and expect him/her to ferret out the pertinent facts. A proper introduction will set the tone for your remarks.

- Give and get business cards.
- Understand what you are there to achieve. Leave the engagement with something tangibly gleaned.
- If the talk will be reported in a subsequent newsletter or will be covered by the media, provide an outline, speech text or press release.
- Follow-up correspondence is always in order.
- If public speaking is an expected part of your management position, seek professional speech and media training.
- Employ a marketing advisor with the skills in procuring and scheduling appropriate speaking platforms, as well as the publicity expertise.

Speakers bureaus are important communications tools for major corporations and community organizations alike. You are competing with many good speakers and must treasure those forums that properly showcase you, your ideas and your company's point of view.

Formulate public speaking, seminars and presentations into your company's formal public relations program. Seek more and better platforms each year. Utilize audiences for third party support building. Get newsletter and press coverage, when appropriate.

7 Categories of Speaker

1. Niche: Knowledge in one subject area. Eager to express ideas and interests to audiences. A mainstay of breakout sessions.
2. Resource: Possess industry expertise, skills, knowledge. Speak in order to network their business, make contacts and share information. Localized toward background and subject area.
3. Motivation: Compile and disseminate other people's material.
4. Chroniclers: It is their career to research, disseminate and convey material from various resources for maximum educational impact. Have areas of expertise and scholarly research, which further enlighten the subject matter. Inject own ideas-philosophies to add value to their writings. Brilliant at inspiring audiences to take techniques, processes and values, for positive actions.

5. Content Speakers: Have amassed a track record in their areas of expertise. Convey case studies, recipes for success and offer encouragement to audiences. These include celebrities. Widely showcased at conferences, workshops and seminars.

6. Senior Speakers: Advanced from the ranks of 3, 4 and 5. Have track record of business successes.

7. Beyond the Level of Platform Speaker: Offer cutting-edge concepts, insights and philosophies, all original material. Create-fulfill their own niche, affording perspective and concepts not available elsewhere. Material is worthy of coverage in the media. Eloquent speaker from the vantage point of having been there, inspiring growth-change and pointing the way toward futurism.

7 Measures of a Successful Speakers Bureau

1. Run a value-added business, a professional operation, practicing fiduciary responsibility. People skills are your strong suit, giving you advantages over vendors. You move swiftly and have developed marketplace sensitivity.

2. Provide for clients speakers and substantive knowledge not easily available. Being creative and finding the perfect fit, bureaus save time and money for clients. Repeat clientele shows your consistency in delivering. Active involvement-expertise of bureau owners puts you in a league above most other businesses.

3. Set industry standards. You're more than the public thinks. You exemplify professionalism, which impacts the way clients do business. Everything you do symbolizes higher commitments than might be evident at first. Continue raising your standards and those of your industry. Clients pay attention to such things.

4. Showcase talent, ideas and concepts. Were it not for bureaus, business would be worse off. You bring them the tools to run their organizations more creatively, effectively and profitably. When you introduce them to speakers and their subjects, you open "new worlds" to client organizations.

5. Raise the bar by introducing new knowledge. Since you're their objective, outside "brain trust," you continually seek and showcase the best new speakers. You recommend and book speakers with cutting-edge ideas to

impart. Clients regularly work with bureaus because you bring the trends and information to them.

6. Exemplify collaborations. Solidify client relationships by being the meeting planners' business partner. Collaborations with other bureaus and speakers create larger business opportunities for all, and it makes good sense for your clients.

7. Profoundly impact client organizations. You affect more aspects of their operation than virtually any other outside supplier-consultant. The fruits of your labor influence their products, processes, policies and profitability. The more that clients understand the multiple benefits and services of speakers bureaus, they will value and repeatedly use speakers bureaus.

Hank Moore delivered the opening keynote address at the ISO 9000 & Audits World Conference on quality management, held in San Antonio, TX. Hank discussed global strategies, teamwork, business trends & challenges, community leadership, his "Big Picture of Business" book series & history of the World's Fair in San Antonio. Pictured: Hank Moore with Robert Freeman, chairman, and with Dr. Sermin Vanderbilt, president of American Quality Institute.

Hank Moore spoke at international conferences in Kuwait, headlining a business outlook summit, corporate event for Kuwait Petroleum and a summit on philanthropy.

Hank Moore in Sao Paulo, Brazil, introduced to super-sphere by international journalist Paulo Enrique Amorim. This economic summit was sponsored by software king SAS for business customers and collaborators.

Hank Moore speaking at conferences, corporate retreats, think tanks. With leadership of the Montana Association of Realtors at strategic planning retreat in Helena, MT.

Chapters in this book stemmed from notes and ideas that I jotted down in public. "The Value You Deserve," the opening chapter of this book, was outlined on a luncheon program in December, 2018, at the Women's Council of Realtors Montgomery County. Two years later, I spoke at that organization and dedicated the inspiration to them, on Nov. 18, 2020, discussing business rebounding strategies & motivation for next business cycles. Hank pictured with WCR leadership, including 2019 President Amber Mesorana and 2020 President Jayce Love.

Memorable speeches as business guru on the international stage. Also spoke at conferences in Mexico, The Netherlands, Brazil, England, plus opening keynotes at conferences across the U.S. (New York, Los Angeles, Chicago, Nashville, New Orleans, Phoenix, Washington D.C., San Diego, Philadelphia, San Antonio, Austin, Denver, Des Moines, Galveston, Seattle, Kansas City, Las Vegas, Tampa, Birmingham, Laredo, Cincinnati, Orlando, Roanoke, Albuquerque, Milwaukee, Houston, San Francisco, Lake Charles, Atlanta, Minneapolis, Corpus Christi, etc.)

Chapter 24

BUSINESS SUCCESS CHECKLIST

W hen you own and operate a business you need to have certain procedures for an efficient and seamless function. Sometimes the difficulty of managing your time makes for a haphazard operation. An inefficient operation results in unproductive activities that often miss the point and worse yet, result in wasted time and wasted resources.

One of the ways in which you can optimize your business activities would be the focus and attention to detail that a checklist can stimulate. Here is my own business success checklist that will help you optimize your activities for a more efficient and purpose oriented endeavor. Success is inevitable.

Having a clearly defined purpose will focus your activities to a customer oriented perspective. When a business loses sight of the customer and what they really need they often run into difficulties. Your clearly defined purpose can also center the attention and be a source of inspiration for your employees.

A leader's purpose and job is to give direction and purpose and motivate his people. Leaders must also provide support for the emotional needs of their employees while they are at work and even sometimes when they bring personal concerns to the working place. The business absolutely needs energetic and emotionally mature leaders for it to prosper.

When a company is content with being merely mediocre it may survive but it will never do extremely well. Put emphasis upon high standards, giving value to customers, accountability and the drive to learn. If these are incorporated into the culture of your company, a culture of excellence in all things will soon be prevalent.

When your business has contingency plans for future scenarios you will seldom be caught by surprise. You never know when the next big recession will hit. Most successful businesses have planned responses to most scenarios because they took the time to think "What If". It is important to identify swings and trends so that innovation is a strength of your business.

The sharp focus and direction on your objectives and goals can only be maintained with constant monitoring of your procedures and processes. Whether your focus is on customer service, profits, investing, marketing or company growth a constant awareness of your current position in relation to where you want to be is essential.

Areas of Focus

1. **The business you're in**
   - Study and refine your own core business characteristics.
   - Understand "The Business You're In" and how it fits into the core business.
   - Design and re-engineering of products-services.
   - Development of technical abilities, specialties and expertise.
   - Utilization of industry consultants or technical specialists.
   - Development of core business supplier relationships.
   - Make investments toward quality controls.

2. **Running the business**
   - Objective analysis of how the organization has operated to date.
   - Formalize the organizational structure.
   - Document practices, procedures, operations and structure in writing.
   - Communicate policies and procedures to employees.
   - Physical plant is regularly studied, updated and modified.
   - Distribution standards are documented, practiced and measured.

- Time management and "just in time" concepts are applied.
- Plans are in writing to address inventories and reducing surplus.
- Legal compliance and precautions plan.
- Outsourcing, privatizing and collaborating plan.
- Purchasing plan.
- Repair and maintenance contracts are routinely maintained.
- Purchase and lease of equipment.
- Continuous quality improvement plan.

3. **Financial**
   - Cost containment is one (but not the only) factor of company operations.
   - Each product-service is budgeted.
   - Long-term investments plan is annually updated, with realistic, measurable goals.
   - Assets are adequately valued and managed.
   - Cash flow, forecasting and budgeting are consistently monitored.
   - Written, consistent policies with payables and receivables are followed.
   - Strategic Plan includes provisions for refinancing, equity and debt financing.
   - Accounting firm utilization plan.
   - Banking and investing plan is annually updated.
   - Payables plan is annually updated, with realistic, measurable goals.
   - Receivables plan is annually updated.
   - Finance charges are negotiated.
   - Insurance plan is annually updated.
   - Benefits plan.

4. **People**
   - Corporate culture reflects a formal Visioning Program.
   - Employees know their jobs, are empowered to make decisions and have high morale in carrying the company banner forward.
   - Top management has as a priority the need to develop and practice People development, skills and team building responsibilities.
   - Human Resources program.

- Incentives-rewards-bonus plan.
- Personnel Policies and Procedures are written, and distributed to all employees.
- Each employee has his-her own Position Results Oriented Description plan.
- Training plan.
- Professional development plan.

5. **Business development**
   - All members of top management have Business Development responsibilities.
   - Company has and regularly fine-tunes a communications strategy.
   - Sales plan is annually updated.
   - Marketing plan is annually updated.
   - Advertising plan.
   - Public relations plan.
   - Research plan.
   - Marketplace development plan.
   - Creative collaborator-vendor plan.

6. **Body of Knowledge**
   - Consultant plan is annually updated.
   - Performance reviews are conducted annually.
   - Company learns how to benefit from changes.
   - Organization predicts and stays ahead of trends.
   - The company leads the industry.
   - Everything that goes on outside our company affects our business in some way.
   - Willingness to invest in research.
   - Commitment toward collaboration and working with other companies.
   - Maintains active government and regulator relations program.
   - Maintains active community relations program.

7. **The Big Picture**
   - Shared Vision is crafted, articulated and followed.
   - Ongoing emphasis upon improving the corporate culture.

- CEO accepts and ideas and philosophies with employees and stakeholders.
- Creative business practices are most welcome here.
- Strategic planning is viewed as vital to business survival and future success.
- Outside-the-box thinking does indeed apply to us and will be sought.
- The organization maintains and lives by an ethics statement.
- Continuous quality improvement processes.

Becoming Your Own Role Model

Amidst these entertaining analogies is a confluence of ideas in each of our heads. Few of us had modeling for life and career. We learned early glimpses of life from the TV. Along the way, we absorbed others, influenced by the misperceptions of pop culture.

It is difficult to inventory all the images, sort perceptions versus realities and look new ways at old business tenets. That is what I've done over the last five years, and that is how this book evolved.

This progression of statements, validations and commitments is the premise of this book, which is just the same approach utilized when I work with corporate clients on strategizing and visualizing their future:

- Examine where you came from.
- Retread old knowledge.
- Apply teachings to today.
- Honestly evaluate your path to progress thus far.
- Affix responsibilities, goals and benchmarks to all intended progress.
- Find creative new ways to approach and conduct business.
- Proceed with zeal, commitment, creative instinct and boundless energy.
- Achieve and reflect upon successes.
- Learn three times more from failure than success.
- Plan to achieve and succeed in the future.

Never stop researching, planning, executing and evaluating. Benchmarks of one phase, project or series of events drive the research and planning for the next phase.

Futurism is not an esoteric concept. After all, it's almost tomorrow. But then, it always is.

Chapter 25

MESSAGING, STRATEGY AND VISION

T here are stages of communications strategy for companies:

1. Basic. There is more information available now than ever before. Most of it is biased and slanted by vendors with something to sell. There exists much data, without interpretation. Technology purveys information but cannot do the analytical thinking.

2. Limited and guarded. The appearance of data leads to initial perceptions, usually influenced by the media in which the information exists. To many people and organizations, perception is reality because they do not delve any further. Thus, learning stops at this point.

3. Brand, not strategy. It is determined more by events-processes than words. Verbal statements are more important when people are suggestible and need interpretation from a credible source. Does not anticipate emergencies, only reacts to them. Many perceptions and opinions are self-focused and affected by self-esteem. Once self-interest becomes involved, opinions do not change easily.

4. Ideas and Beliefs. Formulated ideas emerge, as people and organizations learn to hold their own outside their shells. Two-way communication ensues. Opinion inputs and outputs will craft ideas and beliefs. As people become more aware of their own learning, they tally their inventory of knowledge. Patterns of beliefs emerge, based upon education, experiences and environment.

5. Systems of Thought and Ideologies. Insights start emerging at this plateau. Connect beliefs with available resources and personal expertise. Measure results and evaluate outcomes of activities, using existing opinion, ideas and beliefs. Actions are taken which benchmark success and accountability to stakeholders.

6. Core value, direct. It is shaped by ideas, beliefs, systems of thought and ideologies. Becomes what the person or organization stands for. The company has conviction, commitment and ownership, able to change and adapt. Behavioral modification from the old ways of thinking has transpired.

7. Committed to Excellence and Vision. An informed plateau that few achieve. Able to disseminate information, perceptions and opinions for what they really are. Wisdom focused, an evolving flow of philosophies. A quest to employ ideologies and core values for benefit of all in the organization. Committed to and thriving upon change.

8. It is important to generate ideas and suggestions via writing memos, E-mail messages and internal documents. Their succinctness and regularity of issue have a direct relationship to your compensation and the company's bottom line.

Before presenting ideas to a customer or prospect, consider organizing your approach:

- Predict reasons why someone might oppose your suggestions.
- Seek out supporters, as early as possible.
- Determine the goals. Is the objective to get the idea accepted or get credit for it?

- Understand your audience. Understand differing personality types of your audiences.
- Think of yourselves as leaders, who are good communicators.
- Listen as others amplify upon the idea, which shows their buy-in potential.
- Determine as much accuracy in others' perceptions to your ideas. Don't fool yourself or be blind-sighted to opposition.
- Throw out decoy ideas for others to shoot down, so they don't attack your core message.
- Use language that is easily understood by all. Avoid technical terms, unless you include brief definitions.
- Don't over-exaggerate in promises and predictions.

Other pointers in effectively communicating include:

- Speak with authority.
- Make the most of face-to-face meetings, rather than through artificial barriers.
- Remember that voice inflection, eye contact and body language are more important than the words you use.
- Charts, graphs and illustrative materials make more impact for your points.
- Don't assume anything. If in doubt about their understanding, ask qualifying questions. Become a better listener.
- Sound the best on the phone that you can.
- Use humor successfully.
- Get feedback. Validate that audiences have heard your intended messages.
- Attitude is everything in effective communications.

Strategy and Vision

Most organizations know why they exist and their purpose. Those fundamental elements constitute a Mission Statement.

Most organizations never go past the Mission Statement. Thus, they fail to realize potential. Having a purpose by itself does not make the organization materialize, much less be successful.

Visioning is the process where good ideas become something more. Visioning is a catalyst toward long-term evaluation, planning and implementation. Visioning is a starting point by which forward-thinking organizations ask: What will we look like in the future? What do we want to become? How will we evolve? What does it like when you get there? Vision is a realistic picture of what is possible.

Businesses, communities and organizations will succeed by having, communicating and garnering support for a Shared Vision. Visioning sets the stage for necessary processes, such as growth strategies, re-engineering, training, enhancing shareholder value and organizational development. Without visioning, the community simply performs band aid surgery on problems as they occur. The Vision provides continuous guidance to employees at every level as to how they should manage their respective responsibilities.

Visioning must be Big Picture in perspective. It must creatively focus upon the whole and then the parts of the organization, as they relate to the whole. It is a process by which a Strategic Plan and Visioning program components come off the shelf and alive into action, relative to all levels of the organization:

1. Resource. Equipment, tools, materials, schedules.
2. Skills and Tasks. Duties, activities, tasks, behaviors, attitudes, contracting, project fulfillment.
3. Role and Job. Assignments, responsibilities, functions, relationships, accountability.
4. Systems and Processes. Structure, hiring, control, work design, supervision, decisions.
5. Strategy. Planning, tactics, organizational development.
6. Culture and Mission. Values, customs, beliefs, goals, objectives, benchmarking.
7. Philosophy. Organizational purpose, vision, quality of life, ethics, long-term growth.

The Vision describes what can and will happen, once everyone's energies are focused. Vision is not a financial forecast or a market analysis. Vision is less of a dream and more of a realistic picture of what is possible.

When there is a genuine Vision, as compared to a terse "vision statement," that propels the business for success. In organizations with Vision, people are compelled to learn and excel, not because they are told to but because they want to.

Most leaders have personal visions that rarely get communicated to the organization. By default, Vision has resolved around the values and positioning of one leader. Often, a crisis will rally the organization, but that tends to be short-lived. Personal visions are driven by an individual's deep caring.

Shared visions derive their power via common caring. Truly, people want to be connected together. Shared visions take time to emerge. They grow as a result of successful showcasing of individual visions, with benchmarks for success that are understood.

Visioning needs to take place within each business unit, as well as at the larger organizational level. Too often, management fails to articulate its values or does so imperfectly.

These are the steps toward Strategic Vision, influencing how and why companies get from here to there:

1. Analyze the company's future environment, resources and capabilities. Determine where the Big Picture existed before, if it did at all. Crystallize the core business in terms of viabilities to move successfully forward to some discernible point.

2. Clarify management values. Growth must be conducted in concert with core values. Often, senior management have not yet fully articulated their own individual values, let alone those of the organization. This process helps to define and further develop value systems to carry the organization toward success.

3. Develop a Mission Statement. It is a starting point, not an end in itself. The Mission Statement is rewritten several times, as the planning process ensues. The last draft of the statement is an executive summary of collective ideas of the Visioning team.

4. Identify strategic objectives and goals. I ask clients to do so without using three words: technology, sales and solutions. Most businesses fail to grow because they get stuck in buzz-words and trite phrases that they hear in others' marketing hype. Objectives and goals must be commensurate to your company and its unique position.

5. Generate select strategic options. There are many ways to succeed, and your game plan should have at least five viable options. When the Visioning program matures and gets to its second generation, you'll find that winning formulas stem from a hybrid of the original strategic options. Creative thinking moves the company into the future, not rehashes of the earliest ideas.

6. Develop the vision statement. It will be action-oriented and speaks from the facts, as well as from the passion of company leaders. It will include a series of convictions why your organization will work smarter, be its best, stand for important things and be accountable.

7. Measure and review the progress. By benchmarking activities and accomplishments against planned objectives, then the company has a barometer of its previous phase and an indicator of its next phase.

These are the traits of a successful visioning program:

1. Effective visions are inspiring. They must touch the chords of what the company started out to become. They may compel leaders to renew or multiply their commitments for the future. Their messages can apply to every sector of the company.

2. Effective visions are clear and challenging, involving excellence. There is no such thing as perfection, but incremental levels of excellence are to be attained and bested. Every message must be communicated throughout the organization, acquiring feedback and additional commitments from the rank and file. Thereafter, visions become their brainchildren.

3. Effective visions have marketplace purpose, savvy and flexibility. It is not enough to look good on paper or touch the hearts of some. Visions must squarely place the company in the forefront of its marketplace, customer

base, industry perspective and economic realm. It's all about doing good business and then being a good organization.

4. Effective visions must be stable, yet prudently updated. No "pie in the sky" tenets or trite restatements of other companies' promotions are acceptable. Show how planned, controlled growth will maintain stability for investors, hold interest for the marketplace and propel the organization to break further new ground.

5. Effective visions are role models, when all else is in turmoil. Research shows that only 2% of the world's companies have strategic plans. Visioning programs go far beyond the plan and root the corporate culture into something real and breathing. While most companies meander, your visionary company can chart its own course.

6. Effective visions empower the organization's people and customers. People constitute the largest component (28%) of a successful organization. By nurturing the company's best resource (its people), then productivity, creativity and profitability soar. At all times, what is done and accomplished must focus upon the customer base.

7. Effective visions honor the past and prepare for the future. There are good reasons why the company started. By weathering change and taking new turns, the organization matures. With futures constantly changing, then the art of success comes from re-examining the journey.

These are the levels of visioning programs, determining how far organizations evolve:

1. It was someone's pet idea. A program was initiated to fit a personal or political agenda. It was sold and accepted as such. Therefore, it will be pursued partially because its motivation is transparent or limited. Visioning is more than a "program." It is a process, encompassing change, behavioral modification, focus on growth and positive reinforcement.

2. It was initiated was forced or mandated. A crisis, litigation, merger, loss of market share, government edict, competition with others or a combination of outside factors caused this to begin. Visioning is a response, not a choice.

Support and participation depend upon the circumstances and the spirit with which the mandate is carried out.

3. It was done for show or image. Some organizations think that Visioning will make organizations look good. Actually, it makes them good. Visioning is not a substitute for public relations or marketing. It guides the organization.

4. It was given partial support and resources. It is accorded just enough to begin the process but not quite enough to do it right. It is either the domain of top management or is delegated to the middle of the organization. Visioning must be a team effort and well-communicated in order to hit its stride, gather additional support and sustain.

5. Well Planned. The Visioning process begins with forethought, continues with research and culminates in a Strategic Plan, including mission, core values, goals, objectives (per each key results area), tactics to address and accomplish, timeline and benchmarking criteria.

6. Well Executed. Visioning goes beyond the Strategic Plan. It sculpts how the organization will progress, its character and spirit, participation of its people and steps that will carry the organization to the next tiers of desired achievement, involvement and quality.

7. Well Followed and Benchmarked. Both the Strategic Plan and the Visioning process must be followed through. This investment is one-sixth that of later performing band-aid surgery on an ailing organization.

Chapter 26

TIMELINES, TRENDS AND BUSINESS HISTORY
When Things Happened and Their Impact.

C ommerce was created to advance society's basic needs, wants and aspirations. As time passed, business innovated, gave society more and created opportunities that previously never existed. People shifted attention and priorities as the nation colonized, explored, civilized grew, became a dominant world force and further innovated. The process of adaptation created the American Way.

The history of trade and commerce can be traced to ancient times, even before the Golden Age of Greece and the Roman Empire. Beginning in the 9th Century, the wilderness of Western Europe began populating. Distribution systems were developed, though often interrupted by periods of famine. People built forts at strategic locations for the transportation of goods. The agricultural systems grew to support increased populations. As demands for food products and luxury goods exhibited from town to town, trades, guilds and professional associations were formed to coalesce business opportunities.

Each time that disaster occurred, the rural areas were hurt, and the cities continued to grow. In the 15th Century, trade and business levels rose. Merchants began traveling from town to town to take orders, place goods and move goods. Craft guilds emerged, as cities became viable customers. Improved transportation stimulated the growth of port cities. The Spanish, Portugese, French and English began to search for additional trade in Africa, the Middle East and the New World. The merchants accrued sources of wealth, becoming economic and political influencers.

Christopher Columbus crossed the Atlantic and discovered the New World. Explorers were considered the first entrepreneurs, including Hernando de Soto and Francisco Pizzarro. French exploration affected the development of business history because of its heightened scales and affects on governments. Jean-Baptiste Colbert envisioned the roles of merchants and trade as essential to dominating society. Port cities on the Great Lakes and Gulf of Mexico became funnels to exploring the New World and merchant capitalism.

By the 16th Century, discovery and exploration flourished. The accumulation of capital became a virtue. Materialism became common in advancing societies. From English common law evolved the rights and sanctity of private property. Governments were not based on free enterprise, though they instituted regulations to address potential crises. Successful enterprises are the result of trendsetters, the refining processes, sales to marketplaces, attempts to refine the workforce and the output of goods and services.

British mercantilists established colonies at Jamestown, Massachusetts Bay, New York, Philadelphia, South Carolina and Virginia. Colonial merchants and enterprise systems developed regional characteristics, with trading centers stemming from the kinds of crops, products and goods produced.

Early American manufacturing included weaving, candle making, soap production, leather crafts, iron and copper fabrication, shipbuilding and agricultural markets. Colonists sought protection of property, employment systems, fiscal responsibility, American re-export trade and investments in manufacturing processes.

Settling the continent served to create opportunities for business. During periods of the fights for independence, domestic industries grew, including textiles, farming, ironworks, cotton, food processing and agri-business.

John Rolfe planted and harvested tobacco crops in Virginia in 1612. Tobacco became the main source of revenue for Virginia, Maryland and North Carolina. British tobacco merchants sold the harvested crops for three times the cost to produce them. After the Revolutionary War, the growers established factories for the production of pipe and chewing tobacco. This then inspired the great tobacco empires that grew in the 19th Century.

In the early years of the United States, the building of passable roads and canals were essential to the development of business and commerce. Roads drew the settlements together, then expanded to accommodate the westward expansion.

In 1824, Henry Clay's "American System" proposed a national economic development plan, coupled with protective tariffs to encourage American industry. In 1825, the Erie Canal was completed, resulting in more than 3,000 miles of inland waterways to open up new territories to settlement and commerce.

In the 19th Century, the American states became the largest free-trade zone in the world. Efforts were made to improve transportation, including canals, railroads, national highways, steamboats, the merchant marine and routes to the West. Expanded rail systems moved goods and served as primary consumer transportation.

In 1793, Eli Whitney invented the cotton gin. By 1815, cotton was the dominant Southern crop for export to textile mills being built in the North. In 1860, cotton accounted for two-thirds of the nation's exports.

Electricity was the major factor that transformed business, industrialization and quality of life in the 19th Century. It had been subject of speculation and fantasy until the 16th Century, when scientist William Gilbert studied electricity and magnetism, coining the term "electricus."

In the 18th Century, Benjamin Franklin conducted studies into electricity. In 1791, Luigi Galvani published his study of bioelectricity, with electricity being the medium by which nerve cells pass signals to the muscles. In 1800, Alessandro Volta's battery provided a reliable source of electrical energy. In 1821, Michael Faraday invented the electric motor. In 1827, George Ohm analyzed the electrical circuit. In 1861, James Maxwell linked electricity and magnetism, and light.

In 1835, Samuel F.B. Morse's invention of the electromagnetic telegraph allowed long-distance communication. In 1843, Congress voted to construct telegraph lines. Morse later pioneered the submarine cable telegraph.

Electricity turned from scientific research into an essential tool of modern life, due to the inventions of Thomas Edison, Alexander Graham Bell, George Westinghouse and others. In 1879, Edison developed a successful incandescent lamp. Solid-state components were used in radios in the early 1900's, followed by invention of the transistor in 1947. Delivery of electricity stimulated power plants, municipal delivery stations and ancillary industries committed to powering up society, including Edison Electric Light Company, General Electric, Westinghouse, Tennessee Valley Authority and others.

Early America witnessed the first industrial revolution. As farms could be operated by fewer workers, the people took jobs in factories. Gradually, workers became acclimated to manufacturing schedules, time clocks and the effects of mass employment on family quality of life. By 1860, one-eighth of America's population was foreign born. Immigrants formed company towns in Pennsylvania, New Jersey, Connecticut and Rhode Island.

The gold rush in California in 1848-58 led to business opportunities and a boost to the economy. Shipping companies transported passengers, who stayed and settled the state. Agriculture, commerce, transportation and industry grew. The same was true for the Colorado gold rush a decade later. Gold, silver and copper mining turned into industries dominated by high-stakes capital investors.

Railroads transformed life and business opportunities. The first significant development was in 1865, when the first steel rails were manufactured. In 1893, the gasoline engine was invented. By 1900, there were six principal railroads, navigating 200,000 miles of track, travel industries and shipping services. America grew exponentially along the railroad routes. Cities of commerce sought rail service and depended upon it.

In 1867, Jesse Chisholm mapped out a route for herding cattle to market between Kansas and Canada. The cattle drives created towns and commerce hubs. In 1869, the first transcontinental railroad was completed. Horace Greeley was a newspaper editor who encouraged westward expansion. He set up a model town (Greeley, Colorado) but never visited it. These romanticized periods were factors in settling the Western states.

In 1878, forestry and farmland were big business. Hundreds of sawmills emerged, providing lumber for building communities. Land was given out at cheap prices to encourage building, and fortunes were made in the lumber industry.

Steel was the other building block of modern life, and fortunes were made in that industry too. By 1880, the Kelly-Bessemer process had become the dominant method of manufacturing steel.

The late 19th Century was rich in inventions. Christopher L. Sholes developed the typewriter. I.W. McGaffey invented the vacuum cleaner. John Oliver's chilled steel plow helped develop prairie agriculture. L.H. Wheeler developed windmills to serve areas which were previously uninhabitable. Andrew S. Hallidie invented an underground continuous cable and mechanical gripper. Joseph F. Glidden changed the face of the Great Plains with the invention of barbed wire, as water holes, roads and entire towns were fenced in.

In 1871, Henry Davidson in Great Britain invented the first amusement arcade game. In 1885, William T. Smith invented America's first arcade machine. In 1931, David Gottlieb introduced the first coin-operated pinball game machine. Bumpers were added in 1936 and flippers in 1947. In 1971, Nolan Bushnell wrote the program for the first computer video game. In the 1990s, virtual pinball played on a computer was introduced.

The founding fathers found there were costs associated with modern society, including wars and depressions. As consumption grew, so did the entrepreneurial spirit to create new goods and services. City dwelling gave rise to mass transit, suburbs, infrastructures and modifications to the marketplace. In the industrial age, monopolies led to anti-trust actions, which resulted in decentralization and regulations. Waves of deregulation led to crises, which later led to re-regulations.

The 20th Century was typified by the automobile and its support industries as the most significant factors in commerce growth and development. In 1921, President Warren G. Harding proclaimed in that "the motor car has become an indispensible instrument in our political, social and industrial life."

Ransom Olds introduced the marketing of cars in 1901, produced to be affordable and convenient to operate. Henry Ford built his first car in 1896 and founded Ford Motor Company in 1901. Ford introduced assembly-line production and techniques in 1913. By 1914, the production of automobiles exceeded that of wagons and carriages for the first time.

General Motors was founded in 1908 by William Durant, with mergers of companies in order to offer cars in all price ranges. GM set the pattern of introducing new models each year. Walter Chrysler was president of American Locomotive

Works and then joined GM in 1911, followed by founding his own corporation to make cars in all price ranges.

In 1929, the peak year of the auto boom, more than five million were sold. The industry produced trucks during World War I, and afterward the commercialization of truck production resulted. Bus production followed in the 1920s. Unionization came to the industry in the 1930s. During World War II, the industry retooled its production processes to include vehicles and machinery for military uses. Turmoil produced opportunities and change, which inspired systems of managing change. At each stage were burst of innovation.

Orville and Wilbur Wright did what others said could not be accomplished, developing the first heavy flying machine, thus launching the science of aviation. From the first successful flight at Kitty Hawk, North Carolina, in 1903, they spent years on experiments and refinements to airplanes. In 1909, France's Louis Bleriot flew across the English Channel.

Aircraft was first used by the military during World War I. The airline industry developed to carry mail on a contract basis. In 1927, Charles Lindbergh was the first to fly non-stop from New York to Paris in his plane "The Spirit of St. Louis." His flight increased the sense of adventure attached to airlines. Refinements in planes, safety considerations and dynamics of air travel led to the founding of commercial carriers, along with the building of facilities to accommodate air traffic. Juan Trippe was considered the father of American overseas commercial aviation.

Affordable energy was essential to the operation of automobiles and later aircraft. Over 40 percent of all energy consumption is by industry. In 1870, coal replaced wood as the primary energy for industrialization. In 1910, petroleum replaced coal as the primary energy source.

Leadership in the field of energy meant people of determination and vision, who saw in "black gold" the way of life that we now enjoy. In 1861, the first gusher came in Pennsylvania.

In 1862, John D. Rockefeller went to Ohio to investigate oil as an investment. He bought a refinery. In 1870, he formed Standard Oil of Ohio. By 1875, Standard operated large refineries in New York and Pennsylvania. In 1876, 90% of the oil business was under his control. At the end of his life, he donated generously to charity, at one time handing out dimes on the street to the less fortunate.

In 1901, Joseph Stephen Cullina went into court in Beaumont and got the right in advance to kill any marauder who might oppose his charge to clean up and quiet down in the skyrocketing boomtown. In 1901, oil was discovered at Spindletop, near Beaumont.

In 1903, William Stamps Farish and Robert E. Blaffer met at a boarding house in Beaumont. They joined forces to form a drilling partnership. The next year, they moved to Houston to concentrate on the nearby Humble field where oil was discovered in 1904. In the early years, they were so short of operating money that they lived in a shack in the fields. Blaffer put up his gold watch as security to guarantee payment of a drilling crew's wages. By 1908, they had become comfortably established. Harry Wiess knew the vast benefits of energy from the constant addition of knowledge through chemistry, physics and other sciences that are now applied to every product.

In 1911, Farish, Blaffer and Wiess joined forces with Ross Sterling and Walter Fondren in founding the Humble Oil & Refining Company. Humble became one of the giants in the industry through association with Standard Oil Company of New Jersey. Humble Oil became Enco-Esso, later Exxon and now ExxonMobil Corporation.

In 1902, Texaco was founded. In 1916, Gulf Oil was founded. In 1917, Phillips Petroleum was founded. In 1918, Sinclair Oil was founded.

Oil was difficult to transport on land. So, the pipeline was invented. Oil was difficult to transport by sea. Thus, the tank-ship was invented. Oil was difficult dangerous to refine. The most complex machinery was created to handle oil and gas safely, surely and cheaply.

Oil has grown even harder to find. Even airplane equipment is used to map huge underground areas for prospective oil bearing formations, while drilling in even the rough waters in the Gulf of Mexico and the Pacific Ocean.

Into the shoes of the pioneers of energy stepped such wildcatters as H.L. Hunt, Hugh Roy Cullen, George Strake, Glenn McCarthy and Sid Richardson. To them, the sky was not too high nor the earth too deep to hide oil from them. In 1921, they scoured South Texas reserves. In 1926, the West Texas oil industry was launched. In 1929 came the huge discoveries in Conroe's Cookfield Belt and the Frio sands of the Gulf Coast. In 1926, natural gas was piped into Houston for the first time. It came from a field in Refugio. Up to that point, only manufactured gas had been available.

In 1930, engineer Roger Henquet opened a small office in a walk-up apartment house in Houston, as the only representative for a small radical type of service to the oil industry. The new company was Schlumberger Well Surveying Corporation. In 1930, the U.S. Schlumberger presence consisted of Henquet, one helper and one truck unit. The company that he introduced to Houston oil operators is now spread all over the world and is one of the largest oil service organizations.

Since World War II, the chemical industry has boomed and grown until it is the largest manufacturing employer in Texas. The industry is a complex mixture of companies that produce chemical raw materials, basic chemicals, petrochemicals, agricultural chemicals, plastics, synthetic rubber, metals, drugs and household chemicals.

There were population shifts, typified by moves from farms to cities. Demographic changes led to the influx of women in the workforce. Cities experienced economic supremacy. With rapidly increasing affluence, wages were up, and consumer choices were up. All of these factors inspired business innovations and successes.

The other major business phenomenon of the 20th Century was mass media. In 1891, Thomas Edison was given a patent for the first motion picture camera. The first viewing palace for films was a peepshow in 1893. Movies used a film process developed by George Eastman in 1880. Edison built a movie studio in 1893 in New Jersey. Movies were introduced in European arcades in 1895. The first commercial motion picture exhibition was held in 1896 in New York. Edison developed sound with his motion picture, demonstrated in 1904.

In 1898, the first suggestions made that pictures with sound could be carried across large distances. Within three years, research was begun to carry the moving pictures to distant locations. This early version of television actually preceded the development of radio. In 1920, the first radio sets were sold by Westinghouse to promote its first station, 8XK in Pittsburgh, PA. In 1926, NBC Radio signed on the air. In 1926, Congress created the Federal Radio Commission, later the Federal Communications Commission, as the broadcasting regulatory entity. In 1927, CBS Radio signed on the air.

In 1927, the first television test pictures were sent. In 1928, the first American home got a TV set, to watch the first regularly scheduled TV programs, over WGY-TV and WRNY-TV. The first trans-oceanic TV signal was sent, from London to New York. In 1929, the first public demonstration of a color TV model was made. In 1930, the first closed circuit TV projected on a big screen in a theatre. In 1931, CBS-TV and NBC-TV signed on the air. CBS' first station, W2XAB (later WCBS-TV) began regular daily programming. RCA and NBC put a TV transmitter atop the Empire State Building.

In 1938, NBC covered the first live, breaking TV news story (a fire). In 1939, NBC covered the opening of the World's Fair, as well as the first football game, baseball game and prize fight broadcasts. In 1940, the first basketball game and hockey match were broadcast, as was the first coverage of political conventions.

In 1941, the first licensed commercial television station (WNBT-TV) went on the air. The first TV commercial cost sponsor Bulova Watches a total of nine dollars. In 1944, the first boxing and wrestling matches were broadcast. CBS began its first evening news show, hosted by Ned Calmer. NBC began its TV news show the next year. In 1945, the first public demonstration of a TV set in a department store was held, with 25,000 watching. At this point, nine commercial TV stations were in operation.

In 1946, audiotape was introduced to American network radio. Bing Crosby brought the BASF process from Europe, so he could pre-tape his radio shows and spend more time on the golf course. Soon, most other network radio shows went to tape. This ultimately spelled the beginning of the end of network radio as a primary family entertainment medium.

On TV in 1946 appeared the first televised heavyweight boxing title championship and the first hour-long musical variety show broadcast by NBC, whose network consisted of three stations. In 1947, there were 44,000 TV sets in use and 40 million radios in use. That year marked the first mass production of television receivers.

In 1947, the Dumont Network signed on the air. It was conceived as a vehicle for selling Dumont TV sets. Named for founder Abner B. Dumont. Its flagship station was Channel 5, WABD in New York, and other affiliates provided programming to the network. That year also saw the first broadcast of a joint session of Congress.

Also in 1947 was the first broadcast of a World Series baseball championship. CBS, NBC and Dumont pooled their resources to jointly telecast to an audience of 4 million people.

In 1947, the first kinescopes were created. NBC and Eastman Kodak devised a process for recording programs off a TV monitor and distributing for later broadcast. Kinescopes paved the way for videotape and DVDs later. In 1948, there were one million TV sets in use and 36 TV stations in 19 cities, able to reach one-third of the U.S. population. That year, ABC-TV signed on the air.

In 1948, Columbia Records first issued long-playing record albums on the market. This changed the packaging and distribution of popular music, which gave the rise to a broader audience and music variety shows on television. "The Ed Sullivan Show/Toast of the Town" premiered on CBS. This became the longest-running variety show, lasting until 1974 and syndicated ever since.

In 1948, the "Milton Berle Show/Texaco Star Theatre" premiered on NBC. Berle commanded the highest rating for a single time period, up to 92%. As a show of support, in 1951, NBC signed Berle to an exclusive 30-year contract, which it fully honored. The first Academy Awards ceremonies were broadcast on TV. As an equivalent venue for recognizing its own excellence, the Television Academy of Arts and Sciences was founded, subsequently bestowing its Emmy Awards. The first game show transitioned from radio to TV. It was "Winner Take All" on CBS, the first quiz show developed by Mark Goodson and Bill Todman, who subsequently produced the most game shows.

In 1949, Columbia Pictures was the first major Hollywood studio to enter TV production. Its Screen Gems subsidiary was prolific throughout the 1950s, 1960s and 1970s. RCA Victor Records first issued 45-RPM singles on the market. Laws were passed enabling TV aerials to be perched atop buildings to improve signals. In 1950, Revue Productions entered television, taking over Universal Studios in the 1960s and becoming the most prolific supplier of filmed programming to television. The Korean War became the first living room war, via film footage sent back to networks.

In 1951, RCA unveiled the first community TV antenna system (forerunner of cable TV). Desilu Productions was formed. Its series, "I Love Lucy," was the first to be filmed in front of a live audience. A ratings hit, it set the pace for TV reruns. Desilu's prolific output over the next 16 years included "Our Miss Brooks,"

"December Bride," "The Lucy Show," "The Untouchables," "Star Trek," "Mannix" and "Mission: Impossible." "Hallmark Hall of Fame" premiered on NBC, with "Amahl and the Night Visitors" as its first show. This became the longest-running series of specials and cultural arts show.

In 1952, the coaxial cable was laid, facilitating national broadcast transmissions. 1953 witnessed the first live coast-to-coast broadcast: the inauguration of President Dwight D. Eisenhower, the first worldwide event coverage: the coronation of Queen Elizabeth, the highest rated TV event (the birth of Little Ricky on "I Love Lucy"), the first educational TV station (KUHT-TV, Houston, TX) signing on the air. Also in 1953, TV Guide began publication. RCA tested compatible color TV system on the air for the first time. Leonard Goldenson took over ABC-TV from previous owners, launching a long journey to make the fledgling network a contender to giants CBS and NBC. It took until 1976 for ABC to become #1 in the overall ratings. The network focused upon young viewers, who matured and remained loyal to the network of their youth.

1954 stands as television's Golden Year and the peak of its Golden Age. The first color TV show transmission was "Climax/Shower of Stars" on CBS. Walt Disney entered TV, hosting Disneyland and promoting his theme park concept. His first major mini-series hit was "Davy Crockett," launching a commercial merchandising tradition. In 1955, Warner Brothers and 20th Century-Fox both entered TV with episodic series production.

In 1956, videotape was first used on television production. Originally, tape was used for commercials and portions of programs. By 1958, entire programs were taped and edited for later broadcast. This ultimately spelled the beginning of the end of live television (except for news shows). Desilu Productions acquired the RKO Pictures lot (later selling to Paramount in 1967). MGM entered TV with series based upon some of its movies: "Dr. Kildare," "The Thin Man," "Asphalt Jungle," "Northwest Passage."

In 1957, 40 million TV sets were in use. Jack Paar took over as host of "The Tonight Show" on NBC. The year saw the first coverage of the space exploration program and the entry of Dick Clark into the TV medium that he dominated for five decades. In 1958, the Dumont Network signed off the air, merging into ABC-TV. 1959 saw the Paola investigations into rock n' roll music, the recording industry and plugging of records on radio and television.

In 1960, 90% of all U.S. households had TV. An overhead blimp was utilized for the first time in live sports coverage. The year saw the first Olympics marathon coverage, originating from Rome. The Kennedy-Nixon debates set ratings and precedent for election coverage. JFK was the first TV era President. In 1962, Johnny Carson took over as host of "The Tonight Show" on NBC. Walter Cronkite took over as anchor of the CBS Evening News.

1963's major news event was the assassination of President John F. Kennedy. 1964's top ratings phenomenon was The Beatles on the "Ed Sullivan Show," signaling the major news and cultural icon: the British Invasion (rock music, fashions, fads). 1965 brought the advent of audio cassette tapes. In 1967, Super Bowl #1 was seen by 51 million viewers. The final episode of "The Fugitive" ranked next to the birth of Little Ricky as TV's highest ratings getter.

National Educational Television hence became known as the Public Broadcasting System. In 1967, Ted Turner bought WTCG-TV, a UHF independent station in Atlanta and began programming TV series reruns, movies and sports. WTBS became the flagship for his broadcasting empire (CNN, TNT, etc.). 1968's major news events: assassinations of Martin Luther King and Robert F. Kennedy, plus rioting in the Chicago streets during the Democratic National Convention. 1968 saw the advent of eight-track tapes. 1969's major news event was the landing on the moon.

1970 was the last year for cigarette advertising on television. Satellite, cable and pay TV systems started their aggressive growth, in the beginning carrying clear reception for out-of-town channels. In 1971, the barter syndication strip series concept was introduced. 1972's major news event was tragedy at the Olympics games, as sports and news coverage melded. In 1974, Roone Arledge, head of ABC Sports, also took over as head of ABC News.

In 1976, the cable TV era began. Ted Turner's WTCG-TV in Atlanta became cable TV's first Superstation and changed its call letters to WTBS, the flagship for his broadcasting empire. Barbara Walters moved from NBC over to ABC, with her first stint was as co-host of the ABC Evening News with Harry Reasoner. In 1977, ABC-TV finally hit #1 overall in the ratings. The first home video cassette recorders went on the marketing, selling at $1,700 each. Blank video tapes were selling for $30 each. In 1978, Home Box Office premiered.

In 1980, the concept of videotape rentals was first introduced. The retail cost of VCRs went below $1,000 for the first time. Cable channels BET, Showtime and Cable News Network (CNN) premiered. In 1981 MTV and USA Network premiered. Classic movies and television shows from the 1950s and 1960s began to be marketed on video cassette tapes. In 1982, A&E and TNN premiered.

In 1983, the broadcast of the final episode of "Mash" became TV's highest ratings getter. It knocked the birth of Little Ricky and the final episode of "The Fugitive" down to second and third place. In 1983, home shopping channels and The Disney Channel premiered. In 1985, the cost of blank videotapes dropped below $10 for the first time. VH-1 premiered.

In 1986, compact discs introduced as the newest technology for record albums, playing at 78 RPM (the original phonograph speed). CDs eclipsed vinyl records within the next five years and became the preferred source for music, over cassette tapes. This trend also spelled the beginning of the end for the Top 40 singles market. ABC cancelled "American Bandstand," ending its 39-year run on the network. In 1987, the Fox Network signed on the air.

In 1990, the retail cost of VCRs went below $250 and tapes below $5 for the first time. In 1992, Jay Leno took over as host of "The Tonight Show" on NBC. 1997 saw the advent of the Internet. In 2002, satellite radio was introduced.

In 1958, Congress founded the National Aeronautics and Space Administration to oversee space exploration. NASA sent up its first satellite that year. Manned space flights began in 1961, and they captivated the public. The space program galvanized the adventure of the unknown, the lessons from science and the overwhelming national pride. Astronauts were heroes, and the spaceflights were must-see television viewing.

The space program has brought modern life many inventions. There are 1,800 spin-offs in NASA's Technology Transfer Program, including CAT scanners, computer microchips, cordless tools, ear thermometers, freeze-dried food, insulation reflective techniques, invisible braces for teeth, enriched baby food, the joy stick, light-emitting diodes, memory foam, microwave ovens, scratch resistant lenses, shoe insoles, smoke detectors, solar energy, the swimsuit, powdered lubricants, water filters, space blankets, land mine removal, the soap soaker, flame resistant textiles, the ingestible thermometer pill, workout machines for conditioning, highway safety grooving, artificial limbs, pollution remediation, radial tires, ventricular assist devices, software catalogs and much more.

The 21st Century, in business and in lifestyles, is dominated by technology, from cell phones to wi-fi, from the internet to social media and from modern adaptations of technologies from two earlier centuries.

Technology has influenced so many devices and niche industries, including aircraft navigation, alarm systems, analyzers, automated attendants, automobiles, broadband communications, cable fiber optics, call systems, cellular mobile station equipment, clocks, cloud storage, computers, converters, data management systems, digital test equipment, distributors, earth stations, educational and training systems, fiber optic tools, hardware, headsets, HVAC equipment, key systems, lighting systems, message systems, modems, monitoring systems, paging systems, power supplies, radio telephone equipment, railroad systems, receivers, revenue and billing systems, routers, security systems, semiconductors, signaling systems, storage systems, surge protectors, switches, telecommunications devices, teleconferencing, test equipment, towers, transformers, trucks, video games, video systems, wave guides, wireless equipment, work stations, dust busters, cochlear implants and much more.

Niche areas and industries benefiting from tech innovations include architecture, assistive technologies, banking and finance, construction, energy, healthcare, information technology, manufacturing, medicine, military, nursing, retail, risk management, science, speech and hearing, technology transfer, water treatment, weather forecasting and others.

Chapter 27

THE HISTORY OF VOLUNTEERING
AND COMMUNITY SERVICE

I t has always been part of human nature to help others in need. Colonists banded together to survive the new nation, forming support groups to help each other plant crops, build houses and fight disease. Citizens helped neighbors to bring in harvests, build homes for the aged, maintain roads and raise barns.

Early formal institutions of volunteering were the monastic orders of churches. Monastic orders had as their mission to go into needy communities and serve. Franciscans worked with lepers, who were shunned by all others. During outbreaks of plague during the Middle Ages, it was the Franciscan monks who went into victims' homes and take care of them.

In 1688, after a fire that ravaged Québec City, citizens created the Bureau des Pauvres, an office composed of volunteers, who provided money, food and clothing to the victims.

The earliest volunteers served without pay in militia forces. The original term was coined in 1755, from the French word "voluntaire," defined as "one who offers himself for military service."

Benjamin Franklin founded the first volunteer firehouse in 1736. He took 30 men and formed the Union Fire Company in Philadelphia, PA. Many small towns and cities still have volunteer fire departments. More than 70% of all firefighters today are volunteers.

During the Revolutionary War, the famous "minute men" were a volunteer militia. Volunteers raised funds for the war efforts, showing their philanthropic attitude and patriotism. In the 1830s, young people got involved with outreach work through various religious organizations. Churches operated relief programs, helping the homeless and those victimized by unforeseen circumstances.

Volunteers also played a role in the Civil War. Groups such as Ladies' Aid Societies were created to make bandages, shirts, towels, bedclothes, uniforms and tents.

The American Red Cross began during the Civil War, when Clara Barton took care of wounded soldiers. She recognized the need for medical nursing, supplies at the battlefronts and the need for morale boosts. The international Red Cross organization started in 1863 and encouraged Ms. Barton to create the American chapter. In 1881, she obtained formal recognition and served as its president until 1904. The organization's activities extended to floods, famines, fires and other disasters.

The YMCA was founded in 1844 in London, England, by George Williams, to provide healthy activities for men in cities. By 1851, the Young Men's Christian Association had spread throughout Europe and to the United States. Continued growth saw sports activities, fitness programs and activities geared at the entire family. In 1977, the YMCA was immortalized in a popular record by The Village People, with its accompanying dance becoming a craze that is still shared.

The YWCA was founded in 1855 in London, England, by Mary Jane Kennaird and Emma Roberts. YWCA USA was founded in 1858 and now has 300 associations serving 2.6 million people. Programs include health, fitness, aquatics, career nourishment, early childhood education, housing and shelter, economic empowerment and leadership development.

The Boys' Club was founded in 1860 in Hartford, Connecticut. In 1906, dozens of independent organizations joined as Federated Boys' Clubs. In 1990, they became Boys and Girls Clubs of America, providing after-school programs via 4,000 member clubs. This is the official charity of Major League Baseball. A former club member, actor Denzel Washington, has been the organization's spokesperson since 1993.

The Salvation Army was founded in 1865 by William Booth in England to respond to conditions stemming from the industrial society. In 1880, the U.S. branch was formed by George Railton. The Army has worked to serve those most in need, combatting forces of evil.

Volunteers of America was founded in 1896 by Ballington and Maud Booth. They pledged to "go wherever we are needed, and do whatever comes to hand." In the early-1900s, they moved into tenement districts to care for people in poverty. They organized day nurseries and summer camps, provided housing for single men and women, and established halfway houses for released prisoners. During the Depression of the 1930s, VOA assisted people who were unemployed, hungry and homeless, establishing employment bureaus, wood yards, soup kitchens and food pantries where every food item cost one cent.

During wartime, VOA operated canteens, overnight lodging and meals for soldiers on leave. Affordable housing and child care were provided for defense industry workers. VOA headed community salvage drives during, collecting scrap metal, rubber and fiber for the war effort. VOA has since developed hundreds of affordable housing complexes. VOA operates nursing facilities, assisted and independent living residences.

Most volunteers of the 18th and 19th centuries found their assignments through churches and other private sector entities. People became sensitive to the plights of the disadvantaged. The late 1800s saw the rise of institutions becoming known for voluntary action. All were created to serve the needs of people in crisis of one kind or another. Some actually specialized in addressing specific causes.

Florence Nightingale was a nurse who helped improve hospital practices, which in turn improved patient survival rates. She worked in voluntary action from the Crimean War through World War I. Florence Nightingale's force of skilled nurses brought attention to needs of soldiers and affected healthcare in general.

The Salvation Army focused on unmarried people and alcoholism. The YMCA concentrated on improving men's economic opportunities. The Society of Saint Vincent de Paul developed voluntary services for the poor and homebound elderly.

In the 20th Century, mainstream volunteer organizations began to flourish, shaping volunteer and non-profit organizations with the sole purpose of helping other organizations find their way. America was full of volunteers functioning in every region, giving others the chance at better lives.

Big Brothers and Big Sisters started in 1902 when Ernest Coulter, a clerk in New York Children's Court, befriended kids in need of positive influences. It was chartered in 1904, with each of 39 volunteers agreeing to befriend one child each. In 1934, President and Mrs. Franklin D. Roosevelt became patrons of the Big Brothers and Big Sisters Foundation. In 1958, the Big Brothers Association was chartered. In 1970, Big Sisters International was incorporated. In 1977, both organizations merged.

The Boy Scouts was founded in 1907 in England by Robert Baden Powell. The American scouting program was founded in 1910. Its purpose was to "teach patriotism, courage, self-reliance and kindred values." Learning for Life is a school and work-site subsidiary program of BSA. The NAACP was founded in Baltimore, MD, in 1909 by Moorfield Storey, Mary White Ovington and W.E.B. Du Bois.

The NAACP has addressed segregation, disfranchisement, social barriers, desegregation, civil rights, equal employment opportunities and educational initiatives, building coalitions worldwide.

The Girl Scouts was founded in 1912 by Juliette Gordon Low. That first chapter in Savannah, Georgia, has grown to 3.6 million members throughout the U.S. In 1917, a troop in Oklahoma began selling cookies at their local high school. In 1922, Girl Scouts of the USA recommended cookie sales, and a chapter in Philadelphia organized the first drive. Since then, each council has operated its own sales of cookies each year to raise funds in support of programs.

Camp Fire Girls was formed in 1912, as girls in Thetford, Vermont, watched males participate in outdoor activities through the Boy Scouts. The organization tried to merge with the Girl Scouts but continued as an independent entity. During World War I, Camp Fire Girls sold Liberty Bonds. They planted millions of trees and supported orphans. The name was changed to Camp Fire Boys and Girls in 1975, then in 2012 to Camp Fire.

The United Way was founded as Community Chest in Cleveland, OH, in 1913. There were 1,000 Community Chest organizations in 1948, when they were combined to form the United Foundation. The name United Way was adopted in 1963, modified to United Way of America in 1970. It is an umbrella organization, providing funding and support to thousands of non-profit organizations nationally.

Volunteer organizations drawing from business and citizenry include Rotary International, the Association of Junior Leagues, Kiwanis International, Lions International and the Exchange Clubs.

The first Volunteer Bureau was founded in Minneapolis, MN, in 1919 and became part of the Volunteer Center National Network, reaching 170 million people in thousands of cities across the nation.

Disabled American Veterans was founded by Robert Marx in Cincinnati, OH, in 1921. Marx had been injured during his World War I service. A women's auxiliary was formed in 1922. DAV was given a federal charter in 1932. DAV provides benefits assistance, outreach, research and advocacy.

Environmentalism also found its place during the 1930s, as President Franklin D. Roosevelt raised awareness by creating the Civilian Conservation Corps. The CCC planted 3 million trees in a single decade. Many green initiatives flourished over ensuing decades, a monumental event being Earth Day in 1970.

During World War II, volunteers were active in the military and on the home front. Volunteer organizations collected supplies, cared for the injured, entertained servicemen and supported civilians in a variety of ways.

After World War II, people shifted the focus of their altruistic passions to other areas, including helping the poor and volunteering overseas. The Peace Corps was founded in 1960. President Lyndon B. Johnson declared a War on Poverty in 1964, and volunteer opportunities expanded.

Americorps is a national and community service organization. It has programs that address community needs in the areas of education, environment, public health and safety and disaster preparedness and response. It operates the Volunteers in Service to America (VISTA) program, initiated by LBJ's Economic Opportunity Act of 1964, the domestic version of the Peace Corps. Said Johnson: "Your Pay will be low. The conditions of your labor will be difficult. But you will have the satisfaction of leading a great national effort. And you will have the ultimate reward, which comes to those who serve their fellow man."

VISTA strives to "fight poverty with passion." Programs address illiteracy, health services, housing opportunities, community collaboration and efforts to break the poverty cycle. VISTA members complete the program with lessons learned in teamwork, leadership, responsibility and other life skills, carried with them for the rest of their lives.

National Volunteer Week began in 1974 as a way to recognize and celebrate the efforts of volunteers. Since then, the emphasis has widened to a nationwide effort to urge people to participate and volunteer in their communities. Every April, charities and communities reinforce the week's official theme "Celebrating People in Action" by recognizing volunteers and fostering a culture of service. National Volunteer Week is sponsored by the Points of Light Institute, which began as a foundation, created in response to President George H.W. Bush's inaugural speech in 1989, urging volunteers and community activists to become "a thousand points of light."

Habitat for Humanity was founded in Americus, GA, in 1976. It has assisted more than four million people in the construction, rehabilitation and preservation of more than 800,000 homes. It is the largest non-profit building organization. Programs include A Brush with Kindness, mortgage assistance, Global Village Trips, RV Care-A-Vanners, Women Build, youth programs, recovery efforts along the Gulf Coast and Haiti, Collegiate Challenge and AmeriCorps Build-a-Thon.

In 1987, New York City launched City Cares, a program to get young professionals involved in volunteer service. The name was changed to the Hands on Network in 2004. It includes more than 70,000 corporate, faith and non-profit organizations, delivering 30 million hours a of volunteer service each year.

Volunteer Match, a non-profit organization, was launched in 1998, a merger of Impact Online Inc. and Volunteer America. It utilized the newly emerging internet as an opportunity to match citizens interested in volunteering with organizations in their localities. It bundles enterprise tools with local, regional and national non-profit organizations, facilitating easy connections for those interested in serving. It has won awards as a useful resource and inspired greater usage of the internet by the non-profit sector. Worldwide Helpers is a comparable organization in the U.K.

Volunteer Connections.org was launched in 2000, later becoming 1-800-Volunteer.org. It features an online search for volunteer opportunities for individuals.

The Disabled Veterans National Foundation was created in 2007 by six women veterans and ever since has been helping men and women who have been wounded while on duty or have become sick during or after their service change their lives for the better. The DVNF provides services to disabled veterans and their families, collaborating with various organizations that can provide direct support. They have specific interest in helping those who suffer from Post Traumatic Stress Disorder as well as other brain injuries.

Volunteers, The Art of Volunteering

The Corporation for National and Community Service calculated in 2012 that 64.5 million Americans gave 7.9 billion hours of volunteer service.

All good citizens want to get involved with worthwhile causes. Volunteers are the lifeblood of non-profit organizations and the causes they exemplify. The art of volunteering is in aligning with the community and investing one's time for maximum impact.

Volunteering has the power to improve the quality of life and health of those who donate their time. People must be performing the good deeds from a selfless nature. Volunteering improves not only the communities in which one serves, but also the life of the individual who is providing help to the communities.

Volunteering involves these types of investments:

- Time.
- Knowledge, skills, expertise.
- In-kind reciprocities.
- Political capital.
- Stakeholder relations.
- Social resources.
- Intellectual capital and heritage.
- Financial, directly or indirectly.

People volunteer because they believe in their communities and in specific causes. They want to give back, as time permits. They want to make a difference. Many volunteers get to utilize skills that their jobs do not allow, thus rounding them out professionally. There is a personal fulfillment that comes in unexpected ways. Plus, volunteering constitutes socialization, while doing good work on behalf of important causes.

During the course of each year, 26% of Americans regularly volunteer in their communities. So said the Current Population Survey of approximately 60,000 households that obtains information on the nation's civilian non-institutional population. Volunteers are defined as people who perform unpaid work (except for expenses) through or for an organization.

Volunteering is a core value of citizenship. By giving back, volunteers gain new skills, expand professional networks, stay connected to their community and enjoy physical and mental health benefits.

Chapter 28

MOTIVATIONS TO CARRY ON
What We Were and Where We're Going.

C onventional wisdom told us that each of us has the potential for three careers in us. Recent behavioral studies indicate that the number is now seven. Each professional experiences evolutions in their career. Experiences serve as building blocks to the next plateau of a multi-tiered dynamic life.

Research tells us that people spend 150 hours per year in looking for lost files and data. I submit that the perusing of old files gives you the golden nuggets of ideas in the path to moving forward.

Often, when advising client companies on their Institutional Reviews, we look analytically at what was accomplished. We understand reasons for the successes. We examine the causes and instances of failure, with the contributing factors reviewed.

People are interesting combinations of the old, the new, the tried and the true. Individuals and organizations are more resilient than they tend to believe. They've changed more than they wish to acknowledge. They embrace innovations, while keeping the best traditions.

When one reflects at changes, he-she sees directions for the future. Change is innovative. Customs come and go. Some should pass and others might well have stayed with us.

There's nothing more permanent than change. For everything that changes, many things stay the same. The quest of life is to interpret and adapt that mixture of the old and new. People who fight change have really changed more than they think.

The past is an excellent barometer for the future. One can always learn from the past, dust it off and reapply it. I call that Lessons Learned but Not Soon Forgotten. Living in the past is not good, nor is living in the present without wisdom of the past. Trends come and go. The latest is not necessarily the best. Some of the old ways really work better and should not be dismissed just because they are old or some fashionable trend of the moment looks better.

When we see how far we have come, it gives further direction for the future. Ideas make the future happen. Technology is one tool of the trade. Futurism is about people, ideas and societal evolution, not fads and gimmicks. The marketplace tells us what they want, if we listen carefully. We also have an obligation to give them what they need. In olden times, people learned to improvise and "make do."

In modern times of instantaneous disposability, we must remember the practicalities and flexibilities of the simple things and concepts.

What We Will Be

Build your value. Set levels of values. Respect other people's values. Find places where the values intersect.

Traditions are stories that families write together. Everyone in the family writes a chapter.

Thank you for doing what you do. Keep being an inspiration to us and an engine to the economy and society. What you do makes a difference.

Your success is a beacon to us. Your achievements inspire us to do better. Because you care and do great work, lives are changed.

A person can run away from everything but not from himself. Learn to like people for what they are, not what they've been. Figure a person for what he is, not for something that happened before.

Some people ridicule what they cannot understand. The sad part is if they start thinking that way when they are kids, sometimes the thinking never gets straightened out.

You never really forget words of wisdom. You had them in the back of your head all the time. We all just sort of sidetrack them for a spell. A bruise carried a few days is a great lesson.

A man fears a trick more than a wound because it injures his pride. Man learns that the ideas of a few are not as powerful as the consensus of many.

Friendship cannot live without trust. When wise people speak, who knows what they will say or how long it will take them to say it.

People have always been sure. They were sure that gold could be made out of lead, sure the world was flat, sure that if a mad dog bit them, they would die. Being sure doesn't make you right.

Learning From the Past to Prepare for the Future

90% of firms are out of business by year 10.

The four-year survival rate in the information sector is 38%. The four-year survival rate in education and health services sector is 55%. The average start-up in education and health sector is 50% more likely than the average start-up in the information sector to live four years.

40% of all start-up restaurants fail.

There are 25 million non-employer firms in the United States, and that includes freelancers, contractors and other individuals that work alone. The average that each of these businesses earned was $47,000, which is a good living and one that is indeed higher than the average salary for individuals in employment. However, the profit of those small businesses employing individuals was, on average, $3,000 higher at $50,000.

Change and growth are terms that have been hyped, distorted and used out of context. Many people wrongly believe that the economy changes itself or that technology is the driving factor. They define "change" from their limited perspective and that those who do not subscribe to their perspectives are "anti-change." The reality is that planned business growth and tactical changes are the guiding factors.

To benefit from change and grow, one must understand where you've been and where your organization might go. Research trends and spot opportunities. Take a big picture business approach by looking at the whole, then at the parts as they relate to the whole, then at the whole again. Plan to grow, and grow by the plan.

Signs of Kindness

Kindness is inspiring and contagious. You see signs in yards, spreading positive themes, including:

- We're in this together.
- Spread kindness.
- Heroes work here.
- World's best dad.
- Proud graduate.
- Science is real.
- Black Lives Matter.
- We rise by lifting others.
- Get into Good Trouble.

The phrase "Have a Nice Day" first appeared in the 1948 film "A Letter to Three Wives." The expression was popularized by air traffic controllers in the 1960s. With cute design, it became a catch phrase in the 1970s. "Baby on Board" signs became a fad in 1985.

Encourage friends to hydrate with water and with positive hope. Replenish with historical lessons that inspire tomorrow. Re-fuel with wisdom from others and compassion for humanity. Re-commit to kindness and wishing success for others. Breathe the fresh air of life through a mask. When you say love, you've said it all.

World Kindness Days highlight good deeds, focusing on positive power and the common thread of kindness that binds all of us.

Here are some quotes on kindness:

"Carry out random act of kindness, with no expectation of reward, safe in the knowledge that one day someone might do the same for you." Princess Diana.

"Kindness is the language which the deaf can hear and the blind can see." Mark Twain.

"I've been searching for ways to heal myself, and I've found that kindness is the best way." Lady Gaga.

"For beautiful eyes, look for the good in others; for beautiful lips, speak only words of kindness. Walk with the knowledge that you are never alone." Audrey Hepburn.

There is always reason to be grateful for your blessings. Kindness is everything.

Recalling Teachings from Younger Years

School memories shape our lives. A bunch of great kids with promises they have since fulfilled. Our early years form the basis for contributions throughout life, mentoring others and serving communities. Saluting the current youth, who will do and accomplish magnificent things. The tender years last in our memories forever, just as we share mentorship with the young, as others did with us back in the day. Wishing safe conditions and an atmosphere of positive learning for schools, teachers and students.

Paying tribute to teachers, the men and women who lend their passion and skills to educating our children:

- From Mayna Bode at Brykerwoods Elementary, I learned the art of teamwork.
- From Thelma Henslee at O. Henry Junior High, I learned the art of communicating in different ways to different constituencies.
- From Terri Flynn at Austin High School, I learned how to substitute words to create more colorful narratives.
- From Lafalco Robinson at Austin High, I learned to appreciate and champion all forms of music.
- From Dr. DeWitt Reddick at the University of Texas, I learned that the path to the halls of fame is about more than grades: it's community leadership and professional standing.

- From Dr. Bill Mindak at UT, I learned that being a high-level generalist in business requires much more preparation, research and savvy than being a niche player.
- From Dr. Norman Hackerman at Rice University, I learned that beginning students deserved the best professors. Though a top administrator, he continued to teach Freshman Chemistry.
- My mother taught fourth grade at Travis Heights Elementary School. My grandfather was Dean of Students at the University of Texas at Austin and had a building on campus named for him. Think of the impact that teachers have made on your life.

Volunteering and Gratitude

We honor citizens for their selfless contributions. Volunteers deliver food to citizens, sew masks, offer comfort to seniors and inspire the population by their heroism. Volunteering is worthwhile and enriches lives. Volunteers are the glue to resilient communities. When there are tragedies, there will always be helpers. The more we do, the more we feel the "potlache" of giving to others.

Motivating quote from Dr. Martin Luther King, Jr.: "Everyone can be great because anyone can serve. You don't have to have a college degree to serve. You don't even have to make your subject and your verb agree to serve. You only need a heart full of grace and a soul generated by love."

Giving returns rewards to our lives. The term Potlache means: I give you a gift, especially wisdom. Your receipt of it is my gift. Giving to others multiplies in good feelings. The more you give, the more you are committed to give.

Thank others for their service, often. Get into life-long commitment to community service. Positive energy is returned, the joy of giving gifts.

The wisest people I know assert these principles:

1. Have an early morning gratitude review.
2. Make a gratitude list to neutralize a difficult day.
3. Replace anger with gratitude.
4. Replace criticism with gratitude.
5. Be grateful for challenges.

6. Express gratitude to others at every opportunity.
7. Focus on what you have.

Commit to celebrating our excellence within. Be grateful for what we have earned, more grateful for the achievements and success of others.

The worst disasters bring out the best in caring, compassionate people. Natural disasters do not redefine who communities are. They make communities stronger. Volunteers are the glue to resilient communities.

These are the natural disaster stages: Warning, hit, search and rescue, recovery, rebounding, analysis, danger prevention planning, learning from crisis, community development. When there are tragedies, there will always be helpers. The more we do, the more we feel the "potlache" of giving to others. Regards to first responders and heroes throughout communities.

Labor Day honors workers and their contributions toward the prosperity of the country. There are 20 reasons why people work, including basic physical needs, safe work environment, contact and friendship with fellow workers, acknowledgment for special efforts and contributions, learning from and mentoring others, affirmation, caring for the customers, loyalty to the company, industry expertise, being part of a team, realizing one's dreams and potential, maximizing one's gifts and talents, opportunities for self-development, being one's best, realizing ideals. Labor Day marks the end of summer and beginning of the fall business season.

The Way It Works Out

You always make more at your first garage sale than at the subsequent ones.

Functionaries cannot see beyond their own niche and are most uncomfortable with Big Picture thinking.

Poor workers will become poor managers.

Self-centered people never get enough. There is no appeasing them.

You have to learn to earn. The sooner that one quests to learn and be more in life, the more successful one will be.

The way that one conducts themselves during the lean years indicates how well one can handle success.

Nobody wants you until everybody else does. People are always nice to winners.

The bicycle is one of the most efficient machines. The more complex the machine, the more breakdowns, inefficiencies and problems will occur.

One cannot instantly know who is going to influence his/her future.

Those who change early do it as an act of the heart, not the head. Tell people they cannot do something is a challenge for them to do the opposite. People who remain singular in their own perspective cannot or will not see the other guy's side.

Adapt existing technologies. Reapply past knowledge. Understand the rules. Learn the art of adaptability. Matter and energy are interchangeable. Master the inter-relationship of elements and factors.

Be knowledgeable about paradigms but not controlled by them. We poorly see data that does not fit with our paradigm. New paradigms put old ones at risk.

Good ideas are realities. We see best what we are supposed to see. Out of the box thinking will develop.

Without caring, there can be no quality. Ask someone to do mediocre work, and it kills their spirit.

There will be more moments, life lessons, beacons shining and trees of life. Ignite the joy, interest and commitment.

259

Second volume in this series…

THE BIG PICTURE OF BUSINESS, BOOK 2

Comprehensive Reference for Business Success
Doing Business in a Distracted World

Third volume in this series...

THE BIG PICTURE OF BUSINESS, BOOK 3
Business Strategies and Legends
Encyclopedic Knowledge Bank

Fourth volume in this series...

THE BIG PICTURE OF BUSINESS, BOOK 4

The Value You Deserve

Innovation, Motivation and Strategy Meet Tomorrow

Appendix A

OTHER WRITINGS BY HANK MOORE

This was written in late 2019 as a promo for my high school reunion. It is in the entertaining style of historical chapters in these books.

Everyone grew up somewhere. For me, it was a small town called Austin, TX, which is now a large major city. Its reference to icons of that era is common to everyone who reads their own local histories.

In the interest of nostalgia and warm feelings for historical content, it is included in the Appendix of this book.

Austin High Time Capsule
Memories and Nostalgia from Our School Years
By Hank Moore
AHS Class of 1965.
Author of 14 internationally published books
(five nominated for Pulitzer Prize).
Member of seven halls of fame.

The Stephen F. Austin High School Class of 1965 grew and matured during memorable years.

From our high school years of 1962-1965, we retain many memories, were shaped by events and are products of a rich, robust culture. We followed with college, careers, families and community service. Our lessons learned, life experiences and accomplishments combine for school reunions. We honor those who achieved, those who passed and are Loyal Forever to our roots.

Austin represents many things to many people. This is where people live and work, where we are educated and entertained, where culture and community pride are stimulated and where we learn some lessons in living together with others.

Austin is a growth community. It has seen industries emerge and mature. It boasts generations of healthy families. It encompasses lifestyles, cultures and opportunity that no other world-class city can match.

Austin celebrates the historical, utilize state-of-the-art technology and reflect changing social needs will always be at the forefront of the future. With a sense of pride, reflection and optimism for the future, Austin's legacy is dedicated to identifying, meeting and serving every need of our community.

Our hometown is a collection of neighborhoods, cultures and families. Communities that grow and prosper will analyze and serve the needs of present generations. While honoring the heritage, we planned for the future. Whether in the global sense or on the blocks on which we live, layers of generations comprise our essence. Every community is a collection of lifestyles, inspired through the structures in which they take place are centers of synergy.

During our high school years, the population of Austin was around 200,000. The Lester Palmer Auditorium opened in 1959. That was the venue of our high school graduation in 1965.

How Austin Started

The spirit of the early pioneers took shape in structures and lifestyles attributed to business. Stephen Fuller Austin was the first land developer to bring settlers to Texas. The initial group was 300 families.

Austin had complete civil and military authority over his colonists until 1828, subject to rather nominal supervision by the officials at San Antonio. He allowed them to elect militia officers and local alcaldes, corresponding to justices of the peace in the United States. To assure the uniformity of court procedure, he drew up forms and a simple civil and criminal code. As lieutenant colonel of militia, he planned and sometimes led campaigns against Indians. To meet current costs, Austin's only resource was to assess fees against the colonists.

Austin wrote shortly before his death that his wealth was prospective, consisting of the uncertain value of land acquired as compensation for his services as impresario. Besides bringing the colonists to Texas, Austin strove to produce and maintain conditions conducive to their prosperous development.

Aware of the importance of external trade, Austin consistently urged the establishment of ports and the temporary legalization of coasting trade in foreign ships. He believed that coastal trade would establish ties of mutual interest between the colonists and Mexico and enable Mexico to balance imports from England by exporting Texas cotton. Congress legalized the port of Galveston after a survey of the pass by Austin in 1825. As a result, external trade was confined to the United States.

Austin began the Anglo-American colonization of Texas under conditions more difficult in some respects than those that confronted founders of the English colonies on the Atlantic coast. He saw the wilderness transformed into a relatively advanced and populous state, and fundamentally it was his unremitting labor, perseverance, and foresight. His aim was to promote and safeguard the welfare of Texas.

Austin is the state's fourth largest city. It originated as the riverside village of Waterloo, in a buffalo-hunting region occupied by Tonkawa and Comanche peoples. In 1839 it was selected by scouts as the site for the permanent capital of the Republic of Texas and renamed to honor Stephen F. Austin, father of the republic. Austin was incorporated in 1840, with 856 residents.

Austin High School was founded in 1881. The first classes were held at an Austin Independent School District building at 11th and Rio Grande Streets. The high school moved to its own building in 1900, located downtown at 9th and Trinity Streets. In 1925, the high school moved to 1212 Rio Grande Street, site of John T. Allan Junior High School, which had been built in 1916. AHS was renamed in 1953 as Stephen F. Austin High School, honoring the father of Texas. In 1975, the school moved to its present building at 1715 West Cesar Chavez Street. As part of our 10th reunion in June, 1975, AHS Class of 1965 members got to tour the new campus, which subsequently opened on August 25, 1975. The Rio Grande building has ever since housed Austin Community College.

Restaurant Legends

There were so many classic dining spots in Austin during our school years. House Park Barbecue was built in the shadows of Austin High in 1943. Popular restaurant hangouts near the campus during our era were the Maroon Mill and Maroon Roost. Also popular were the Holiday House restaurants operated throughout the city by Ralph Moreland, known as the hamburger king of Austin.

John Martin opened Dirty's in 1926. Harry Akin opened The Night Hawk Restaurants and The Frisco Shop in 1932. The Hoffbrau Steakhouse opened in 1932. Hut's was a burger joint and bar, opened in 1939.

Cisco's Bakery was opened on East 6th Street in 1943. That was Lyndon Johnson's power breakfast place, serving bloody marys by the pitcher and platters of Mexican bread.

Classic restaurants of the past included Lung's Chinese Kitchen, Youngblood's Fried Chicken, El Patio, Hill's Café, Dale Baker's Barbecue, 2-J Hamburgers, Kirschner's Fried Chicken, Irving's Steakhouse, Salt Lick Barbecue, Les Amis, G-M Steakhouse, Piccadilly Cafeteria, Lim Ting, Villa España, The Hitching Post, La Tapatia, The Barn, Green Pastures, Chicken Shack, Zuider Zee, the Terrace & Villa Capri Steakhouses, Toddle House, Burger Chef, Tarrytown Cafeteria, Christie's Seafood. Also, the Big Four Mexican restaurants operated by Monroe Lopez: El Matamoros, El Toro, El Charro and Monroe's to Go.

And, for the sweet tooth, there were Mrs. Johnson's Donuts, Frost Top Root Beer, Scotty's Bakery, Lamme's Candies and the Spudnut Shop. Sandy's Hamburgers, custard stand, opened in 1946 on Barton Springs Road. Amy Simmons opened Amy's Ice Cream on Guadalupe in 1981.

The original places to get pizza in Austin were Rome Inn, Victor's Italian Village, Shakey's Pizza and Buzzy Buck's Pizza Kitchen.

Randy Goss, Ed Norton, Skeeter Miller and Bruce Walcutt opened County Line Barbecue in 1975. Patricia Atkinson and David Ayer opened Kerbey Lane Café in 1980. Mike Young and John Zapp opened Chuy's in 1982.

Chains based out of Austin include Mr. Gatti's Pizza, Whole Foods, Schlotzsky's Deli and Thundercloud Subs.

Entertainment Meccas

Scholz Garten, a German beer hall, was opened in 1866. It is Austin's oldest restaurant and bar.

The Hancock Opera House was built in 1893. It evolved in the 1920s into the Capitol Theatre.

Kenneth Threadgill opened a gas station in 1933. It became a nightclub, and a folksinger named Janis Joplin sang the blues there in 1960. Threadgill's was converted into a restaurant in 1981.

KTBC signed on as Austin's first TV station in 1952. The second station was KLRN-TV, signing on in 1961, with its longest running program, "Austin City Limits," which debuted in 1976. The third station was KHFI-TV (now KXAN), signing on in 1965. The fourth station was KVUE-TV, signing on in 1971.

The Vulcan Gas Company opened in 1967. Armadillo World Headquarters opened in 1970.

Memorable clubs of years past included Charlie's Playhouse, The Checquered Flag, the New Orleans Club, Cotton Club, Torch Club, Nero's Nook, the Broken Spoke, Splitrail, Donna's Club, Show Bar, Punch's Lounge, the Austin Outhouse and the Living Room Piano Bar. The Torch was a teenage nightclub.

Sporting venues included Dart Bowl and Bobby Layne's Bowl-arama.

HemisFair was the San Antonio World's Fair, held in 1968.

There were record labels in Austin in the 1950s and 1960s. These included Domino, whose artists included The Slades, Ray Campi, Clarence Smith & the Daylighters and Joyce Webb. Sonobeat Records recorded Johnny Winter, the Lavender Hill Express (featuring Rusty Wier), Wali & the Afro Caravan, the Sweetarts, 13th Floor Elevators, Bill Miller Group, Lee Arlano Trio, David Flack Quorum, Plymouth Rock and Fast Cotton.

Austin recording artists who appeared on national record labels included Stevie Ray Vaughn, Cactus Pryor, Jerry Jeff Walker, Marcia Ball, Ray Wylie Hubbard and New Riders of the Purple Sage. Also on the music scene were other Texans who were Austin transplants, including Janis Joplin, Waylon Jennings, the Skunks, Doug Sahm, Willie Nelson, Beto and the Fairlanes, Charlie Sexton, Shiva's Headband, Ernest Tubb, Ray Peterson, Bob Wills, the Fabulous Thunderbirds, the Gatlin Brothers, Joe Ely, The Pflugerville Five, Eric Johnson and Johnny Dee & the Rocket 88's.

Retail Legends

In the 1960s, Austin housed many exciting retail stores and shops. They reflected and served a dynamic lifestyle and culture.

Scarbrough & Sons was the dominant department store. Academy Super Surplus started as Austin Army-Navy Surplus. The first modern shopping center to open was Capital Plaza, and the second was Hancock Center.

Popular retail stores of our youth were Dacy's For Shoes, Michael's The Colony, Karavel, Studtman Photo Service, Evelyn's Jacobson's, Slax, Reynolds-Penland, Studer's, Bill Gaston Boats & Motors, Goodfriend's, Studio Gilmore, Comal Cottons, Berkman's Typewriters, Calcasieu Lumber Company, Renfro's Drugstore, T.G. Murphy's, Sheftall's Fine Jewelry, Firm Foundation Bookstore & Publishers, Jack Morton's, Sanford's Shoes, Fred's Fruit Stand, Louis Shanks Furniture, Finn Jewelry, Bob Wilson Dance Studio, Oscar Snowden's, Winn's, Don Weedon's, The Steck Company, Career Girl Shop, Woolworth's, The Towne Shop, Texas Lumber Company, Hemphill's Book Store, S.H. Kress & Co., Bill Bunch Flowers, Wesley Pearson True Fit Seat Covers, Cabaniss-Brown Furniture, Kruger's Jewelers, Leon's, Harold Eichenbaum Displays, Austin Coin & Stamp Center, University Studio, Rawls Lumber Company, Nau's Drugstore.

Grocery stores of old included Rylanders, Kash-Karry, Minimax, Handy Andy, Sam Slaughter Stores, Moyer's and Shoppers World. There were two local suppliers of milk, Superior Dairies and Hillcrest Farms. Austin had two local baking companies for bread, Pan Dandy and Buttercrust.

There was a time that record sections were everywhere. They were in department stores, grocery stores, convenience stores, auto stores and drug stores.

J.R. Reed Music Company, Caravell's and The Record Shop were dedicated music retailers downtown. One found the largest selection of music at record stores, with small listening booths, and you could spend hours there previewing anything. Then came Waterloo Records and other stores in the UT, 6th Street and other areas. Half Price Books & Records debuted in Austin above a laundry plant on Lavaca Street, and its corporate office had debuted in a dry cleaning plant in Dallas.

Momentous Events During Our School Years

The Austin Aqua Festival was created in 1962 to promote Austin and the Texas Highland Lakes as a top vacation area and to boost the local economy in what was normally a slow period. The first Aqua Fest occurred Aug. 3-12, 1962. Art Linkletter was the headliner for the event. It was held up through 1998 on the shores of Town Lake, now known as Lady Bird Lake. It paved the way for such other events as South by Southwest, Austin Water Lantern Festival, Austin Urban Music Fest, Art City Austin, Indie Fest, Witch Fest, Stand Up for Schools, Urban Music Festival and Austin City Limits Festival at Zilker Park.

In the fall 1962 semester, the school to 8:00-3:00 and 9:00-4:00 staggered schedules, adjusting to the student "population explosion." Students were offered expanded job training skills through the Industrial Cooperative Training Program, Data Processing and Distributive Education.

Football was robust, as our district grew and expanded. Honors came to the band, essay contests, scholarships, speech programs, Interscholastic League competitions, future farmers, science programs and arts groups. Trustee Awards for academic excellence were presented. There were many organizations for student participation, including the Red Jackets, Girls' Intramurals, Red Dragon Players, Debate Squad, National Forensic League, Equestrian Club, Future Teachers, National Merit Scholarship Semi-Finalists, National Honor Society, District X Science and Mathematics Fair and the Comet yearbook,

The I.I. Nelson Athletic Field was dedicated. The Austin Maroon newspaper published its first full-color issue on Sept. 20, 1963, a national first.

Space flights by NASA were high on the attention span of the public. From 1961-1965, school classes had TV sets, where students could watch the early journeys into space. These included:

- Mercury Redstone 3—May 5, 1961—Earth Suborbital (Alan Shepard)
- Mercury Redstone 4—July 21, 1961—Earth Suborbital (Gus Grissom)
- Mercury Atlas 6—February 20, 1962—Earth Orbiter (John Glenn)
- Mercury Atlas 7—May 24, 1962—Earth Orbiter (Scott Carpenter)
- Mercury Atlas 8—October 3, 1962—Earth Orbiter (Wally Schirra)
- Mercury Atlas 9—May 15, 1963—Earth Orbiter (Gordon Cooper)
- Gemini 3—March 23, 1965—Earth Orbiter (Gus Grissom, John Young)

Friday, November 22, 1963, was an unforgettable day. President John F. Kennedy came to Texas, appearing in San Antonio, Houston and Fort Worth.

While in a parade route in Dallas, he was assassinated. Austin was to have been the final event on the evening of November 22. Our school was already scheduled to be let out at 1:00 p.m., so that students could go see the afternoon parade downtown. That was the time that our principal came on the sound system and announced that the President had been shot. The scheduled evening dinner was cancelled.

At the end of our senior year, our principal, Lipscomb Anderson, left the school after 12 years, promoted to a supervisory post in the Austin Independent School District. Our high school memories keep as Loyal Forever.

Appendix B

OTHER WRITINGS BY HANK MOORE

This second Appendix entry is the Foreword that I was asked to write by Bill Nash. He is a talented singer, humanitarian and ordained minister.

Bill Nash's book is "Saint, Singer, Singer. An Unexpected Redirected, Resurrected Life."

Foreword by Hank Moore

Music is life. Music provides purpose. Music brings you up, and it makes you reflect. Music is a major part of people's being.

Purveyors of music are important beacons to the public. They tap their talents and energies, thus inspiring audiences of one and many.

One of the great beacons of the Music of Life is Bill Nash. I discovered him in 1974 and remain enthralled by his versatility and understanding of the creative art.

I've known many people in the entertainment world. Some have talent but lack direction. Some have fallen victim to life matters. Others have risen and came back.

What strikes me about Bill Nash is his immense talent, his humble nature and the way in which he genuinely connects with people. His ministry of the best in all of us is done through music and is reinforced by the magnitude of community stewardship.

This book is about widening the scope much further. Whenever we review what made relationships and lives successful, we see that Big Picture thinking occurred. The potentiality of people and organizations is a progressive journey from information to insight to knowledge.

Bill Nash has impacted me because of his warmth, sincerity, know-how, determination and the ability to make you seem to be the most important person in the room, the society and the world.

That's the essence of this humanity-focused book. It had its genesis with making music. It has been articulated by the involvement with Champions Kids Camp and its impact on others.

Much of the wisdom to succeed lies within. People under-perform because they are not given sufficient direction, nurturing, standards of accountability, recognition and encouragement to out-distance themselves. Societies start to crumble when their people quit on each other.

Happy people absorb all the knowledge and insight they can, embracing change, continuous quality improvement and purpose in life.

This book and its author, Bill Nash, embrace the heart and soul of the music of life. Chapters are written in such a way as to be interpreted on several levels. Part common sense and part deep wisdom, they are intended to widen your focus and inspire the visionary that exists within you, the reader.

Bill Nash says that he is an average person who is trying to make a difference. I say that he is an exemplary role model, with advice and insights well worth hearing and taking to heart. I say that he brings out the greatness in us.

Hank Moore
Corporate Strategist™
Author of 14 books, nominated five times for the Pulitzer Prize.
Member of seven halls of fame.
Community steward and humanitatian.
Big fan of Bill Nash, Kim Nash and Jimmy Nash.

Cover wrap for Bill Nash's book.

At Champions Kids Camp: Hank Moore, Joan Wilhelm Moore, Kirby Lammers and Bill Nash.

Appendix C

OTHER WRITINGS BY HANK MOORE

This third Appendix entry is a magazine article that I wrote for TV Guide in 1973. It is an interview with Roy Disney.

25 years later, Roy Disney became my client, as I advised Disney Corporation in Corporate Strategy. I had met his uncle Walt Disney in 1965 and was brought in as a trusted advisor to the company.

Roy Disney's endorsement appears in the front of this book: "Hank Moore provides fresh approaches to heavily complex issues. His step-by-step study of the business layers makes sense. It shows how much success one could miss by trying to take shortcuts. There cannot be a price put on that kind of expertise."

Roy Disney Interview
By Hank Moore

Being brought up in the world's most prolific family of creativity, Roy E. Disney wanted to carve his own niche. His uncle was the legendary Walt Disney. His father, Roy O. Disney, runs the business aspects of the corporation of family entertainment and films.

After graduation from college, he went to work as an NBC-TV page, later as film editor on the "Dragnet" TV series. He later joined Disney Studios when he felt he could lend his own talents rather than cash in on nepotism.

Roy is vice president of 16MM production, a member of the board of directors at Walt Disney Productions and produces many of the animal and nature segments for NBC-TV's "The Wonderful World of Disney."

He is simultaneously working on six projects for the 1973-74 and 1974-75 seasons. "They tend to take a little longer. So, we need a little longer lead time," Disney told me in a chat at his Burbank CA offices. He doesn't foresee ratings keeping his staff from planning shows years ahead.

"It's always seemed to me that nature shows get higher ratings than anything else," claimed the producer who films them at a lower budget than live-action segments. "We do spend from six months to a year shooting on the thing," he explained for the factor that equalizes costs. He has never been attacked by an animal while filming."

Crews who don't know what they are doing will tend to get desperate early in the game," Disney noted. He advocates photographing nature in the wilds and never faking scenes or cajoling animals into action. "Our basic thesis is that the animal is the star, and we had better take pretty good care of him. Otherwise, you're going to pay for it the next morning."

His upcoming segments include a two-parter for fall airing, "Mustang," filmed in New Mexico, an 1880s saga. A crew is in Africa doing one on an antelope brood, "Bongo." There is another two-parter about a boy and his pet wolf. A crew in Florida is now doing a documentary on the brown pelican, an endangered species.

Foremost in his selection of topics are ways and means to film them. "I've been trying to figure a way to do a story about the Indian tiger for a long time," Disney observed. "Unfortunately, we haven't been able to make the right connections with the Indian government at this point."

He is constantly seeking to get fresh footage. "It gets harder all the time, partly because we've made enough of these shows that we've covered just about every American animal there is," he admitted. "We're finishing up a story about a raccoon, and I think it's the third raccoon show that we have made. But it's a new approach to it."

Once upon a time, Roy E. Disney aspired to write drama and actually did a script for the "Zorro" TV series. "Writing is more hard work than anything else," he confessed for becoming a producer and limiting his writing to staff memos and some occasional film narratives. Jumping from one project to another "keeps your mind a lot busier."

His father's end of the business bored young Roy. "I was always a bit of a rebel, like most sons who say 'I won't do what my father does.'"

He was strongly influenced by the Disney legend. "In terms of trying to use common sense when it was needed, that was my dad's strongest point. I'd rather participate in the creative end, where Walt inspired me."

Roy is a boating buff, and his wife is a horsewoman. Strong attachments to nature are with him. "You have to be in love with animal you're going to do a story about. Sometimes, you tend to fall in love with them as you go," he told of a falcon. "We did one this year about a skunk, which is harder to love." And there's his present star, a wolf. "That's an animal I don't know whether you say love but admire tremendously."

To Roy E. Disney, the best part of his job is traveling all over the world, scouting out unique locations for extraordinarily fresh film footage. He tries to take the family along as often as possible, but for even a Disney, traveling costs can sometimes be too prohibitive.

"We've branched out to include people stories as well as animal stories," Disney explained for making his documentaries something more than an instructional experience. "You've got a storyline to keep people interested, but you're still exposing them to new information. When you say documentary flat-out, I think it tends to turn people off. First, they've got to be entertaining. As soon as people are entertained, they're going to find out something they didn't know before."

A typical Disney, he thinks that you meet the nicest animals in the wilds of nature and on the home TV screen."

The Disney Legacy

Walt Disney started his career as an artist at a newspaper in Kansas City. He met cartoonist Ubbe Iwerks, and they formed a company. They made advertisements, and Disney was inspired into a career in animation. Disney produced the "Newman Laugh-O-Grams," followed by "Alice Comedies" and then "Oswald the Lucky Rabbit." Losing the rights to Oswald, Disney and Iwerks developed a new character, Mickey Mouse, who soon topped "Felix the Cat" as the most important cartoon character.

With the success of Mickey Mouse came the "Silly Symphonies" series, which later inspired the feature-length film "Fantasia." The Symphonies spawned The Three Little Pigs, Donald Duck, Goofy and Pluto. "Snow White and the Seven Dwarfs" in 1937 was Disney's first feature film. Later came "Three Caballeros," "Alice in Wonderland," "Peter Pan," "Lady and the Tramp," "Sleeping Beauty," "Sword in the Stone," "Bambi," "101 Dalmations," "The Aristocats" and many others. Disney produced spirit films during World War II and later true-life adventure features. Some features included animated and live-action scenes, including "Song of the South" and "So Dear To My Heart."

This quote summarizes the Disney philosophy: "When you wish upon a star. Makes no difference who you are. Your dreams will come true." Voiced by Jiminy Cricket, in the Disney movie classic "Pinnochio" (1941).

The 1950's brought Disney Studios into live-action scripted movies, including "Treasure Island," "20,000 Leagues Under the Sea" (starring Kirk Douglas), "Old Yeller" (starring Tommy Kirk), "The Great Locomotive Chase" (starring Fess Parker) and "Light in the Forest" (starring James MacArthur and Carol Lynley). The 1960's brought audiences "Polyanna," "The Parent Trap" (Hayley Mills starring in the original, Lindsay Lohan starring in the remake), "Mary Poppins" (starring Julie Andrews), "Babes in Toyland" and "The Monkey's Uncle" (starring Annette Funicello).

Disney conceived a theme park in California, Disneyland, which would embrace his studios characters, stories and fans. While raising money to build it, he agreed to produce a television series, "Disneyland," later retitled "Walt Disney Presents" and "Walt Disney's Wonderful World of Color." The park opened in 1955 and was a hit, inspiring in 1971 Disney World in Orlando, Florida.

The Disney TV series remained a popular attraction for decades, running on the ABC and NBC networks. The show was a mix of recycled material from his shorts and movies, original dramas, promotions for new Disney films and compilations of subject material. It spawned Davy Crockett, a major craze that in turn spawned feature films, coon skin caps, toy merchandising, recordings and personal appearances for stars Fess Parker and Buddy Ebsen. Disney produced two other TV series, "The Mickey Mouse Club" and "Zorro." Sub-series within "Disneyland" included Davy Crockett, Andy Burnett, The Swamp Fox, Elfego Baca, Spin & Marty.

Walt Disney hosted himself, added credibility to the program and became everyone's surrogate uncle. Nobody seemed to balk at the obvious commercialism, in the context of the show, all the promos were part of the mosaic.

Walt Disney was a creative genius and spent far more on each show than first-run network TV budgets could afford. Like independent producers Dick Powell and Desi Arnaz, he exceeded budgets, knowing that the quality would bode well in endless TV reruns, the real cash-cow market. Case in point: he filmed everything in color, though the first six years of Disneyland's broadcasts were shown in black and white.

Business extensions have included Buena Vista Distributing, Disneyland Records, vacation resorts, water parks, Imagineering services and cable networks.

Inspired by Disney, other entertainment companies specializing in children and the family trade have operated successfully. They have brought us movies, TV shows, merchandising, theme parks and a lot of great memories.

In later years, Disney became more of a corporate success, grew its scope of operation and eventually purchased the TV network to whom it went for funding back in 1954.

Roy Disney

Appendix D

OTHER WRITINGS BY HANK MOORE

This fourth Appendix entry is a group of essays that I wrote for the popular "Chicken Soup for the Soul" books.

Neighborhood Oriented Policing

I came home to find my house burglarized. Such a discovery brings a feeling of violation, and dealing with a non-caring police team simply compounds the anger, discomfort and disgust in "the system." I had been burglarized before, because that's life in the better residential neighborhoods.

This time, I was impressed with the professionalism with which the police handled it. My community (Houston, Texas) had recently appointed a new police chief, Lee P. Brown, who had done great things previously with the Atlanta Police Department and had gotten acclaim for handling a rash of child muggings and killings.

I wrote a complimentary letter to the chief, affirming how positive changes were already being felt in perceptions of safety. That letter launched a 20-year friendship, as well as 900 of the best volunteer hours that I have ever given. Chief Brown personally called me, stating how rare such complimentary letters were received. We agreed to meet for lunch and discuss a new concept called Neighborhood Oriented Policing.

For citizens to care about our safety, we should find worth in our people. In a city that was terrorized by youth gangs, negatively influenced by corrupt police administrations of past years and self-oriented toward commercial growth, it was clear that convictions toward caring for public safety must emerge.

During that first lunch meeting with the chief, I recalled the elements of public awareness and fund raising campaigns that had worked best for other causes. I told the chief that esoteric concepts would not work unless they are marketed to the consuming publics.

We positioned police cars as roving billboards, soliciting citizen warmth, rather than create suspicion. I asked a graphic artist friend to donate service in creating five sample renderings. One was chosen, and all other graphics of the department subsequently followed the style that we develop. Flashy graphics and slogans by themselves do not constitute organizational vision and corporate culture. Yet, communications and stakeholders must be considered when visionary concepts are developed. We spent the next year in planning, getting support and communicating the benefits of Neighborhood Oriented Policing.

Over the next two years, we held town hall meetings to ascertain public sentiments and issues. Among those attending were grandparents scared of their safety, merchants whose stores were regularly vandalized and educators without a firm grasp on the changing conditions. I was most touched by the pains of teenagers, calling out to contribute to society but somehow rebuffed and caught in a web of neglect and apathy.

A law enforcement community must be a source of information, help and respect. Resulting in the hurt and fears communicated by the public, a series of educational campaigns were created to address the issues. From teen suicide prevention campaigns to child seat restraint initiatives, our volunteer advisory board made sure that cohesion, fair-play and compassion marked this initiative.

Chief Brown subsequently went to New York City, where, as Police Commissioner, he enacted numerous Neighborhood Oriented Policing initiatives. Subsequently, as drug czar under President Bill Clinton and later as Mayor of Houston.

From a letter of appreciation that I wrote in 1982 came many lunches, creative brainstorm sessions and ceremonies. I attended many ceremonies and town hall meetings, just to hear and be touched by hundreds of citizens whom I would have never otherwise met.

It was an interesting journey that resulted from my house being burglarized. And the police recovered most of the stolen property too. But now, I saw the difference between caring peace officers and the guys who just filled out burglary report forms. I saw it through the eyes of citizens who were less frightened and had a little more hope for life.

Doing Your Best Work for Free

Seymour Cohen was an unpretentious, kind-hearted man. He ran a successful local advertising agency, along with his partners, Adie Marks and Larry Sachnowitz. To him, no meeting needed ever be longer than 20 minutes to handle anything truly important.

Mr. Cohen didn't like to trumpet his community service. He just quietly contributed and inspired others through his understatement. He always gave more gifts than he received. Compliments were always reflected positively upon you, rather than toward him.

The most important quote that I learned from "Slugger" Cohen was, "You always do your best work for free." That meant that you give your all for any project, especially for the ones that pay nothing.

To Mr. Cohen, people are consistent in all aspects of their lives. If they renege on charity or civic promises, then their attentiveness toward family and work are comparably bad. Colleagues and family will support your volunteerism endeavors because you do the right things for the right reasons, and it is indicative of your character overall.

From the joy, accomplishment and glow that we get from pro-bona activity come the glimmers of the potential within. We pick community service projects based upon the good that it will do for others. The passion from within must fuel every task that we voluntarily perform. The body of accomplishments are in the heart, not on the awards in plaques.

As Slugger advised me, when recognition for volunteer service comes, you are propelled to do more the next time, for other causes, in unique ways and to light the torch for others to give their best work for free.

As I meet people in the business world, they recall activities that I performed in community service. They recall boards that you served on or causes associated with your name. I respond by recounting the commitment and how it touched me or made me a better person, as Mr. Cohen always did. As he also told me, "You often credit for good deeds that others did. Be sure to spread the credit around."

I understand and appreciate what Seymour Cohen said, how he exemplified it and how each of us inspires ourselves to reach further as a community steward. Successful people are products of mentorship. So are our communities. I've remembered and recorded most of the worthwhile advice that I've been given. Again, thinking about volunteerism as Slugger did, we make and honor our commitments, nurtured by our responsibility to mentor others. If we're going to be called role models, we show it without fanfare and inspire others to lead.

Learning Hidden Skills, Literacy Foundations

I was entering a new business area, having had great success in others. I crammed, researched and asked questions of those with knowledge of this new field. I told my friend that I felt like a "Johnny come lately" in this new sphere and didn't want the stakeholders to feel uneasy.

I was reminded that I was taking the effort to do the groundwork that my competitors were not, concluding with some of the best advice of my life, "It's not when you learn. It's that you learn." I learned that sage wisdom at the ripe old age of 34.

Years later, I was devoting volunteer talent to creating a literacy provider umbrella organization. Talking with recipients of tutoring services recalled Pam's career advice and put deep soul into what became my commitment to create and transfer knowledge.

Maria was a 43-year-old mother of five who survived on domestic's wages. She almost died because she couldn't read prescription labels and mistook doses. At age 43, she took a community center course and now had a literacy diploma, which she proudly read to her children and grandchildren.

Ursula worked as a hospital orderly and knew the symbols and jargon, enough to keep her job. She bought food for her family by choosing recognizable pictures on cans at the supermarket. Her graduation from a literacy program, at age 51, meant that she could now admit to employer and family what she hadn't known and which she still sought to learn.

Alejandro was a 23-year-old cashier at fast food restaurants. He couldn't make change or take orders without the assistance of computer buttons. Because the systems never crashed, he kept jobs and never was "found out" until he had to fill out forms for a child seeking health care. His decision to seek literacy counseling was an affirmation that he would "read his way" out of button-pushing and attain jobs where he could think and reason.

From the literacy educators, I learned that 60% of the American public is functionally illiterate. But tutoring the underprivileged across town was not enough in the fight against illiteracy. We are all literate and need to accelerate our skills.

Workplace illiteracy is more rampant than we believe. College-educated people never developed thinking and reasoning skills and now cost their employees with wrongly pushed buttons, inattentiveness to detail, poor workmanship and other signs of a neglected work ethic. 37% of all high school graduates never read another book for the rest of their lives. 16% of all college graduates never complete another book. 50% of Corporate America is functionally illiterate.

I advocate workplace literacy programs, better known as training. Research shows that today's workforce will require three times the amount of training that it needs in order to remain competitive. And training is not just defined as computer skills. It must include developing our potential as thinkers, leaders and role models to others.

It all comes back to what we were not taught and what more we can learn, as Maria, Ursula and Alejandro took the effort to learn and share with others. Thousands like them put the pride aside and learn, thus becoming mentors.

I heard the term "workplace literacy" for the first time at age 40. Since that time, I was inspired by those whom I met in the literacy programs to write more than 200 publications for the business world. My quest now is to enlighten business leaders on aspects they were never taught in college and which I wish that I had learned years before.

As I learned from others during my literacy agency volunteerism, including Maria, Ursula and Alejandro, it's more important what you do with what you've learned, to whom you pass it on and how your soul improves because of newly processed knowledge.

ABOUT THE AUTHOR

Hank Moore is an internationally known business advisor, speaker and author. He is a Big Picture strategist, with original, cutting-edge ideas for creating, implementing and sustaining corporate growth throughout every sector of the organization.

He is a Futurist and Corporate Strategist™, with several trademarked concepts of business, heralded for ways to remediate corporate damage, enhance productivity and facilitate better business.

Hank Moore is the highest level of business overview expert and is in that rarified circle of experts such as Peter Drucker, Tom Peters, Steven Covey, Peter Senge and W. Edwards Deming.

Hank Moore has presented Think Tanks for five U.S. Presidents. He has spoken at seven Economic Summits. As a Corporate Strategist™, he speaks and advises companies about growth strategies, visioning, planning, executive-leadership development, futurism and the Big Picture issues affecting the business climate. He conducts independent performance reviews and Executive Think Tanks nationally, with the result being the companies' destinies being charted.

The Business Tree™ is his trademarked approach to growing, strengthening and evolving business, while mastering change. Business visionary Peter Drucker termed Hank Moore's Business Tree™ as the most original business model of the past 60 years.

Mr. Moore has provided senior level advising services for more than 5,000 client organizations (including 100 of the Fortune 500), companies in transition (startup, re-engineering, mergers, going public), public sector entities, professional associations and non-profit organizations. He has worked with all major industries over a 50-year career. He advises at the Executive Committee and board levels, providing Big Picture ideas.

He has overseen many strategic plans and corporate visioning processes. He has conducted performance reviews of organizations. He is a mentor to senior management. This scope of wisdom is utilized by CEOs and board members at the corporate level..

Types of speaking engagements which Hank Moore presents include:

- Conference opening Futurism keynote.
- Corporate planning retreats.
- Ethics and Corporate Responsibility speeches.
- University—college Commencement addresses.
- Business Think Tanks.
- International business conferences.
- Non-profit and public sector planning retreats.

In his speeches and in consulting, Hank Moore addresses aspects of business that only one who has overseen them for a living can address:

- Trends, challenges and opportunities for the future of business.
- Big Picture viewpoint.
- Creative idea generation.
- Ethics and corporate responsibility.
- Changing and refining corporate cultures.
- Strategic Planning.
- Marketplace repositioning.
- Community stewardship.
- Visioning.
- Crisis management and preparedness.
- Growth Strategies programs.
- Board of Directors development.
- Stakeholder accountability.
- Executive Think Tanks.
- Performance reviews.

- Non-profit consultation.
- Business trends that will affect the organization.
- Encouraging pockets of support and progress thus far.
- Inspiring attendees as to the importance of their public trust roles.

Making pertinent recommendations on strategy development.

Hank Moore has authored a series of books:
The Big Picture of Business, 4-book series
The Business Tree™ (with international editions)
Pop Icons and Business Legends
Non-Profit Legends
The High Cost of Doing Nothing. Why good businesses go bad.
Houston Legends
The Classic Television Reference
Power Stars to Light the Flame
Pop Music Legends
The $50,000 Business Makeover
Plus monograph series for the Library of Congress Business Section, Harvard School of Business, Strategy Driven and many publications and websites.

Follow Hank Moore on:
Facebook: http://www.facebook.com/hank.moore.10
Linkedin: http://www.linkedin.com/profile/view?id=43004647&trk=tab_pro
Twitter: https://twitter.com/hankmoore4218
YouTube: https://www.youtube.com/watch?v=jFax7XZvz0U
Pin Interest: http://www.pinterest.com/hankmoore10/
Google+:https://plus.google.com/u/0/112201360763207336890/posts
Atlantic Speakers Bureau: http://atlanticspeakersbureau.com/hank-moore/
Business Speakers Network: http://directory.espeakers.com/buss/viewspeaker16988
Silver Fox Advisors: http://silverfox.org/content.php?page=Hank_Moore
Facebook business page: https://www.facebook.com/hankmoore.author/?fref=ts
Additional materials may be found on Hank Moore's website: www.hankmoore.com

A free ebook edition is available with the purchase of this book.

To claim your free ebook edition:

Visit MorganJamesBOGO.com
Sign your name CLEARLY in the space
Complete the form and submit a photo of
the entire copyright page
You or your friend can download the ebook
to your preferred device

Morgan James BOGO™

A **FREE** ebook edition is available for you
or a friend with the purchase of this print book.

CLEARLY SIGN YOUR NAME ABOVE

Instructions to claim your free ebook edition:
1. Visit MorganJamesBOGO.com
2. Sign your name CLEARLY in the space above
3. Complete the form and submit a photo
   of this entire page
4. You or your friend can download the ebook
   to your preferred device

Print & Digital Together Forever.

| Photo | Free ebook | Read anywhere |

CPSIA information can be obtained
at www.ICGtesting.com
Printed in the USA
JSHW040756180921
18825JS00002B/97